.NET & J2EE Interoperability

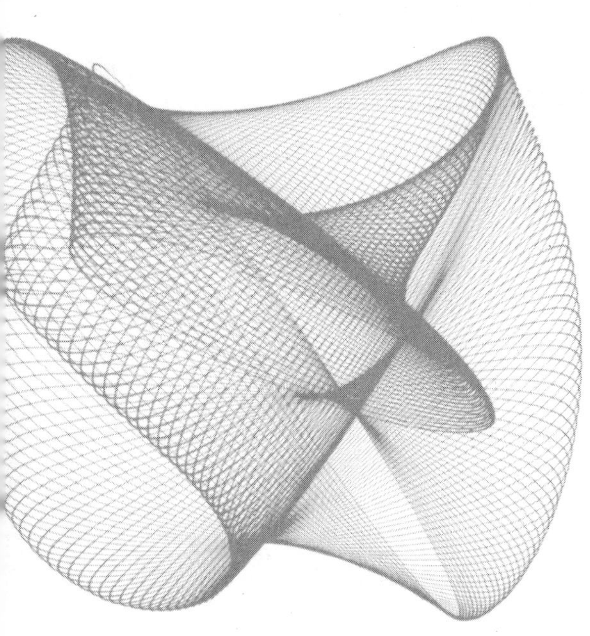

About the Author

Dwight Peltzer has extensive experience as a professor of computer science, developer, lecturer, and author. Presently a member of the faculty in the School of Engineering and Computer Science at C. W. Post, Long Island University, he has held Visiting Chair positions at several universities. They include the Fulbright Visiting Professor Chair at Keele University in Staffordshire, England, Southern Illinois University, and the New York Institute of Technology. He teaches seminars in C++, Visual Basic .NET, C# .NET, SQL, ASP.NET, and J2EE-related technologies such as JAXP, Java Server Pages, and XML.

Dwight lectures regularly at universities throughout the United States, Canada, and England. He also presents lectures for the Canadian Broadcasting Corporation, the British Broadcasting Corporation, and National Public Radio.

During the past several years, Dwight has served as consultant to Sheridan Software Inc., A. C. Nielsen, TRW, and Interboro Corporation.

Dwight is also the author of *XML: Language Mechanics and Applications* (Pearson Addison Wesley, 2003).

.NET & J2EE Interoperability

Dwight Peltzer

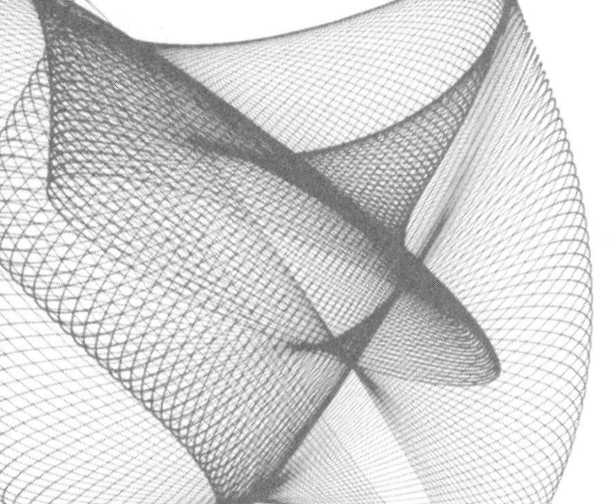

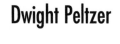

McGraw-Hill/Osborne

New York Chicago San Francisco
Lisbon London Madrid Mexico City Milan
New Delhi San Juan Seoul Singapore Sydney Toronto

The McGraw·Hill Companies

McGraw-Hill/Osborne
2100 Powell Street, 10th Floor
Emeryville, California 94608
U.S.A.

To arrange bulk purchase discounts for sales promotions, premiums, or fund-raisers, please contact **McGraw-Hill**/Osborne at the above address. For information on translations or book distributors outside the U.S.A., please see the International Contact Information page immediately following the index of this book.

.NET & J2EE Interoperability

1234567890 CUS CUS 019876543

ISBN 0-07-223054-1

Publisher Brandon A. Nordin
Vice President & Associate Publisher Scott Rogers
Editorial Director Wendy Rinaldi
Project Editor Janet Walden
Acquisitions Coordinator Athena Honore
Technical Editors Karl Hilsmann, Jonathan Bruce
Copy Editor Judith Brown
Proofreader Karen Mead
Indexer Valerie Robbins
Composition George Toma Charbak, Jim Kussow, Kelly Stanton-Scott
Illustrators Kathleen Edwards, Melinda Lytle, Michaell Mueller, Lyssa Wald
Series Design Roberta Steele
Cover Series Design Greg Scott
Cover Illustration Akira Inoue/Photonica

This book was composed with Corel VENTURA™ Publisher.

This book is dedicated to my lifetime companion and source of inspiration, Marla, and to my two sons, Jonathan and Christopher. They are all shining lights in my life and are constantly encouraging me to keep writing.

Contents at a Glance

Contents

Acknowledgments

I want to especially thank Wendy Rinaldi, my acquisitions editor, for her encouragement and for making it possible to write this book. I also want to thank Dr. Steven Heim for his beautiful graphics. He is a soul mate and inspiration to me. Judith Brown, a fantastic copy editor, is an inspiration to all writers. Janet Walden was a wonderful editor to work with by keeping me on schedule. Thank you to all who contributed to producing this book.

Introduction

In today's digital economy, it is becoming imperative to integrate legacy systems, business applications, and code with emerging new technologies. Interoperability, the subject of this text, explores the two major platforms—Microsoft .NET. and J2EE *.NET & J2EE Interoperability* provides an in-depth examination of how these two major platforms interact with each other from a developer's point of view. Numerous examples demonstrate how .NET and J2EE provide application integration. For example, Chapter 5 examines the Common Language Runtime (CLR) and explains how it serves as a web container, similar to IBM's WebSphere. It provides low-level services such as memory management, automated garbage collection, and security to ASP.NET, ADO.NET, and all languages targeting the .NET Framework.

The first four chapters focus on J2EE technologies, and Chapters 5, 6, and 7 concentrate on .NET. Chapter 8 introduces JNBridgePro, an innovative business solution providing true cross-platform interoperability between J2EE and .NET. JNBridgePro technology allows developers to generate proxies that facilitate two-way integration. A Java developer can access .NET functionality directly, just as .NET developers can leverage Java technologies. JNBridge business solutions represent a significant advance in facilitating interoperability.

.NET & J2EE Interoperability: A Guided Tour

Chapter 1, "Interoperability in the Enterprise," serves as an introduction and chapter-by-chapter overview of internal and external integration between the two major platforms. For example, the discussion on technology interoperability between J2EE and .NET and their mutual support for web services introduces the central theme of this book.

The chapter introduces a case study intended to serve as a focal point for illustrating particular concepts in Java or .NET. A finance corporation called

International Finance Corporation Exchange (IFCE) buys and sells foreign currency. The study focuses on business *process*; for example, IFCE checks the status of a customer to determine whether he or she has established an account. In the final chapter, a project built in Visual Basic .NET illustrates how to create a currency converter. A currency amount entered in the dialog box, for example, in British pounds, can be converted to the euro, or to German marks, or another currency.

Chapter 2, "J2EE Servlets, Java Server Pages, and Web Services," begins with a brief description of Sun Microsystems' three development platforms, namely, Java 2 Platform, Micro Edition (J2ME); Java 2 Platform, Standard Edition (J2SE); and the Java 2 Platform, Enterprise Edition (J2EE).

The three technologies discussed in this chapter are *communications* between applications, the *presentation* layer, and the *business applications* layer.

A detailed discussion focuses on Java servlets, Java Server Pages, and their respective roles in creating a distributed enterprise application. Topics include a servlet's life cycle, management of session state with servlets, Java Server Pages (JSPs), and JSP page directives and how to apply them when returning requested results to a client.

Chapter 3, "Enterprise JavaBeans, Interfaces, and JDBC Persistence," begins with a review of the Enterprise JavaBeans development and deployment phases, followed by an introduction to two types of JavaBeans—synchronous and asynchronous. Next is an in-depth examination of session and entity beans. In order for the reader to better understand Enterprise JavaBeans, a discussion ensues on EJB interfaces with a detailed description of an EJB's life cycle.

The next section in Chapter 3 focuses on containers and their services. IBM's WebSphere serves as the container model. The chapter explains the process whereby Enterprise JavaBeans live within a container and receive the full range of services that containers provide.

The chapter presents Enterprise JavaBeans from a client's perspective and explores technologies necessary for accessing services supported by the EJB container.

Chapter 4, "RMI-IIOP, the JNDI, and Deployment Descriptors," begins with an examination of Remote Method Invocation (RMI) calls on objects distributed throughout a web farm or an enterprise network. Originally, RMI technology was used to execute remote object access by importing the java.rmi package. RMI offers distributed garbage collection and object activation. However, J2EE uses RMI-IIOP and the Java Naming and Directory Interface (JNDI) for access to remote objects.

The next topic of interest covered is the role played by deployment descriptors in deploying J2EE applications. Entity bean authors indicate within the deployment descriptor how the container should manage the Enterprise JavaBean. They specify whether a bean is a *session* bean, the type of session bean (stateful or stateless), or one of the two types of entity beans. The author should indicate whether the bean is *container-managed persistent* or *bean-managed persistent*. The deployment descriptor should further indicate whether the bean is message driven. If so, the deployment descriptor should indicate that the message-driven bean has no interface. The final section of Chapter 4 describes how to deploy JAR files to a container for distribution.

Chapter 5, ".NET Language Integration Components," provides detailed information about the Common Language Runtime (CLR). Similar to a J2EE web container, the CLR serves as the .NET Framework manager and provides services ranging from verifying the validity of data types before compiling, to ensuring that the application conforms to both the Common Type Specification (CTS) and Common Language Specification (CLS), to managing security. The chapter also contains a discussion and examination of program executable (PE) files and introduces the concept of an assembly that contains all program binaries and file references required to execute the application.

Chapter 6, "ASP.NET Architecture," examines ASP.NET's infrastructure and begins by listing ASP.NET's benefits and new features. The features include a *code-behind* model to separate HTML from program logic, an event-driven program model that allows developers to write events and create handlers for them, and server controls that manage client state by using *view state.*

The chapter examines ASP.NET namespaces with a description of System.Web.UI classes. A description of an ASP.NET page's life cycle is accompanied by examples demonstrating how an ASP.NET page interacts with the CLR and the Framework to provide a user-friendly experience in developing ASP.NET applications.

A section in Chapter 6 examines web forms and explains how to add server-side controls to the form both declaratively and programmatically. A subsequent chapter section provides detailed instructions on how to create *user-defined* controls and add them to a web form. The chapter concludes with a discussion on security and error handling.

Chapter 7, "ASP.NET and Web Services," provides a detailed overview of web services as they relate to ASP.NET. The chapter begins by posing the question: "What is a web service?" and proceeds with an examination of a service-oriented architecture. It explores XML and how it is integrated with web services.

A section is devoted to exploring how a client accesses web services by employing Simple Object Access Protocol (SOAP) and HTTP. It further explains how a Web Services Description Language (WSDL) file is generated and provides a detailed description of Universal Description, Discovery, and Integration (UDDI) and its use in discovering a web service.

Chapter 7 also provides information on object-oriented programming and describes best practices in programming to interfaces, a methodology that supports component reuse. Another chapter section discusses .NET's architecture and explains how the framework consists of a series of components and interfaces. This examination further underscores how the ASP.NET infrastructure and .NET CLR collaborate to provide flexibility and support the development of scalable web services.

Chapter 8, "Interoperability Solutions from Third-Party Vendors," introduces JNBridgePro. This software package enables developers to achieve true cross-platform interoperability. JNBridgePro generates proxies that allow developers to access .NET functions and methods from J2EE as though they were written in J2EE and vice versa. A user-friendly interface permits developers to select the classes and interfaces they desire and then generate proxies to facilitate application and method interoperability.

Chapter 9, "Best Practices, Design Patterns, Security, and Business Solutions," concludes the text with a review of both J2EE and .NET technologies and how they achieve interoperability internally and externally. The chapter provides a section on best practices, on how to apply them, and when it is appropriate to use them in context. A section is devoted to selecting a business model, such as the MVC model, and knowing how to use it effectively in application design.

Applying security measures and managing application state in a distributed environment are also discussed and accompanied with examples demonstrating how to achieve these tasks. The chapter concludes with an example written in Visual Basic .NET to demonstrate multilanguage interoperability in the IFCE case study.

Appendix A provides a brief overview of J2EE's Java Connector Architecture (JCA). Connectors facilitate access to Java-based Enterprise Information Systems (EISs) and legacy data stores. The appendix tells developers where they can obtain more information about connectors and download the JCA specification.

And to conclude, Appendix B provides a list of recommended reading, as well as the main sources for various specifications relevant to the book.

Who Should Read This Book

Chapter 1 serves as an introduction to interoperability and points to individual chapters and what they cover. Chapters 2 through 4 are useful for IT professionals, developers, and students who wish to learn how J2EE technologies achieve application integration both internally and externally.

Chapters 5 through 7 introduce the reader to the .NET Framework and explain in detail how .NET technologies support multilanguage integration, one of the more significant advances in technology in recent years. This section is appropriate for those who are already familiar with J2EE, but want to concentrate on .NET technology.

In Chapter 8, J2EE and .NET come together in the cross-platform solution provided by JNBridge. This chapter should be of interest to IT professionals, developers, and students who want to begin working with both platforms. Chapter 9 focuses on best practices and offers a currency converter solution created in Visual Basic .NET to demonstrate how an application can be written in any language and on any platform.

About the Companion Web Site and Downloads

All source files are available at *http://www.osborne.com*. Please follow instructions provided by McGraw-Hill/Osborne to locate specific links to the book.

PART I

J2EE Interoperability Inside and Out

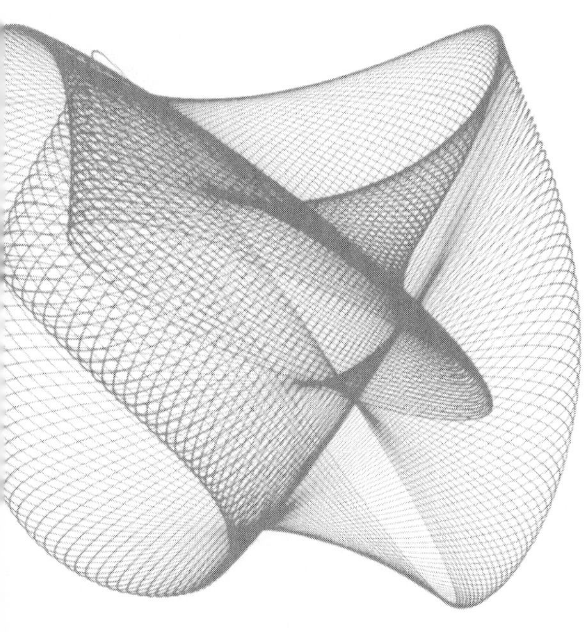

CHAPTER

1

Interoperability in the Enterprise

IN THIS CHAPTER:

Introduction to Distributed Application Development

Interoperability in the Enterprise

J2EE Servlets, Java Server Pages, and Web Services

Enterprise JavaBeans, Interfaces, and JDBC Persistence

RMI-IIOP, the JNDI, and Deployment Descriptors

.NET Language Integration Components

ASP.NET Architecture

ASP.NET and Web Services

Interoperability Solutions from Third-Party Vendors

Best Practices, Design Patterns, Security, and Business Solutions

Java Connector Architecture (JCA) Specification

Case Study: International Finance Corporation Exchange (IFCE)

The main objective of this book is to serve as a guide for achieving integration between the two platform-independent technologies, Sun Microsystems' Java 2 Platform, Enterprise Edition (J2EE 1.4) and Microsoft's .NET. Cross-platform communications between business partners and transmission of mission-critical data in the enterprise are the central themes. The material covers *why* interoperability is essential for success in today's digital economy, but also *how* to achieve integration between diverse technologies. Web services and remote procedure calls in a distributed environment require tight security measures in order to maintain integrity of data across multiple servers. The discussion focuses on services provided for developers by J2EE and .NET.

This chapter introduces the concept of technology integration between J2EE and .NET, with their mutual support for web services, and summarizes the main points covered in subsequent chapters. Many of the headings match the chapter titles and are meant to direct you to a specific chapter for an examination of that particular topic. For example, Chapter 2, "J2EE Servlets, Java Server Pages, and Web Services," begins an examination of J2EE with an introduction to servlets, Java Server Pages, and web services. Chapter 5, ".NET Language Integration Components," begins the section on .NET, with a look at its key components.

This chapter also describes the case study that will be used throughout the book to demonstrate the various technologies supporting interoperability between J2EE and .NET in a real-world example.

Introduction to Distributed Application Development

Sun's Java 2 Platform, Enterprise Edition (J2EE 1.4) provides an extensible framework for designing multi-tiered solutions. J2EE technology consists of numerous specifications rather than a downloadable set of technologies. These specifications, or contracts, define how a technology such as J2EE Connectors or the Java API for XML (JAX) functions. This applies to all J2EE technologies. For example, business partners must agree to a specified contract or specification before they can utilize a specific set of services offered by a J2EE technology.

Sun has a well-established history of reliability, maturity, and support for building server-side applications. It comes as no surprise that they spearheaded an initiative called the Java Community Process (JCP) for purposes of soliciting suggestions from major corporations to improve all Java platforms, including J2ME, J2SE, and J2EE. This applies to standardizing key Java technologies as well. Giving third-party vendors the opportunity to have input and a say on future direction and Java implementations is a wise move on Sun's part. Rather than keeping the source code proprietary, Sun has permitted thousands of people to view the same code; consequently, all Java platforms continue to improve. Sun has a stake in bringing an improved technology to market and offering their customers better service. Community involvement encourages open source application development.

Recently, Sun included support for building XML-based web services. They have also added the Java Connector technology to their impressive array of specifications. (See Appendix A for an overview of the JCA specification.) Sun offers frequent releases of the Web Services Developers Pack (WSDP). They recognized that support for web services is fundamental to conducting cross-platform, distributed, interactive business transactions in the enterprise. One of the most important features offered by J2EE technology is the ability to compile applications only once and deploy them on any platform.

Microsoft's .NET Framework and Visual Studio .NET's suite of tools have generated considerable discussion and debate in both Java and Microsoft camps. Most of the discussion centers around platform maturity and stability, and capturing market share. The question most frequently asked is, "Can Java and Microsoft .NET coexist?" It is significant that while Microsoft is experiencing increasing adoption of its integrated suite of products, Sun's added support for web services is resulting in the evolution of a fruitful development environment benefiting all developers. The Gartner group recently predicted that within the next three years, 90 percent of medium and large corporations will be leveraging the benefits of both Java and .NET. Employing a mixture of both technologies is a win-win situation for both business and consumers.

Microsoft entered the enterprise arena with Windows Server 2003, the Microsoft .NET Framework, Visual Studio .NET, and programming languages hosted by the framework. Their product suite includes Microsoft Transaction Server (MTS), COM +, their flagship SQL Server 2000 database, and the Microsoft Message Queue (MSMQ). The .NET architecture is web services–centric. This paves the way for interoperability between technologies residing within the .NET platform. Web services are the glue that binds diverse web-enabled applications. The ability to build applications utilizing any programming language targeting the Framework is a major plus for Microsoft-oriented developers. Languages include Visual Basic .NET, J# .NET, managed C++ .NET, and C# .NET. Developers can write a distributed application in the language of choice, compile it, and subsequently deploy it. Unfortunately, to date, the Microsoft .NET applications run only on the Windows platform. Let's hope that Microsoft will soon recognize the need for modifying their servers and suite of tools for use on other platforms and operating systems.

The .NET infrastructure presents a component-based, multi-tiered approach to distributed programming, and designates Simple Object Access Protocol (SOAP) as the primary technology for supporting web services. The components consist of classes and member functions designed to modify data and provide object-oriented functionality. The .NET Framework hosts these components. In a distributed environment, it is essential to layer services. For example, it is a good idea to separate the presentation layer containing Active Server Pages from the middle tier components. These contain business logic and enforce the business model. The third tier consists of low-level components for managing and providing services such as database access, connecting to legacy applications, and so forth.

The .NET Framework uses HTTP as the communications protocol for messaging and exchanging documents via the Internet. This protocol allows any programming language, platform, or middleware to be an interactive participant in cross-platform interoperability. XML serves as a .NET architecture core component and provides the means with which to construct XML-based SOAP messages.

Increasing demands for distributed applications in the enterprise have serious implications for developers. Those who are normally accustomed to designing, building, and implementing systems for either one platform or the other, but not both, are finding it necessary to become familiar with all options and technologies available in order to service a client's needs.

Microsoft .NET and Java's Web Services Share a Similar Architecture

The .NET web services architecture is similar to J2EE 1.4. The .NET platform facilitates the construction of web-enabled applications for the enterprise. The web service container hosts the .NET Framework and contains .NET-managed components such as ASP.NET. One of the keys to interoperability in this environment is leveraging services provided by the Host Integration Server 2000 by facilitating legacy system integration with Microsoft's Message Queue (MSMQ), Microsoft Application Center Services, Microsoft Transaction Server (MTS), SQL Server 2000, and other such technologies.

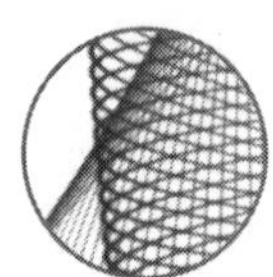

NOTE

Various .NET Enterprise Servers do not yet have full .NET Framework integration. However, developers can still interact with them and other products using COM+ interoperability.

Client tier components include web service technologies such as SOAP, UDDI, WSDL, Disco (Microsoft's proprietary methodology for discovering web services), and BizTalk Server. Web browsers and wireless devices access .NET-managed components via HTTP. The back-end systems include Microsoft's flagship database, SQL Server 2000.

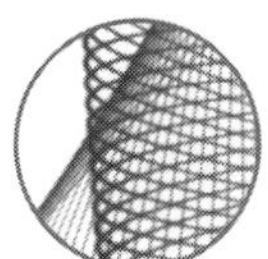

NOTE

Significantly, the current version of SQL Server 2000 and the pending release of Yukon recognize XML as a native language to the database.

Specifically, Microsoft supplies a SQL data provider to create a new instance of the Connection object and communicate directly with the server. This eliminates the necessity for setting up a server connection through a generic ODBC driver. Clients can also leverage the numerous benefits ADO .NET offers for database operations.

Within the Microsoft environment, the .NET Framework offers a unified API between all Framework targeted languages, courtesy of the Common Language Runtime (CLR). Through this runtime service, maintainable, sophisticated server applications receive support via a robust programming environment for classes, methods, interfaces, exception handling, just-in-time compilation, and garbage collection, without compromising server process integrity. Integration enforces secure access to system resources from user code via .NET Code Access Permissions in conjunction with Windows security.

Interoperability in the Enterprise

Interoperability between components exists on various levels. In other words, independent technologies residing within a platform such as J2EE can communicate with each other through interfaces designed expressly to allow for application integration. These technologies can also interact across platforms with diverse protocols on other platforms.

The web services container (for example, IBM's WebSphere Application Server) hosts the application. These containers consist of a number of components that manage transactions, persistence services (saving and storing data to your repositories or hard drive), and application security. The components include servlets, Java Server Pages, and Enterprise JavaBeans. The beans contain business logic and perform business processes when invoked. A container interacts with relational data stores by utilizing the JDBC API Data Access API, or optionally, SQL/J. With the inclusion of the new J2EE connectors, the container also provides connectivity to legacy systems. J2EE leverages SOAP, UDDI, WSDL, and ebXML web services through Java APIs for XML (JAX APIs).

Clients access J2EE applications through web services. Servlets accept web service requests, whereas applets access the Enterprise JavaBean layer through a technology called Internet Inter-ORB Protocol (IIOP).

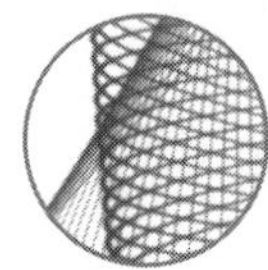

NOTE

J2EE uses RMI-IIOP and Java Naming and Directory Interface (JNDI) for access to remote objects. They can also leverage the much simpler lightweight Remote Procedure Call (RPC) request-response technology, provided the client is sending parameters rather than objects to the server. Also, RPCs usually interact with procedural applications, whereas RMI-IIOP provides true interoperability with applications written in non-Java languages.

Web browsers and wireless devices interact with Java Server Pages (JSPs), which provide HTML, XML, or WML user interfaces.

J2EE Servlets, Java Server Pages, and Web Services

Chapter 2 focuses on server-side servlets, Java Server Pages (JSPs), and web services. Servlets function as a mediator between client calls and JavaBeans or Enterprise JavaBeans (EJBs), and interaction with the data source and database. The Model, View, Controller (MVC) is the business development model selected for J2EE distributed enterprise application development in Chapters 2, 3, and 4.

Enterprise JavaBeans, Interfaces, and JDBC Persistence

Chapter 3 covers development of Enterprise JavaBeans, and how to employ the *home* and *remote* interfaces. A set of rules defines the path for creating EJBs. Java Database Connectivity is examined in detail and demonstrates how JNDI (Java Naming and Directory Interface) and RMI-IIOP are used to connect with repositories in a distributed environment.

RMI-IIOP, the JNDI, and Deployment Descriptors

Chapter 4 discusses the RMI technology and how it accesses remote objects across platforms. Deployment descriptors and XML play a significant role in deploying an enterprise-distributed application. Deployment of JAR files is also examined.

.NET Language Integration Components

The .NET Framework offers internal interoperability between programming languages supported by Microsoft. Three specification components, discussed in detail in Chapter 5, define the .NET Framework:

- Common Language Runtime (CLR)
- Common Type Specification (CTS)
- Common Language Specification (CLS)

Common Language Runtime Tasks

The CLR's primary task is to generate a .NET assembly as well as metadata that describes every data type residing within the assembly's binary. The CLR also identifies the assembly's version. This allows COM binaries and assemblies to coexist side by side without causing an exception. Once it has read the assembly's metadata, the Intermediate Language (IL) code compiles to a platform-specific set of application instructions.

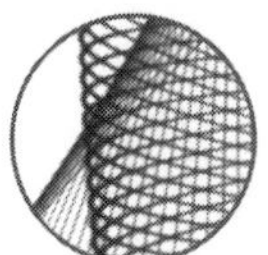

NOTE

This is similar to Java's method of compiling code into bytecode, a cross-platform intermediary. At runtime, the Java Runtime Environment (JRE) interprets the bytecode and then executes it.

All programming languages targeting the .NET Framework must adhere to base class libraries provided by the Framework in order to achieve interoperability. Additionally, the CLR supports cross-language exception handling and debugging.

The .NET assembly manifest includes a detailed assembly description as well as identifying a list of externally referenced assemblies required for application execution. The CLR generates both single-file assemblies and multi-file assemblies. The first type is a single binary, whereas the multi-file assembly contains more than one binary.

CTS Supports Data Type Interoperability

The *Type* refers to a collection of classes, interfaces, structures, delegates, and enumerations supported by the runtime engine. An alternative is to build custom data types and place them in a unique namespace, thereby eliminating name conflicts between assemblies. For those who are VB 6 developers, the Common Type System

Structure replaces VB 6.0 *Types*. VB 6.0 supported the *Type* keyword, allowing for the creation of user-defined types. However, in the .NET environment, *Structure* defines numeric types such as complex numbers. The CTS provides information on all data types supported by the runtime. Through reflection, the CTS describes how data types interact with each other.

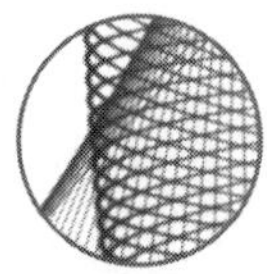

NOTE

Structures can implement any number of interfaces but cannot derive from other base types. Rather, they are sealed. (A sealed modifier prevents a derived class from further overriding a specified method.)

The Common Language Specification

The CLS provides a set of guidelines explaining rules that a .NET-aware compiler must follow in order for generated code to be eligible for support by the CLR. The CLS permits all languages supported by the .NET Framework to share Intermediate Language (IL) code.

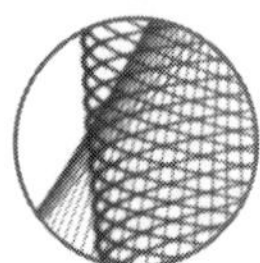

NOTE

Write your applications with CLS-compliant data types to ensure interoperability with other .NET-targeted languages.

Private variables declared within a function or subroutine can use nonsupported data types and still achieve interoperability.

ASP.NET Architecture

Web services offer the potential for achieving seamless interoperability across disparate type platforms, programming languages, and applications. ASP.NET, discussed in Chapter 6, facilitates web-based application development. The .NET Framework infrastructure provides the basic services supporting ASP.NET as well as Windows web form development, the new rich client development technology. An attractive feature of ASP.NET is the ability to create web applications in any .NET-compliant language, whereas the older ASP technology restricted developers to programming with scripting languages. Another ASP.NET benefit is code that is compiled rather than interpreted, which considerably improves performance. Although it is preferable to write web applications within the new Visual Studio .NET IDE, you can create an ASP.NET page in Notepad, save it with an .aspx extension, and let the ASP.NET runtime compile the page dynamically when called for the first time. When coding pages in Visual Basic .NET, C#, or J# .NET, the Microsoft .NET Framework comes bundled with command-line compilers for each individual language.

ASP.NET retains many older classic version features from its previous ASP version. Request and Response remains, as well as the Application, Session, and Server objects. You can still use the familiar `<SCRIPT RUNAT="Server">` or the `<% %>` ASP script delimiter. ASP and ASP.NET applications can run side by side, courtesy of the Common Language Runtime, which utilizes reflection to gather assembly information from the manifest rather than registering the application in the system registry. Referencing an assembly rather than the registry has eliminated DLL hell, something all developers have experienced.

Here are several new ASP.NET features:

- **Server controls** These controls offer convenient server-side programming. They map easily to HTML elements and can output HTML code designed especially for Internet browsers.
- **Web forms** Drag web forms onto a page and write code to facilitate interaction with objects, such as calling them.
- **Web services** Developers can provide services to clients and other developers. Web technology based on SOAP allows for cross-platform interoperability.
- **Configuration file improvements** ASP.NET uses a new methodology for storing XML-based configuration information for web applications. Typically, this information is stored in an IIS database.
- **Caching** ASP.NET has improved methods for enhancing performance by restricting database server and web server processing loads to a minimum.
- **State management improvement** ASP.NET offers support for persisting application state information in SQL Server. This technology also enables state management without using cookies.
- **Security** ASP.NET offers new authentication methods, improved code access security, and role-based authorization.

In order to receive full support from the .NET Framework, do the following:

- Web-enabled applications should not be tightly coupled to specific platforms or programming languages.

- Developers should leverage Internet-supported standards rather than creating custom solutions.
- Avoid solutions displaying dependencies on any particular component.
- Create web applications so they can accept any type of distributed infrastructure.
- Make sure the application uses data types compatible with both the Common Type Specification and Common Language Specification.

The .NET Framework facilitates web application development in more than one programming language. Just design your application to adhere to the .NET Framework specifications. ASP.NET utilizes HTTP and Simple Object Access Protocol (SOAP). During the design phase, determine how a client and server will communicate with each other. For example, consider a scenario where both client and server reside within the same LAN. The client will most likely interact with the server via HTTP and the Internet. This means the transport protocol should function equally well within both a LAN and Internet environment. HTTP and SMTP are excellent choices for web-enabled applications.

HTTP is popular because it is intrinsically stateless and not connection oriented. If a client and server lose their connection, rerouting ensuing calls to another server carries neither risk nor loss of information. CORBA and DCOM are not good candidates for web services because the developer must write extra code to preserve state, which is not a natural function of CORBA and DCOM. You cannot simply reroute a client's call. For this reason, HTTP is the platform-agnostic protocol of choice.

ASP.NET Preserves Application State Between Calls

Many times, it is important to preserve application state (units of data) across a series of requests between multiple users sharing the same application. Preserving state in web applications is complex and challenging because HTTP is stateless. Fortunately, ASP.NET preserves state by providing a collection of key-value pairs that developers can apply to their web-enabled applications. The .NET *HttpApplicationState* class supplies state storage by representing the class as an instance of the Application property of the *Page* class. Every ASP.NET page inherits from this class. ASP.NET facilitates the ability to add items to the collection using the Add() method as well as clearing items from the collections by applying the Clear() method. The Application object provides the Lock and Unlock attributes to ensure that only a single user can update the application state.

Frequently, it is important to provide metadata along with messages. HTTP offers a mechanism for including specific header information along with the message body embedded within a SOAP envelope. The framework lends support for processing SOAP header files. Set them with the CallContext object. Additionally, the framework provides two APIs, called GetHeaders and SetHeaders, to set and retrieve the SOAP headers for a specific call. The GetData and SetData static methods set and retrieve data transmitted within the SOAP request message. Specify routings by defining the destination for a message or placing a time restriction for message delivery. ASP.NET supports two encoding styles, Document and Remote Procedure Calls (RPCs). By default, Document facilitates text-based messages between client and server. In contrast, RPC is the protocol of choice for machine-based exchanges. Additionally, the ASP.NET Framework offers a mechanism called SOAP extensions. This technology allows you to modify the contents of SOAP messages transmitted between client and server.

ASP.NET provides a rich set of services for building web applications, including security control. Within the ASP.NET domain, a web service contains an .asmx file, and serves as an endpoint for the web service. A class contains the web service implementation and can reside within either an .asmx file or dynamic link library (DLL). The runtime locates and consumes information contained in the .asmx file in order to locate the class. Each individual .asmx page carries directions specifying a defined format and implementation location. Subsequently, the runtime utilizes this directive to bind the web services to a particular class. The page contains an attribute that defines the fully qualified name of the class implementing the web service.

Although there is potential for creating web services and achieving interoperability across different platforms, SOAP has its problems because incompatibilities exist between releases. As an increasing number of specifications attempt to resolve incompatibilities and other issues, interoperability challenges increase. Fortunately, the SOAPBuilders community has developed interoperability test labs and discussion forums to resolve numerous problems standing in the way.

ASP.NET and Web Services

ASP.NET and web services are a perfect match. Chapter 7 places special emphasis on how .NET and ASP.NET support web services.

Both J2EE 1.4 and .NET supply APIs for accessing diverse types of repositories. For example, .NET employs ADO.NET to access SQL Server data, whereas J2EE uses JDBC for storing and retrieving data in Oracle, DB2, and other repositories. Some problems come immediately to mind when employing these approaches:

- **Data storage location** Proprietary solutions must provide information on data location. Support must be provided for both parties on their respective platforms.
- **Performance issues** Serialization of data on the submitter's platform and deserialization of data on the recipient's end are problematic. The code must be updated on both platforms in the event either participant changes the format or protocol. Additionally, ensuring validity of data is another problem because data conversion is risky.

One of the problems facing Sun, Microsoft, and third-party vendors is the lack of a consistent industry-wide standard for multi-tiered, distributed software development.

Participating business members must agree on a common set of methods and a specified protocol before they can share processes, resources, and achieve true application integration. This scenario frequently exists when trading business partners use legacy systems dissimilar in methodology and protocol. They require a customized solution. A proprietary solution may work in one context, but not be reusable in another. Proprietary solutions are too expensive to maintain. This is the case with both ODMG's CORBA and Microsoft's DCOM. Both technologies represent attempts to provide methods for developing protocols to facilitate interoperability between incompatible technologies and platforms. Unfortunately, they are limited to applications and components installed within their respective platform's environment. Both technologies use tightly coupled proprietary protocols and are connection oriented, limiting their use as distributed services.

DCOM, CORBA's counterpart, is Microsoft's initiative to make legacy application and platform integration possible. It encounters the same problems as CORBA. Written expressly for Internet use, DCOM assumes that interacting applications on both ends are implemented as COM objects. DCOM allows an application to invoke COM components installed on different servers. Employing reusable components in a loosely coupled environment is a necessity when programming enterprise-distributed applications, something tightly coupled components do not allow. Unfortunately, clients face numerous barriers when communicating with the servers. Firewalls restrict the use of open ports, making calls in an open environment difficult.

Another problem DCOM displays is its connection-oriented architecture, thereby limiting its use as distributed services. DCOM cannot easily manage interruptions such as external calls from other clients. When a client makes calls via the Internet, it cannot control the connection. Although the connection may succeed, the next call may fail if an interruption occurs. Designing load-balanced connections between client and server is difficult. It is not possible to reroute a new request to another server. In order to maintain integrity of the currently processed transaction, the connection must be preserved. *Remoting* implies communication between objects existing within different application domains. This is true whether the objects reside on the same machine or exist on machines connected by a network. Recognizing the difficulties encountered using CORBA or DCOM, the developer should consider several criteria for accommodating Remote Procedure Calls:

- **Interoperability** Clients on other platforms must freely use a remote service.
- **Strongly typed interfaces** Data types transmitted to and from the client must map easily to data types defined by most procedural programming languages.
- **Support for any language** The implementation of a remote service should use existing Internet standards, thereby eliminating the need to reinvent the wheel. Java, Perl, C#, Visual Basic, and managed C++ must all have access to the web service.
- **Support for any distributed component infrastructure** Avoid tightly coupled components.

Interoperability Solutions from Third-Party Vendors

Chapter 8 takes a look at how third-party vendors, such as JNBridge, LLC, and Intrinsyc Software, are writing Java–Microsoft .NET interoperability solutions for heterogeneous environments. The vendors achieve this through various unique approaches. Recently, JNBridge released JNBridgePro to update its existing interop solution. It allows Java code to retain its cross-platform portability and conformance to standards written to accommodate the Java language. The following list itemizes the benefits of JNBridgePro version 1.3:

- Support for both J2SE and J2EE.
- Support for all major J2EE application servers, including BEA WebLogic, IBM WebSphere, iPlanet, Oracle9*i*, JBoss, and Borland Enterprise Server.
- Support for transactions managed by thread-true classes ensuring data integrity.
- Support for J# .NET.

- The 100 percent pure Java code residing on a Java Virtual Machine is available on all Java-enabled technology platforms.
- The option for passing objects by value or by reference enhances performance. JNBridge suggests various methods for increasing efficiency and performance, and they have made this information available at http://www.JNBridge.com/performance.htm.
- Direct mapping between J2EE and .NET classes guarantees better efficiency among distributed applications.
- Strong naming of proxy assemblies permits better security.

JNBridgePro distinguishes between service-level integration and class-level integration. *Service-level integration* is defined as Java components exposed to .NET as a collection of services. Service-level interoperability occurs when developers expose a component (set of individual classes) as a single service. This approach does not expose individual classes because the single component provides the basic functionality. In contrast, *class-level integration* means Java classes interact in cross-language development, just as .NET classes do. Exposing class interfaces facilitates class inheritance because individual classes are exposed rather than viewed as a single component containing more than one class. This allows developers to develop .NET code based on preexisting Java classes, thereby facilitating interoperability between the two platforms.

Although web services are becoming increasingly popular for moving large blocks of data via SOAP and HTTP, they carry considerable overhead because XML is text based. Additionally, web services do not support callbacks since callbacks allow Java code to call .NET code without having to modify Java code. Another disadvantage to using the traditional web services approach is that the web services do not support passing objects by reference.

Approaches to Java–Microsoft .NET Interoperability

Porting the complete .NET platform to Java and reimplementing the entire framework as a set of Java packages is less than satisfactory. Although this solution allows Java to call .NET APIs, it does not permit either Java or .NET classes to call each other. A solution to this problem requires that a cross-compiler translate all .NET source code or binary code. This translation allows all .NET classes and Java classes to interact seamlessly with each other.

Compiling Java Code to .NET Code

The chief advantage to compiling Java code to .NET code solution is cross-platform interoperability, primarily because it makes .NET code interoperable:

- **Cross-compilation** This solution results in no overhead for interplatform communication. Unfortunately, the API for Java must be reimplemented for .NET, an unsatisfactory solution.
- **Bridging** JNBridgePro manages communications between Java and .NET. Proxy classes provide access to the actual classes they represent. JNBridge prefers this because they bypass the conversion factor completely. As JNBridge explains, .NET classes run on a CLR, while Java classes run on JVM. Proxies created in .NET emulate the interfaces of corresponding Java classes. Microsoft .NET classes can inherit from a Java class by inheriting from the class's proxy, and vice versa.

Because Java runs on a JVM or J2EE platform, it does not require source code if the binary is available. JNBridgePro lends support for passing objects by value or by reference. Depending on context, if the Java runtime components are installed on a J2EE application server, the execution speed is faster than an RMI implementation. However, JNBridge explicitly states that if the runtime components are installed on the client side, there will be some overhead because SOAP and the HTTP protocol are required.

Visual Studio .NET includes Visual J# .NET, a development tool for Java language developers who want to develop applications on the .NET Framework. JNBridge has issued a comparison between JNBridgePro and J# .NET to demonstrate the versatility of JNBridgePro. Whereas J# .NET uses proprietary extensions to the Java language, JNBridgePro allows developers to create applications with standard Java. The JNBCore component of JNBridgePro allows applications to run on any JVM-supported platform, thereby permitting the Java segment of distributed applications to run in any environment. However, .NET classes interacting with Java code must run on the .NET platform.

Intrinsyc Software has much in common with JNBridge Software. They both recognize the need for providing interoperability between J2EE and .NET. Both offer the following features:

- Support for enterprise application servers, including WebSphere, BEA WebLogic, Oracle9*i*, Borland Enterprise Server, and JBoss

- Support for HTTP and TCP/IP protocols
- Support for SOAP
- Support for binary messages
- Client-activated and server-activated objects
- Invocation of methods on Java objects from the CLR
- Invocation of methods on CLR objects from Java
- Support for passing Java/CLR objects by reference and by value as parameters/return values
- Marshalling objects by value or by reference
- Callbacks

Intrinsyc's Ja.NET bridges the gap between Java and .NET. It is possible to write clients for Enterprise JavaBeans in a .NET language targeting the .NET Framework. Using any language hosted by the framework in conjunction with Ja.NET facilitates interoperability between Java objects or Entity JavaBeans. Additional features permit reusing components written in Java within the .NET environment or vice versa. In essence, Ja.NET Java components act as though they were Microsoft .NET, and vice versa, because Ja.NET leverages .NET remoting.

Ja.NET provides a tool called GenJava to generate a Java proxy for .NET components. For example, access to an Internet Information Server (IIS) component from Java is easy. The Janetor tool configures the Ja.NET runtime. Then, Java clients can use the proxies to access a remote CLR component as though it were a local Java component. The tool can also generate a .NET component bearing proxies for Enterprise JavaBeans client-side classes. Then, Janetor generates a web application archive (WAR) file containing all web server–deployable files. Another nice feature permits the CLR client written in any language to access Enterprise JavaBeans as though they were local CLR components.

Intrinsyc has another interop tool called J-Integra. It is a COM-Java tool employed for accessing ActiveX components as though they are Java objects. Conversely, accessing Java objects as though they are Microsoft .NET components is allowed. J-Integra works seamlessly with any Java Virtual Machine on any platform and requires no native code. Additionally, J-Integra speaks native DCOM and is layered over Remote Procedure Calls. J-Integra requires no JVM or additional software installs on the COM platform.

Best Practices, Design Patterns, Security, and Business Solutions

The final chapter, Chapter 9, discusses a variety of issues in enterprise application development. In Chapter 2, the MVC development model is introduced and discussed, and Chapter 9 explains why the MVC model is frequently used—it shields the user from the implementation, and the developer can modify the code without redesigning everything within the model.

Java Connector Architecture (JCA) Specification

The discussion on Java connectors is located in Appendix A. This information is in the appendix because the main emphasis of this book is on web services and distributed application interoperability. Enterprise Information Systems (EISs), Enterprise Application Integration (EAI), and legacy applications are not the focus in this text.

Connectors provide a set of contracts describing how EISs can interact with enterprise applications and servers. The contracts reside between J2EE applications and the EIS. The Java connectors also supply a client interface API for purposes of allowing J2EE application reusable components to access EISs in a heterogeneous environment.

A Java connector defines two contracts:

- A *system-level* specification between an application server and a resource adapter (a system library provides connectivity to a specified EIS)
- An *application contract* between an application server and a resource adapter

The system-level contract defines a standard methodology for use by developers to support connectivity to multiple EISs. This contract comprises three subcontracts:

- **Connection management contract** This allows an application server such as WebSphere to pool connections to an EIS. Pooling connections is significant when large numbers of clients request access to the underlying EIS.

- **Transaction management contract** This specifies the conditions under which the transaction manager supports transactions across Internet spaces.
- **Security contract** This enables tight security access to multiple EISs.

The application contract defines a client API that an application component utilizes for access to a specified EIS. For example, a client API for a relational database (JDBC) is an example of a resource adapter. Another example would be the Common Client Interface (CCI) API. The dataset could be IBM's DB2, or MySQL.

What Is Enterprise Application Integration?

Enterprise Application Integration (EAI) facilitates integration between legacy systems and applications. EAI enables enterprises to interoperate with new, emerging technologies and provides innovative solutions whereby enterprises can accommodate new methodologies and retain their existing systems. This eliminates the necessity for application and system redesign in addition to being cost effective.

As web services and business-to-business (B2B) applications continue to evolve and coalesce, XML, web services, and Java connectors are now commonplace in our digital, interconnected world. More frequently, new web-based applications are designed to plug into preexisting legacy systems and data-driven applications. In order to achieve interoperability, both off-the-shelf applications and in-house developed software systems must be compatible with J2EE specifications. Developers know how J2EE, in partnership with Java connectors, consists of a set of specifications and contracts between application servers and other enterprise servers and systems. When businesses start to merge their systems and applications, incompatibilities begin to emerge. However, a synergy between Java and XML exists. Therein lies the power of J2EE and Java's J2EE connector architecture.

It is important for enterprises to share both data and business processes without modifying their existing applications. One of the main challenges facing developers is how to deal with a lack of industry-wide standards. Before application integration can exist, business partners must agree on both a communications protocol and a set of specifications and contracts. Java connectors fulfill this role by presenting a methodology and standard set of specifications (contracts) that business partners can utilize to communicate with each other.

Many real-world examples of EAI exist, for example, Amazon.com, Fidelity Investments, and Dell—all successful business models. As their software architecture evolves, they are the supply chains. Their success demonstrates how they have recognized the need to integrate their applications in order to stay competitive. Java connectors answer this need.

As businesses succeed, new challenges arise. For example, web-driven integration places additional security requirements on the enterprise. An application server must be both transactional and secure in order to maintain data integrity. Additionally, as systems grow and interact, the applications must be scalable. Considering the large number of Internet users requesting web services both hourly and daily, both systems and applications must be able to respond to consumer demands in a flexible and timely fashion. Adhering to this fast evolving concept of EAI is imperative. Traditionally, legacy systems managed the front end and back end separately, whereas now, web-enabled applications integrate both front end and back end as a single entity. Integrating applications and systems is only one piece of the puzzle. Enterprise Information System integration also requires attention.

What Is an Enterprise Information System?

An *Enterprise Information System (EIS)* places emphasis on business processes and its data in order to run and grow its business. This comprises both the business process and information technology (IT) infrastructure. The enterprise processes include applications for inventory management, delivery fulfillment, financial accounting, and other such system management tasks. The process may also include security, transaction services, and load balancing.

EISs must also integrate their infrastructures with existing web services. This entails both the data and business process. In many cases, these are legacy applications and systems, databases, and so forth.

EIS Approaches Vary

EIS approaches to enterprise architectural design are many and varied, as the following list demonstrates:

- Two-tiered client-server architecture
- Application server–based approach
- Synchronous adapter approach
- Asynchronous adapter approach
- Message broker approach

Typically, a two-tiered client-server approach does not base its design on web services. The EIS provides an adapter that defines API for data access and basic component functionality. The adapter's task is mapping a reusable set of APIs to a vendor-specific EIS. Communications between adapter and EIS utilize a protocol applicable to the EIS. This may include support for transactions and security. A C library can function as an adapter, thereby enabling use of the Java Naming Interface (JNI) to access the library.

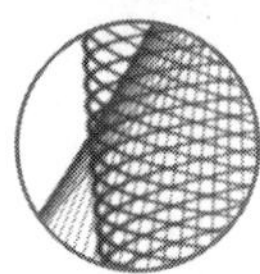

NOTE

There are numerous advantages to programming within the Java VM environment. However, because a huge investment exists in legacy code, the JNI interfaces permit invocation of binary code.

Employing the *application-based server* approach is particularly appropriate because it provides a platform for development, deployment, and maintainability for web-based enterprise applications. This is especially true for building multi-tiered applications. The application architecture contains three levels: a client tier, a middle tier, and an EIS tier. The middle tier consists of business logic components, whereas the EIS tier contains the low-level systems that run enterprise applications and access databases. The client tier offers different kinds of functionality. It can, for example, be a web browser–based HTML-type client.

The application server functions as a component-based business model. It can host either business components, web components, or both. Business components contain the Enterprise JavaBeans for processing business logic, whereas the web components represent reusable components relevant to providing presentation web services such as servlets and Java Server Pages. The application server provides support for the following services:

- Security
- Transaction support
- Distributed communications
- Database access
- Connection pooling
- Distributed transactions
- Load balancing and failover
- Asynchronous messaging
- XML
- Web protocols

Components deployed on application servers can also utilize *synchronous resource adapters* to connect and access EISs. (A *resource adapter* is a system library designed to provide connectivity and access to a specific EIS.) One drawback to synchronous calls is that once the client makes its call, it waits for a server to process and fulfill its request, thereby blocking all other activity until it receives the server's response.

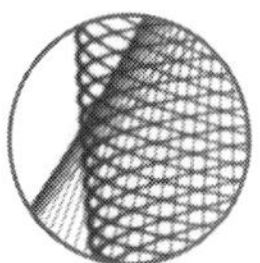

NOTE

It is imperative that the resource adapter runs within the application server's namespace. Additionally, application components can offer a Java Message Service (JMS) provider to a message broker for purposes of integrating with EISs based on asynchronous messaging.

Asynchronous message-based communication allows enterprise applications and EISs to interact. In this scenario, two formats exist: publish-subscribe and queue-based messaging. The case study is a valid candidate for receiving stock quotes and publishing updated stock prices to subscriber applications. Message *publishers* broadcast messages, while message *subscribers* register their interest in specified messages. A separate message facility functions as a facilitator for receiving and distributing messages to subscribers.

In queue-based communications, an application sends messages to a message queue. Subsequently, a receiver application receives messages from the same queue and distributes them to interested subscribers.

Case Study: International Finance Corporation Exchange (IFCE)

International Finance Corporation Exchange provides the following foreign currency exchange services for clients:

- Managing currency exchanges
- Ordering foreign currency
- Processing payment
- Checking availability of requested foreign currency at all local bank branches
- Providing convenient locations throughout the United States, Canada, United Kingdom, France, Germany, Switzerland, and Scandinavia

Buying and selling foreign cash and travelers checks based on current exchange rates is IFCE's sole business. International Finance Corporation Exchange services customers with and without accounts. For customers without an account, they provide cash-only services, whereas bank customers may use credit cards, personal checks, and other forms of payment. All branch offices receive individual country currency reports. These include information about country currency name, the denominations of both cash and travelers checks, and currency restrictions for each type of currency. Account executives and cashiers not only provide customers with currency information and exchange rates, but also place orders for currencies. Throughout the day, cashiers and account executives receive updates on individual foreign currency price quotes and currency availability at each branch. The system rejects requests for currencies in cash exceeding individual country restrictions. The following categories exist for fulfilling orders:

- Pending orders
- Processing orders
- Completed orders

Pending orders occur only if currency is not available in cash drawers or in local branches. The standard procedure for such an occurrence is procuring requested currencies from regional branches. The system notifies the customer via email when the currency is available at the user's local branch. An audit performed on a cashier's drawer completes the transaction. The system reconciles any discrepancy. If currencies exist beyond normal limits, the central branch stock receives the overage. A balance shortfall prompts a request for currency replenishment from central bank stock.

Product Perspective

The IFCE project will capture user inputs and visual outputs with added printing capabilities. Microsoft SQL Server 2000 and IBM's DB2 contain business logic and serve as repositories for data storage and retrieval. The project employs the web services XML, SOAP, WSDL, and UDDI for data transmission and communication with Credit Card Services for payment processing. Reuters and Bloomberg serve as data sources for transmitting updated currency quotes.

General Information

The following abbreviations are used in discussions of the case study:

- **IFCE** International Finance Corporation Exchange
- **MDC** Main data center
- **MTBF** Mean time between failure

The following assumptions and dependencies exist for our case study examples:

- The IFCE main data center resides in the United States.
- IFCE links to the National Credit Card Services for noncash transactions.
- IFCE points to the Federal Reserve System for up-to-the-minute currency rate information.
- Account and non-account customers interact with the system through a local branch.
- Each regional bank reserves the privilege of selecting the most cost-effective hardware for a particular location. This privilege comes with the understanding that the hardware meets some defined criteria such as X86 Intel compatibility, power redundancy, or acceptable MTBF.

The following software platforms and application servers are present in the system:

- Java 2 Enterprise Platform (J2EE 1.4)
- Java 2 SDK Version 1.4.0_02
- Microsoft Windows XP Professional
- Microsoft Windows 2000 Advanced Server 2000
- JNBridge Pro Enterprise Edition
- Microsoft .NET Framework V.1
- Microsoft Visual Studio .NET
- Apache Server 2.0
- Microsoft SQL Server 2000
- SQL Server 2000 for XML Version 3

Extensible Markup Language (XML), Simple Object Access Protocol (SOAP) Toolkit 3.0, WebService Description Language (WSDL), TCP/IP, and HTTP are employed for data transmission and exchange between different financial entities such as the National Credit Card Services and Reuters.

IFCE deals in the following currencies:

Abbreviation	Currency	Location
EUR	Euro	Europe
USD	U.S. dollar	United States
CAD	Canadian dollar	Canada
GBP	British pound	Great Britain
DEM	German mark	Germany
FRF	French franc	France
CHF	Swiss franc	Switzerland
NOK	Norwegian krone	Norway

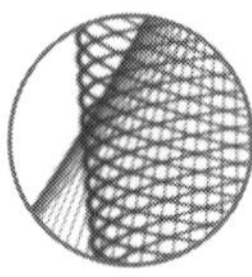

NOTE

The overall architecture for this case study will remain static. The application servers are modified when appropriate to demonstrate a particular technology.

CHAPTER

2

J2EE Servlets, Java Server Pages, and Web Services

IN THIS CHAPTER:

The J2EE Specification

Developing a J2EE Application

The MVC Business Development Model

Servlet Design

Java Server Pages

Initially, a developer examines various application development models and tools before deciding on a specific platform for developing a web services–centric distributed application. Usually, several criteria exist for developing an enterprise solution from the point of view of both application- and infrastructure-related issues.

Application-related criteria might be defined as follows:

- An e-commerce site should contain a shopping cart–type methodology that allows customers to interact with a service such as International Foreign Currency Exchange as well as to buy and sell foreign currency with a credit card, and use other options depending on whether they do or do not have an account.
- The site should provide a way to process and fulfill the customer's orders.
- The site should facilitate the ability to manage currency inventory and interface with suppliers, such as Bloomberg or Reuters.
- The site should provide customer notification functionality, such as email.

Infrastructure-related criteria determine how your application will run:

- Select a programming language, such as Visual Basic .NET, C, Perl, or Java.
- Choose an operating system, such as Windows 2000, Unix, or Linux.

Once the development model has been established, there are several enterprise-computing platforms to choose from, for example, .NET and Java's Enterprise Edition (J2EE).

.NET is the most recent architectural release from Microsoft for building distributed enterprise applications. This release contains many exciting new features, including multilanguage support. Currently, .NET supports applications written in 27 different languages. The applications compile to Microsoft Intermediate Language (MSIL) code. At runtime, MSIL executes to an application-specific runtime machine. The drawback to selecting this option is that .NET is platform dependent and only runs on the Windows operating system; nevertheless, it is a viable alternative to J2EE.

CORBA is a vendor-independent, language-neutral, operating-system-agnostic environment. CORBA applications compile to the Interface Definition Language (IDL). Four separate components exist: ORB, CORBAservices, CORBAfacilities, and the business application objects. The Object Request Broker (ORB) enables objects to submit requests and receive responses from local or remote objects. The CORBAservices component is made up of a collection of system-level services.

The CORBAfacilities consist of a number of application frameworks designed to be used directly by business objects. The business application objects encapsulate the business logic and utilize the CORBA services and frameworks. CORBA facilitates interoperability with applications written on other non-Java platforms, a major plus for application developers.

J2EE, the technology selected for application development in this and the subsequent two chapters, is the enterprise specification. Here are the three editions:

- Java 2 Platform, Micro Edition (J2ME) supports PDA application development, and access to cable services and other business devices with limited memory capabilities. In essence, J2ME facilitates the development of portable applications for the consumer market.
- Java 2 Platform, Standard Edition (J2SE) accommodates desktop applications that incorporate GUIs and other presentational components.
- Java 2 Platform, Enterprise Edition (J2EE) is the platform of choice for building mission-critical, server-side, distributed applications. It is component based and contains an extensive collection of interfaces that allow developers to implement those interfaces according to an application's specific requirements.

The Java 2 platforms are Java-language centric but present a platform-independent architecture, one that is portable and can run on Windows, Sun Solaris, IBM AIX, and HP HP/UX, to name only a few.

The J2EE Specification

In addition to defining the interfaces required for building an enterprise-distributed application, the best feature about the J2EE specification is that it describes *what* is required from vendor providers, but does not suggest *how* interfaces should be implemented. Therein lies the formula for success: flexibility, scalability, and making provisions for J2EE and the other specifications' growth by receiving input from other major third-party vendors and the entire Java community. J2EE is the obvious choice for developing secure distributed applications.

The J2EE's multicomponent infrastructure is defined as five functional technologies. The first three technologies listed here are discussed in this chapter, the last two in Chapter 9 and Appendix A:

- Communications
- Presentation

- Business applications
- Security (Chapter 9)
- Enterprise information system enabling technologies (Appendix A)

Table 2-1 lists the Java technologies, their acronyms, and current version.

J2EE Specification	Acronym	Version
Communication Technologies		
Java Message Service	JMS	1.0.2
Java Mail	JavaMail	1.2
JavaBean Activation Framework	JAF	1.0
Java Interface Definition Language (part of J2SE 1.3)	JavaIDL	1.3
Remote Method Invocation-Internet Inter-ORB Protocol	RMI-IIOP	1.0
Extensible Markup Language	XML	1.0
Java Naming and Directory Interface	JNDI	1.2
Java Authorization and Authentication Service	JAAS	1.0
Presentation		
Java servlet	Servlet	2.3
Java Server Pages	JSPs	1.2
Java API for XML Parsing	JAXP	1.1
Business Applications		
Java Database Connectivity Extension	JDBC	2.0
Enterprise JavaBeans	EJBs	2.0
Java Transaction API	JTA	1.0
Java Connector Architecture (Appendix A)	JCA or Connector	1.0

Table 2-1 *J2EE Technologies*

The Communication Technologies

The eight Java technologies that make up the communications component facilitate client-side business component communications. They are described briefly in the following sections.

Java Message Service (JMS) 1.0.2

Business enterprise applications require facilities for exchanging messages. JMS offers a unified-standard messaging API for supporting several different messaging formats, including XML. The JMS API supports two types of messages:

- Point-to-point
- Publish-subscribe

Java Mail (JavaMail) 1.2

Email pervades our professional and personal lives every day. An email is both platform and protocol agnostic.

JavaBean Activation Framework (JAF) 1.0.1

The JAF represents a "smart" application framework. It is capable of analyzing new data, abstracting the data's operations, and making them available to other application components. This is essential where new data formats are evolving. The JAF is somewhat comparable in functionality to Microsoft .NET's Framework v.1.1. *Frameworks* are where all application-centric functionality is defined and managed. As new technologies evolve, and as new data types and development languages emerge, they rely on the framework to support and manage the new technologies.

Java Interface Definition Language (JavaIDL) 1.3

Typically, business applications contain legacy applications that need to be integrated with newly created Java applications. The Java IDL is an Object Request Broker that comes bundled with the Java 2 Standard Edition (J2SE) and allows J2EE components to invoke requests on external CORBA objects using IIOP as the protocol.

Remote Method Invocation and Internet Inter-ORB Protocol (RMI-IIOP) 1.0

All interaction between components in a distributed environment consists of client calls to remote objects residing on different machines. RMI uses the Java Remote Method Protocol (JRMP) for communications with remote objects. RMI works only in a Java environment, whereas the Internet Inter-ORB protocol (IIOP) represents a CORBA-based standard, which is independent of the underlying protocol. CORBA is the glue that facilitates interoperability with non-Java and CORBA clients. Subsequently, RMI and IIOP were merged to provide cross-platform communications, a real win-win for developers.

Extensible Markup Language (XML)

XML is the markup language of choice for enabling businesses to define object behavior and provide data-format-independent representations in an extensible manner. XML facilitates transmission of data over the wire and penetrates corporate firewalls seamlessly.

This explains why XML is a core component of every enterprise application in both Java and .NET-oriented web services. For example, all distributed applications employ XML for creating web-config files, for creating deployment descriptors, and for providing metadata to applications via a methodology called *reflection.*

Java Naming and Directory Interface (JNDI) 1.2

In a distributed environment, services and objects require a standard, uniform, and transparent method for locating objects residing on different servers on a network. JNDI provides this methodology. It enables applications to access resources distributed throughout the network. J2EE uses JNDI and RMI-IIOP for finding the remote objects.

Java Authentication and Authorization Service (JAAS)

Security-enabling technologies facilitate J2EE application security implementations by providing authentication and authorization services to users before accessing enterprise resources. JAAS is the primary technology for supporting these services. A container such as WebSphere automatically provides them.

The Presentation Technologies

The three presentation-oriented technologies include Java servlets, Java Server Pages (JSPs), and Java API for XML Parsing (JAXP).

Java Servlets 2.3

Servlets represent server-side Java objects that function as an intermediary between web clients and other business objects (JavaBeans or Enterprise JavaBeans). The beans support the execution of business logic and interact with database objects. In essence, servlets implement the presentation logic and manage requests from web browsers to business components.

Java Server Pages (JSPs) 1.2

Java Server Pages are a servlet extension designed to construct dynamic presentation-oriented applications. A JSP page consists of directives and code fragments that provide functionality similar to ASP.NET pages. Once the servlet accepts a client request and delegates the requested task to a business logic–oriented JavaBean or EJB, it designates a Java Server Page for returning any requested business result to the client via HTTP and HTML. JSPs can interact with business components.

Java API for XML Parsing (JAXP) 1.1

JAXP is the technology employed for parsing and transforming XML documents into an appropriate format using the standard Java APIs. JAXP supports the Simple API for XML (SAX 2.0), Document Object Model (DOM), and XSLT, the XML designated transformation language.

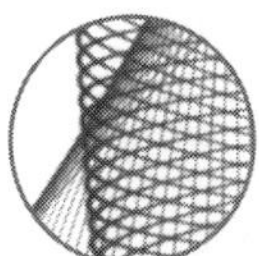

NOTE

For an extensive treatment of the DOM, SAX 2, and XSLT, refer to my book, XML: Language Mechanics and Applications *(Pearson Addison Wesley, 2003).*

The Business Application Technologies

The business applications are discussed separately in later chapters of the book (JCA and its specification are covered in Appendix A). Here, I will concentrate on Enterprise JavaBeans (EJBs) 2.0, which is the focal point for the J2EE platform.

J2EE is component centric, providing an extensive collection of reusable interfaces for developing distributed applications for the enterprise. The business application component consists of an EJB container that provides the runtime environment for Enterprise JavaBeans. The container (such as WebSphere or BEA's WebLogic) supports and implements tasks such as automatic garbage collection, memory management, application server start-up and shutdown services, user authentication and authorization, and other container-managed services. The various components are embedded with the container. Figure 2-1 displays a physical layout of a J2EE component container and its hosted standard protocols.

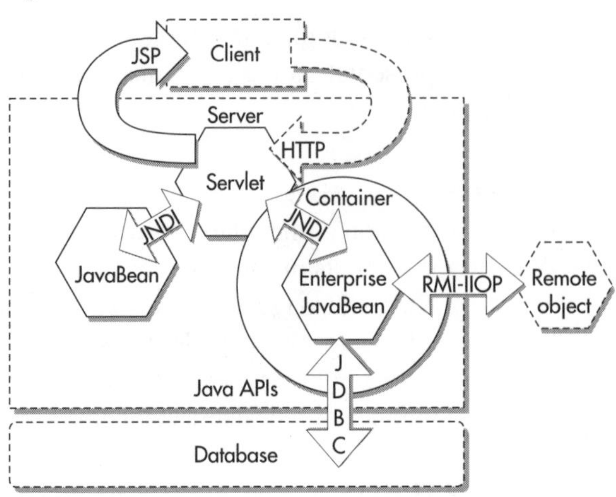

Figure 2-1 *A J2EE web container*

The Client Tier

A *rich client* can be both proprietary standalone Java applications and non-Java applications. Rich clients are capable of accessing both RDBMS and ERP services directly via JDBC connectors. They may also access the EJB web container residing within WebSphere or BEA's WebLogic. The web container contains both servlets and JSP pages that can access the Enterprise JavaBeans.

A *thin client* residing on a client tier supports the HTML container (browser), HTML, and applets. Thin clients access the web container via HTTP/HTTPS, XML, and HTML. They are also capable of using JDBC connectors to access a relational database and ERP applications.

The Presentation Tier

This tier hosts the web container that supports Java servlets, Java Server Pages, and Java API for XML Parsing, and the XSLT transformation services. These technologies employ both RMI-IIOP and vendor-proprietary protocols for accessing the remote objects.

The Business Tier

This tier hosts the EJB container and provides support for business transactions executed by EJBs. The business beans utilize the JDBC and JTC connectors to interact with an RDBMS and ERP business solution.

The Enterprise Information Services Tier

This tier facilitates cross-platform interaction with enterprise legacy systems. It separates data, including the database, enterprise resource planning, and mainframe transaction processing, from the business and client tiers. J2EE designates two technologies for providing portable access to the EIS tier: JDBC and the Connector technology.

Developing a J2EE Application

Developers must implement a strategy and design that offers flexibility, scalability, and reuse of application components. Application responsibilities include application start-up and shutdown, accessing external properties, error handling, and applying interface preferences.

Developing and deploying a J2EE application requires three distinct phases: development, assembly, and deployment. During development, web component providers and developers build components that encapsulate presentation logic. The reusable components are deployed as *WAR* files. EJB component developers create the EJB components that encapsulate business logic, and subsequently deploy them as EJB-JAR files.

In the assembly phase, an assembler puts together both the WAR and EJB-JAR files and merges them into an *EAR* file. The assembler is responsible for examining both types of files and customizes fields in the deployment descriptor file.

Finally, the deployer examines the EAR file, resolving any external dependencies, and configures the application to execute and deploy in an operational environment.

Several different development models exist within the Java environment. They include the time-tested traditional *client-server model*, which is similar to the web services client-server model. A client submits an HTML-based request to the server for processing server-side business logic. This process typically involves submitting updates, deletes, storing, and retrieving data to a relational database. Other traditional development models include the following:

- Remote presentation model
- Distributed logic model
- Remote data management model
- Distributed data management model

Web-Based Remote Presentation Model

In the remote presentation model, commonly referred to as the thin client paradigm, the only tool a client needs for communicating with the server is a web-enabled browser for submitting HTML-based requests via the HTTP transmission protocol to the server. This model represents a simple request-response solution. All business logic sits on the server. The user invokes the desired web service, which redirects the client request to a service provider. This development model offers the following benefits:

- All server-side components, including business logic, servlets, Java Server Pages, and data management components, reside on the server.
- The server-side controller (a servlet) provides dynamic content to a client.
- The only tool needed is a web browser.

Developers face minimal challenges when utilizing this model. They must deal with exception handling and noncompliant user agents—that is, the inconsistencies between Netscape, Mozilla, Opera, and Internet Explorer. For example, an HTML presentation in Internet Explorer differs from a servlet streaming HTML raw output to a Netscape browser. Presenting a consistent display to the client requires extensive testing and making provisions for outputting the correct formatted data in different browsers by querying a browser for its version, for example.

Figure 2-2 represents a client-side presentation model and demonstrates how it interacts with servlets, Java Server Pages, and their access to the business model layer, containing both traditional JavaBeans and Enterprise JavaBeans. The EJBs reside within a web container. The figure also shows how business beans access the data source layer.

The web server is a server-side program that invokes a servlet to manage and execute a server application. The servlet's chief task extends the functionality of a web server and functions in two separate capacities. It can stream HTML to a client as a response to its request, or it can serve as manager by receiving client requests and delegating the task to the appropriate JavaBean or Enterprise JavaBean for business logic processing. Once the task is complete, the servlet calls a Java Server Page to stream the results via HTML back to the client. The latter role is preferable because it separates presentation data from business logic.

Servlets interface with existing JavaBeans or Enterprise JavaBeans. In either case, they access databases or transactional systems, providing such core services as user authentication, authorization, and session management. The servlet's life cycle

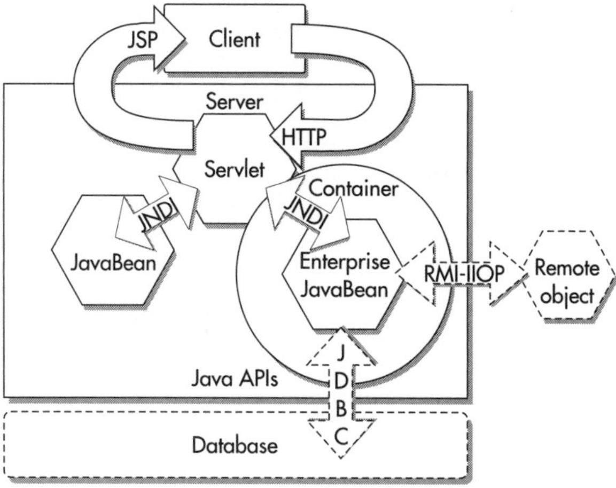

Figure 2-2 *Applying a filter to the J2EE's infrastructure*

defines the business process by loading the servlet into memory, executing the servlet, and finally, unloading it from memory. The client provides a URL that identifies a specific servlet in order to access the servlet and leverage its services.

Servlets offer excellent security by running within the context of a container such as WebSphere's application server. The container is responsible for providing low-level application services such as automated garbage collection, memory management, user authorization, and authentication.

Distributed Logic Application Model

Distributed logic business solutions divide the application roles between client and server. This solution offers application flexibility and features both Remote Procedure Calls (RPCs) and messaging services.

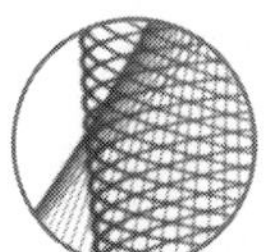

NOTE

The more traditional RPCs are invoked on procedural-type applications rather than on object-oriented web-based applications.

RPCs are synchronous, and using them has a significant drawback. Synchronous calls mean the calling program is blocked until the procedure returns a response. The Remote Method Invocation (RMI) solution allows developers to transmit messages remotely to an object. RMI includes a naming registry, which tracks instances and associates them with remote objects. Remote objects use the *activation service* to activate a server object at the behest of a client when it requests the service.

All distributed object protocols are built using the same architecture. This design makes an object residing on one computer look as though it sits on a local machine. This model contains three components: the business object, the stub, and the skeleton.

The *stub* resides on the client, whereas the *skeleton* exists on a middle layer that contains the business logic. Every business object contains matching stub and skeleton classes constructed specifically and designated for an identified business object. For example, a business object called Widget would have a matching Widget_Stub and a Widget_Skeleton. The following example demonstrates how a small distributed business model called WidgetServer implements the Widget interface:

```
public interface Widget {
   public int getSku()throws Throwable;
   public String getName()throws Throwable;
  }
```

The interface implementation contains both business logic and state for the Widget:

```
public class WidgetServer implements Widget {
  int sku;
  String name;
  public WidgetServer (String name, int sku){
// perform initialization here
     this.sku = sku;
     this.name = name;
  }
public int getSku() {
   return sku;2345  }
public String getName () {
   return name;
   }
}
```

The next step is providing a way to make the WidgetServer accessible to a remote client. The Widget_Stub and Widget_Skeleton are logical choices for this task. The Widget interface describes the concept of a Widget independent of the implementation. The WidgetServer implements the interface to support both business logic and state; the Widget_Stub implements the interface so it can represent the Widget object on the client and send requests to the skeleton, which forwards requests to the object. Here is the stub:

```
import java.io.ObjectOutputStream;
import java.io.ObjectInputStream;
import java.net.Socket;

public class Widget_Stub implements Widget {
  Socket socket;
  public Widget_Stub throws Throwable {
 /* Create a connection to the skeleton.
    Select either local host or the skeleton's IP address if it resides
    on a remote computer. */
     socket = new Socket("localhost" 9000):
public int getSku() throws Throwable {
   ObjectOutputStream oStr =
     new ObjectOutputStream(socket.getOutputStream());
   oStr.writeObject("sku");
   oStr.flush();
   ObjectInputStream inStr =
     new ObjectInputStream(socket.getInputStream());
   return inStr.readInt();
   }
 public String getName() throws Throwable  {
   ObjectOutputStream oStr =
       new ObjectOutputStream(socket.getOutputStream());
       oStr.writeObject("name");
       oStr.flush();
   ObjectInputStream inStr =
       new ObjectInputStream(socket.getInputStream());
   return (String)inStr.readObject();
   }
}
```

A String token is created and streamed to the skeleton when a method is invoked on the Widget_Stub. The token identifies the specific method invoked on the stub. Next, the skeleton parses the token and calls the corresponding method on the business object, and subsequently streams back the result. When the stub reads the skeleton's reply, it parses the value and returns it to the client. This process actually makes the stub look as though it were processing the request locally.

Here is the skeleton code:

```
import java.io.ObjectOutputStream;
import java.io.ObjectInputStream;
import java.net.Socket;
```

```
import java.net.ServerSocket;

public class Widget_Skeleton extends Thread {
   WidgetServer myServer;
   public Widget_Skeleton(WidgetServer server){
   //this establishes a reference to the object this skeleton wraps
   this.myServer = server;
}
   public void run(){
      try {
      //generate a server socket on port 9000
      ServerSocket servSocket = new ServerSocket(9000);
      Socket socket = servSocket.accept();
      while(socket != null){
         //create an input stream to receive requests from the stub
         /*remember, the skeleton sits on the middle tier and listens
           for requests from the stub */
       ObjectInputStream inStr =
           new ObjectInputStream(socket.getInputStream());
       //Read the next stub method request.
      String method = (String)inStr.readObject();
      if(method.equals ("sku")){
    int sku = myServer.getSku();
    ObjectOutputStream oStr =
       new ObjectOutputStream(socket.getOutputStream());
    //send results back to the stub
      oStr.writeInt(sku);
      oStr.flush();
  }else if(method.equals("name")){
   //invoke business method on the server object
   String name = myServer.getName();
   //Create an output stream to send return values to the stub
   ObjectOutputStream oStr =
      new ObjectOutputStream(socket.getOutputStream());
   //return the results to the stub
   oStr.writeObject(name);
   oStr.flush();
   }
  }
 }catch(Throwable t) {t.printStackTrace();System.exit(0);}
}
 public static void main(String args[]){
   WidgetServer widget = new WidgetServer("DLink100", 2345);
```

```
    Widget_Skeleton wSkel = new Widget_Skeleton(widget);
    wSkel.start();
    }
}
```

The Widget_Skeleton directs requests received from the stub to the business object, WidgetServer. The Widget_Skeleton functions solely as a listener awaiting stub requests. When it receives a request, the skeleton parses it and delegates the task to the corresponding method on the WidgetServer. The business object's return value is streamed back to the stub, returning the result and making it look as though it were processed locally rather than remotely.

The final step in describing the roles of both stub and skeleton is creating a client that utilizes the Widget:

```
public class WidgetClient {
    public static void main(String [] args){
      try {
          Widget widget = new Widget_Stub():
          int sku = widget.getSku();
          String name = getName();
          System.out.println(name+" is "+sku+ " hub product ");
          }catch(Throwable t ) {t.printStackTrace();}
      }
}
```

The client application demonstrates how the stub is used on a client machine. Note how the client is unaware that the Widget business object is in reality a network proxy to the business object on the middle tier.

RMI represents the basis for distributed object systems. Its primary task is making distributed objects *location transparent.* This means a server's actual object location is always unknown to the client.

Summarizing the functionality for this example, the developer creates an interface that extends the *java.rmi.Remote interface.* This interface describes all remote methods that a client object can invoke. Then, the developer creates a server class to implement the newly declared subtype that extends the java.rmi.Remote interface. The final step involves using the RMI compiler (rmic) to accept the subtype of the remote interface as an input parameter and generate both a client stub class and server-side skeleton class, in addition to creating object instances of them. These two classes then interact with the RMI reference layer.

Remote Data Management Model

The remote data management model provides a consistent methodology for clients to access remote databases sitting on networked servers distributed over the Internet. The Java Database Connectivity (JDBC) API offers a shared interface to various relational dataset implementations. The JDBC API provides the following benefits:

- Retrieve and scroll through query results returned by a server.
- Treat database results as JavaBeans.
- Manage and pool database connections.
- Persist objects in relational databases.
- Forward SQL statements to the database server.

The following steps are required for establishing a database connection and manipulating data:

- Initialize and allocate drivers and database connections.
- Create and prepare statements for database execution.
- Navigate and process query results.
- Perform any cleanup tasks before disconnecting from the data source.

Distributed Data Management Model

Replication is the key to distributed data processing. This business solution requires data management on both client and server. The administrator must synchronize both client and server databases. The drawback to this scenario is that it is a proprietary solution. Concurrency is also an issue.

The MVC Business Development Model

Recall from Chapter 1 that the MVC model consists of three kinds of objects: the *model* is the application object, the *view* represents the screen presentation, and the *controller* determines the manner in which the user interface responds to user interaction. The main benefit derived from employing this model is the way MVC decouples views and models by establishing a *subscribe-notify protocol* between them.

A view must always reflect the model's state. For example, if the model's data changes, the modifications are posted back to views that are dependent on the model's state. After receiving a notification of change, the views must update themselves.

MVC allows you to alter the way a view reacts to user input without changing its visual presentation. For example, it encapsulates the response mechanism for a controller object by enabling the principle of substitution, thereby allowing the developer to create a new controller as a variation on an existing one. This is consistent with the object-oriented concept of an interface. As long as the developer adheres to an interface's signature, one object instance may be replaced with another object instance without altering the overall structure.

In a J2EE component-based set of interfaces, the servlet is synonymous with the MVC controller object. When the servlet receives a client request, it determines whether a JavaBean, an Enterprise JavaBean, or other object is required to fulfill the client's request. Once this determination is made, the servlet directs a specific object to execute the business logic and encapsulate the results. Subsequently, the servlet directs a Java Server Page to deliver the content back to the client.

The MVC model is consistent with the object-oriented model. The controller component consists of servlets that mediate among various parts of the view by managing navigation and error-reporting tasks.

VC Layering

Traditionally, the MVC model embraces the concept of *layering* and divides the functionality of an application into separate vertically stacked layers. Each layer interacts only with the layer beneath it. The presentation layer objects interact with domain objects, the layer where the business logic resides. The data access layer objects access repositories at the request of a domain object. The layered structure concept was designed to incorporate a decoupled design that involves the appropriate indirection in support of layer substitution.

The MVC concept represents a component-based set of interfaces. Interfaces are designed to support the object-oriented concept of object substitution.

Presentation Layer

This layer consists of objects defined to accept user input and present application output. They include GUI objects, HTML, Java Server Pages, and servlets that act as a controller. They may also include applets, using the Abstract Windowing Toolkit (AWT) or Swing.

Controller/Mediator Layer

The MVC concept of layering incorporates the *mediator* design pattern. The controller object implements the mediator design pattern. (For a complete description of this pattern, refer to *Design Patterns*, by Gamma, Erich, et al.; Addison-Wesley, 1996.) The mediator pattern ensures that domain-specific logic is not bundled with presentation object methods, but rather is obtained from a mediator-referenced domain object. The purpose of employing the mediator pattern is to be able to define an object that encapsulates how a collection of objects interact with each other. *Loose coupling* is the mechanism that prevents objects from referencing each other directly. A mediator serves as an intermediary to keep objects separate. In fact, child objects only know the mediator, but not other objects. Only the mediator knows its child objects.

The Servlet's Role A servlet is a Java class that extends the functionality of a web server. The web server loads a servlet into memory where it intercepts client browser–based requests. Once the servlet parses the object, it creates a new thread and executes code within the thread. The servlet plays many interesting roles. Although the servlet is capable of generating raw HTML tags to the PrintWriter, it facilitates the production of dynamic HTML content by providing an entry point (the servlet) into the server-side Java Virtual Machine through a web server. Servlets also provide session management, user authentication, and authorization. More importantly, servlets function as an MVC controller to provide a convenient way of storing user-defined application session objects. Servlets are covered in detail a little later in the chapter.

Domain Layer

The domain layer implements objects as standard Java classes and interacts with traditional JavaBeans. Another option exists for developers, namely, the ability to implement domain objects as Enterprise JavaBeans. The advantage here lies in making distribution easier, receiving transaction support, and facilitating object persistence.

Data Mapping Layer

A major obstacle facing developers is the problem of mapping data to a relational database. The added mapping layer facilitates moving data from domain objects to back-end data sources and vice versa. Although this action requires some careful planning, the developer has the option of taking advantage of the automatic services provided by a container such as WebSphere. The EJB container in WebSphere includes an intuitive user interface for supporting data persistence for EJBs.

Data Source Layer

Sun offers the JDBC (Java Database Connectivity) API for accessing data stores such as DB2, Oracle9*i*, and Sybase.

EJB containers perform mapping and persistence operations for storing and retrieving data. Servlets and JavaBeans may also use JDBC directly for accessing enterprise data.

Servlet Design

A servlet represents a Java class running within a Java Virtual Machine (JVM) related to a web server. Servlets interact with a collection of JavaBeans or Enterprise JavaBeans (EJBs) to execute any described business logic. As previously stated, servlets add functionality by providing session management and other related functions such as user authentication and authorization. The following topics provide a framework for understanding a servlet's responsibilities:

- HTTP essentials
- Servlet life cycle
- Servlet primary classes

HTTP and Servlets

HTTP, which provides the basic services for the Web, is built on the TCIP/IP protocol and is employed for application-level data transmission. One of the primary beneficial characteristics of HTTP is its *request-response protocol*. It is the transmission protocol of choice because it facilitates transmission of data through corporate firewalls. It also allows requests and responses to exist as MIME-like messages.

From an application-level perspective, HTTP has its drawbacks. It is both stateless and connectionless. It is based on a web server and has the following format: it receives client requests and sends a response back to the client. It is important to understand that neither the client nor server retains any state information whatsoever. Incidentally, servlets take over where HTTP is unable to preserve state. Servlets support session state. A client can be one of the following:

- A web-enabled browser
- A Java applet

- Another web server
- Another web-enabled application

A servlet is accessed through a Universal Resource Locator (URL). A URL is specific to the HTTP scheme, but a URN is not. URLs exist as simple formatted strings that identify an object via name, location, or any other resource characteristic. HTTP does not place any limitations on a URL's length. For example, in order to access a specified HTML page such as index.html residing on a web server such as *www.dps.com*, the absolute URL would be *http://www.dps.com/index.html.* The basic format for the URL is as follows:

```
protocol://hostname<:port>/identifiers
```

Servlets make extensive us of GET and POST requests. Let's examine them. A GET request can be made in several ways:

- Enter a URL in the URL line of a web browser.
- Click on a link that appears inside an HTML page, for example, <A HREF=url . . .>.
- Select a form button to submit your request. The form would specify a GET method with the following syntax: <FORM method=GET action= url…>. After receiving a client request, the web server maps it to a file residing on a web server file system (for example, *C:\www.html\index.html*) and then responds by returning the payload of that file to the browser. This transaction involves exactly one connection to the web server and a single response back to the client.

The POST round-trip request is as follows: Let's say the request is for the URL *http://webserver/servlet/Register.* The user clicks the form's button designated specifically for accessing a servlet in the format <FORM method=POST action=url…>. After receiving the request, the web server maps it to the servlet's class file residing on a web server, or servlet engine file system such as *C:\WebSphere\AppServerf\servlets\Register.Class.* The web server then runs the servlet. Next, the server or servlet engine parses the posted data, utilizing a second connection and performing the requested POST operation. Finally, the servlet engine or web browser responds with a result. This operation requires two separate connections to the web server with an immediate response.

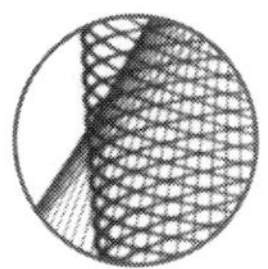

NOTE

Sun Microsystems provides a reference implementation for the Java Servlet API named Tomcat. You can download Tomcat from http://www.apache.org. *IBM's VisualAge for Java supports servlet testing. It contains the WebSphere Test Environment (WTE), a servlet development and test environment based on IBM's WebSphere. The WTE can be used in VisualAge for Java instead of Tomcat for developing and testing servlets.*

The Servlet Life Cycle

The process of loading a servlet into memory, executing the servlet, and then unloading the servlet from memory is the servlet life cycle. For example, a servlet is accessed by typing the following URL: **http://localhost/servlet/GreetingsServlet**. Typing the keyword **servlet** in the URL path informs the web server that the client request is designated for a particular servlet and not an HTML page.

Creating a servlet requires the following steps:

- Create a GenericServlet subclass, essentially the class *javax.servlet.http.HttpServlet*, meaning you invoke the servlet via HTTP.
- Supply the minimum doGet() or a doPost() method to make the servlet workable. When the servlet is requested for the first time, the web server asks the servlet engine to load the designated server class and all of its methods into memory on the servlet engine node.
- Pass control to the init() method. Note that GenericServlet provides a default empty init() method. Here is where you perform any initialization tasks, such as connecting to a database. The init() method receives only one initial call, which occurs immediately after the servlet is loaded into memory. The following code demonstrates how to write the init() method:

```
public void init(javax.servlet.ServletConfig config) throws ServletException
{super.init (config);
// place your code here to perform any initialization tasks
}
```

Each time a servlet is called, a new thread is created, and that thread executes over the service() method.

- Override the service() method in order to perform any work. This method is where a servlet performs its multifarious tasks. Because the service() method is always executed within a new thread, make sure that everything executed within this method is reentrant (thread safe).

- Finally, call the destroy() method when the web server senses that the servlet's tasks are complete. The destroy() method unloads the servlet from memory. Typically, tasks such as closing database connections, closing files, and other administrative tasks are performed in this context.

A Small Servlet

Every text presents a HelloWorld example. Why display a complex example when simplicity is both more efficient and more informative? So let's plunge in and examine this servlet:

```
/**
 *This class is an example servlet
*/
import java.io.*;
import javax.servlet.*;
import javax.servlet.http.*;

public class HelloServlet extends HttpServlet{
/**
 *this method handles an HTTP GET request and outputs
 *HTTP to print "Hello World" to the browser
*/
public void doGet(HttpServletRequest req, HttpServletResponse res)
throws ServletException, IOException{
   PrintWriter out = null;
   res.setContentType("text/html");
   out.println("<html>");
   out.println("<head><title>A Servlet example</title></head>");
   out.println("<body>");
   out.println("Hello World!");
   out.println("</body>");
   out.println("</html>");
   }
}
```

Assuming the localhost is properly defined, and the web server and application server are properly configured, type the following code in your browser: **http://localhost/servlet/HelloServlet**.

The servlet class extends the class *javax.servlet.http.HttpServlet*. The main point to remember here is that HTTP servlets typically handle GET and POST requests. The HttpServlet subclasses override either the doPost() or doGet() method. In our example, we're overriding the doGet() method.

An object that implements the HttpServletResponse() method achieves the following:

- Procures a PrintWriter for output with getWriter(). This is preferable because PrintWriter performs like an output stream. An alternative to this is using the getOutputStream().
- Sets the HTTP header values with setHeader(String, String). The chief benefit of this method is that it enables the developer to disable both browser and server page caching for a response page.
- Redirects the browser to a different page using the following directive: sendRedirect(String).
- Sets the content type with setContentType(String).

Servlet Interfaces and Classes

The Java Servlet API 2.1 offers developers an extensive set of classes and interfaces with which to develop web applications. APIs are contained within three distinct packages. The developer is required to supply implementations for these interfaces:

- javax.servlet
- javax.servlet.http
- javax.servlet.jsp

The javax.servlet Package

The javax.servlet package represents a collection of basic APIs for servlets. However, they are not bound to any particular schema or protocol that defines how they should be implemented. Table 2-2 lists the classes and interfaces in the javax.servlet package.

Servlet Interface The Servlet interface defines the essential APIs for servlets that include the init(), service(), and destroy() methods.

Classes	Interfaces
GenericServlet	RequestDispatcher
ServletException	Servlet
ServletInputStream	ServletConfig
ServletOutputStream	ServletContext
UnavailableException	ServletRequest ServletResponse SingleThreadModel

Table 2-2 *Classes and Interfaces in the javax.servlet Package*

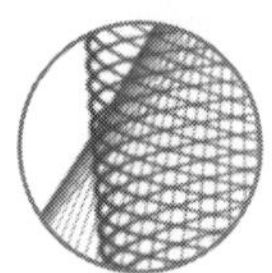

NOTE

All servlets implement this interface by subclassing the GenericServlet class or, alternatively, the HttpServlet class.

ServletContext Interface For each servlet, a context is required because communication must be established with a servlet in a *nonrequest-specific* manner. Requirements for this include locating path information, accessing different servlets running on a web server, and writing to the server log file.

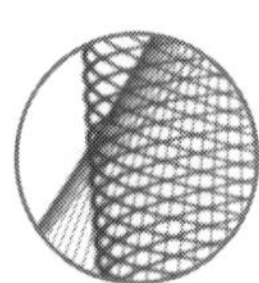

NOTE

If a server supports multiple virtual hosts, the ServletContext object must be unique. The ServletContext object resides within the ServletConfig object. You can access this object by employing the Servlet.getServletConfig() method.

GenericServlet Class This class is abstract and provides the primary behavior for the Servlet interface. This class also implements the ServletConfig interface, thereby offering a convenient way to access the ServletContext and initialization parameters. It also implements the init() and destroy() methods. All subclasses should override both the init() method and destroy() method and call the super-class implementation for the GenericServlet class.

ServletRequest Interface The ServletRequest interface prescribes an object as the first parameter passed in a call to the service() method for a GenericServlet. This provides the servlet with metadata about the request originating from a client call. It includes data, parameter name, values, attributes, and an input stream. For example, the HttpServletRequest provides HTTP data. Furthermore, a servlet request represents a MIME body request. Conversely, the response provides a MIME body response. It is always wise to use the getReader() method when the body contains text. If the body contains binary data, use the getInputStream() method.

ServletResponse Interface This interface defines an object used in transmitting MIME-encoded data from the servlet to a client. The servlet engine creates a ServletResponse object and transmits it as an argument in the servlet's service method. Always call the SetContentType() method before calling either the getWriter() or the getOutputStream() method.

RequestDispatcher Interface This interface defines an object that receives requests from a client and forwards them to a resource, such as a servlet, an HTML file, or a JSP file on the server. The servlet engine creates a RequestDispatcher object, which wraps a server resource residing on a specified path. The intent is wrapping servlets. However, a servlet engine can create RequestDispatcher objects to wrap any type of repository resource.

A RequestDispatcher is obtained from the ServletContext by utilizing the ServletContext.getRequestDispatcher("resource-name"). Once the dispatcher is obtained, a servlet can forward the request to the named resource in getRequestDispatcher(). An alternative is to use RequestDispatcher() for sending a request to a Java Server Page for display.

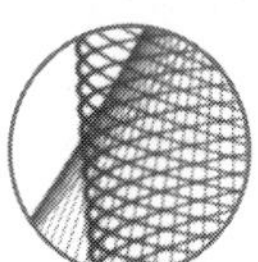

NOTE

The RequestDispatcher() interface provides a convenient way for servlets to communicate among themselves.

The javax.servlet.http Package

This package hosts the APIs for servlets used as servlets. Table 2-3 lists the classes and interfaces in the javax.servlet.http package.

Classes	Interfaces
Cookie	HttpServletRequest
HttpServlet	HttpServletResponse
HttpSessionBindingEvent	HttpSession
HttpUtils	HttpSessionBindingListener
NoBodyOutputStream	HttpSessionContext
NoBodyResponse	n/a

Table 2-3 *Classes and Interfaces in the javax.servlet.http Package*

HttpServlet Class The GenericServlet provides the basic behavior for a servlet. However, a separate mechanism for processing HTTP requests is essential. The HttpServlet, a subclass of GenericServlet, provides the additional behavior for HTTP requests. The GET and POST methods are most commonly used. HttpServlet includes the doGet() and doPost() methods for handling both HTTP GET and HTTP POST.

When an HttpServlet is requested via a URL, the service() method examines the HTTP header and determines which HTTP method to invoke. The programmer must provide overrides for doGet() and doPost() in order to achieve the servlet's requested tasks. Both the service() and do() methods require two parameters, which represent instances of the HttpServletRequest and HttpServletResponse interfaces.

These versions of the request and response objects contain HTTP-specific items such as cookies, headers, and sessions.

HttpServletRequest Interface This interface extends the ServletRequest interface by defining a request object associated with the HTTP request. Special items included in this category are authentication through the getAuth() method, the list of cookies through the getCookies() method, and the query string through the getQueryString() method. The servlet engine implements this interface.

HttpServletResponse Interface This interface extends the ServletResponse interface and defines a response object corresponding with an HTTP response. This interface permits the servlet's service() method both to access and set HTTP headers and to return data (HTML) to a client.

HttpSession Interface This interface establishes an application-level connection between the web browser and the web server. Utilizing sessions enables the developer to store session-specific data in the servlet engine. The session persists for a specific time period spanning more than one connection or page request from the user. Typically, a session corresponds to a single user who may visit the same site repeatedly. The server can maintain a session by leveraging the services of a cookie or by rewriting URLs.

HttpUtils Class This interface represents a concrete class providing a collection of methods that a developer can use when creating HttpServlet subclasses. The getRequestURI() method, a static method, facilitates the ability to reconstruct the request URI for use by the server.

Nonstatic methods include parsePostData(), for parsing the parameters of a POST, and parseQueryString(), for parsing a GET request's query string.

Managing Session State with Servlets

As a developer, one of the biggest challenges is maintaining an identity with users as they revisit your site multiple times. The information collected during these visits is called *session data.* Making the distinction between session data and *transaction data* is easy. Session data is temporary, whereas transaction data is persisted in a repository such as DB2 or Oracle. You can easily convert session data to transaction data by using an interface provided by the Java Servlet API. As each session is created, it is assigned a unique identifier. The ID is subsequently associated with the user and becomes the key ultimately used for locating the proper session for subsequent visits.

The HttpSession interface facilitates both storing and retrieving application state information. To begin, an instance of the HttpSession is procured through the HttpServletRequest interface. The required interface method is the HttpSession getSession(boolean). The Boolean argument, if determined to be true, creates a new session. Many times, it is desirable to ascertain whether the HttpSession returned was in fact a newly created session or one previously created. Accomplish this by using the HttpSession interface method boolean isNew(). It returns a Boolean to indicate whether the sessionID was returned in the current HttpServletRequest object. It is also possible to discard a session by using the void invalidate() method.

An alternative to storing key-value pairs is placing objects in a session instance by employing the void putValue(String, Object) method and retrieving objects from the current session by using the Object getValue(String).

Here is an example demonstrating how to employ these methods. International Foreign Currency Exchange maintains a staff of employees for implementing the business model. In this example, IFCE has designed an Employee Editor set of servlets to facilitate changing employee attributes. The user first enters an employee ID on an HTML page, followed by another HTML page displaying the current values of the employee's attributes. They are modifiable and should be resubmitted with new values. The first servlet called is the DisplayEmployeeValues, where an employee ID is retrieved.

```
public void doPost(HttpServletRequest request,
                   HttpServletResponse response)
                   throws ServletException, IOException{
String id=request.getPararameter("id");
Employee emp = Employee.getEmployeeFor(id);
```

```
HttpSession session = request.getSession(true);
/*check to see if the session is new.
If not true, invalidate the current session and create a new session */
if(session.isNew()==false){
  session.invalidate();
  session=request.getSession(true);
}
session.putValue("employee",emp);
}
```

Assume the user has decided to submit the changes. Clicking the Submit button invokes another servlet to process the modifications and persist any data modifications.

```
public void doPost(
  HttpServletRequest request,
  HttpServletResponse response
  )throws ServletException, IOException{
HttpSession session =request.getSession(false);
if(session== null)
   handleError();
else {
   Employee emp =(Employee)session.getValue("employee");
   if(emp != null)
   {
     session.invalidate();
    }
   //send a response
}
```

The preceding example demonstrates how to procure an existing session from the request object. The *false* parameter in the getSession() method specifies *not* to create a new session if one is not located in the request object. If so, a null is returned. The getValue() method return type is Object, so the value must be cast to the appropriate type before the value is usable.

Determining How a Session Is Located

When the HttpServletRequest.getSession() method is invoked, the application server ascertains which HttpSession instance is associated with the current user by assigning a session identifier. This identifier is stored in a specified cookie in the user's browser.

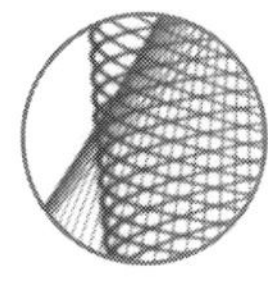

NOTE

Session cookies are not in permanent storage and expire when the browser closes. An application server's JVM initially holds the HttpSession in memory. Only the identifier is stored in the client's browser.

As long as cookies are enabled in a client's browser, they serve as the conduit for transporting the session identifier between browser and server. On the other hand, if cookies are not available, *URL rewriting* is a viable option. In order to accomplish this, employ the encodeURL() or encodeRedirectURL() method from the HTTPResponse interface. The former method appends the unique session ID to the URL in any links generated by your servlet. For example, when a user invokes a servlet using the modified URL, the server strips the ancillary information from the URL and utilizes it as the new session ID for retrieving the session data.

Another high-scale solution for persisting session data is storing HttpSessions in a third-tier relational database shared by multiple JVMs. Here is how it works. Each HttpSession represents a transaction in a third-tier relational database. The transaction begins with a call to the HttpServletRequest.getSession(). The session is terminated when either the servlet's service() or sync() method is called on the class that implements HttpSession in a container such as WebSphere.

Java Server Pages

JSPs represent a Java-based technology that allows the development of dynamic web sites. A major strength of JSPs is that they allow programmers to produce dynamic content using an HTML-like syntax. A JSP container is similar to a servlet container, except that it provides support specifically for JSPs.

Java Server Pages not only offer developers automatic servlet generation, but also eliminate the need for manually writing doGet() and doPost() methods. Additionally, the JSP model separates presentation tasks from back-end tasks.

The JSP Life Cycle

JSPs begin life as a text file and are translated to servlets. The translation involves conversion of JSP source code into servlet source code by the JSP container. This process is commonly referred to as *compilation* of a JSP page into a servlet.

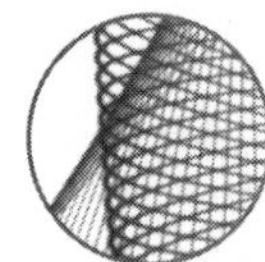

NOTE

Don't confuse the process of converting JSP source code to servlet source code with compilation of Java code into bytecode.

After the conversion process is complete, the servlet is subsequently compiled. Because JSPs are converted to servlets, they inherit a servlet's dependence on the request-response model. When the JSP container translates the body of a JSP page into a servlet, it creates a new class that implements the *javax.servlet.Servlet interface*. This new class contains a method called _jspService() and is constructed from the body of a JSP page. In addition, the container bases the newly generated class on a class whose service() method calls _jspService(). A JSP page is translated to a method that maps requests to responses based on the JSP's page contents.

How are contents translated? The simplest part of the JSP source file is translating template text. This means translation of the page segment that does not contain page directives, a scripting element, an action, or anything else related directly to a JSP page. Template text can be HTML or XML. For example, a simple text could be converted into a call that looks like the following. Initially:

```
<p>Template plain Text</p>
```

is translated to this:

```
out.println("<p>Template plain text</p>");
```

Scripting expressions are easy to translate into servlets. This is because the Java code is translated as is with no modification.

Page Translation and Execution

Processing JSP pages consists of two phases, the translation phase followed by the runtime phase. First, the JSP page is converted to a servlet. The second phase occurs when the container receives a request. Then, the servlet runs.

Execution Implications

The translation occurs only when required. For example, if the JSP page is not altered in any way, there is no justification for generating a new servlet. On the other hand, if the page is modified, a new translation is required.

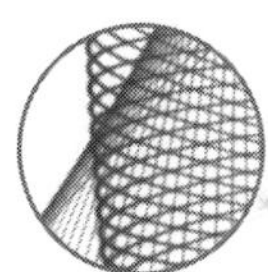

NOTE

JSP also supports precompilation of JSP pages into servlets. This method enhances performance by avoiding the time-consuming compilation of a page when first requested.

JSP Specialized Tags

Table 2-4 presents several JSP tags.

The JSP specification also includes standard tags for bean use. The *usebean* directive creates an instance of a specific JavaBean class. If an instance is present, it is retrieved; otherwise, it is created. The *setProperty* and *getProperty* tags allow you to manipulate properties of a given bean. In summary, most Java code becomes part of the servlet's service() method when the JSP page is compiled to a servlet. However, this does not include code contained within declaration tags. The service() method is always called whenever a client performs a GET or POST operation.

Syntax	Description
<%code fragment%>	A *scriptlet tag* contains a code fragment and one or more lines of code. No method needs to be declared because the code fragments become part of the servlet's service() method when the JSP is compiled.
<%!declaration %>	This is a method or variable declaration. The complete method must be contained within the tag. It is subsequently compiled into a method or variable declaration in the servlet.
<%- - comment - -%>	This represents a JSP comment that is never passed to the browser.
<%= expression %>	This represents an expression and contains any valid Java expression. The result is displayed where the expression lies on the page.
<%@ taglib uri="path to tag library" prefix="tag prefix" %>	This is a taglib directive. It makes a tag library available for use in the JSP by specifying the location of the tag library and the prefix to use with its associated tags. Directives like this should always be the first lines in a JSP page.

Table 2-4 *JSP Tags*

The following examples demonstrate how to use the JSP tags described in Table 2-4. The code fragment:

```
<html>
<head>
<title>
CodeFragment
</title>
</head>
<body bgcolor="#ffffff">
<h1>
<%= "Greetings, IFCE New Customer" %>
</h1>
</body>
</html>
```

The output occurs directly at the point where the expression is positioned on the page.

A JSP declaration:

```
<%! int i = 0; %>
```

A comment:

```
<%--This comment is never passed to the browser --%>
```

An expression:

```
<%= "2 * Math.PI * radius"%>
```

A taglib directive makes the tag library available for use in the JSP by specifying the location of the tag library and the prefix to use:

```
<myTagLibrary:customAction attribute="%= value %>" />
```

This particular example is interesting because the JSP scripting expression specifies the value of a JSP action's attribute. Here is another example:

```
<jsp:setProperty name="login" property="visits"
value="<%= previousVisits + 1 %>"/>
```

The following example presents a simple JavaBean class to display a JSP that uses it:

```
package com.taglib.dpsjsp.firststeps;
public class HelloBean {
```

```
  String name = "world";
  public String getName(){
    return name;
  }
  public void setName(String name){
    this.name = name;
  }
}
```

Although this is a primitive Java class, it contains a single instance variable, *name*, which refers to a string. The value of this string is "world." External code can retrieve the name using the getName() method. The following Java Server Page can consume this JavaBean using the following page directives:

```
<html>
<body>
<p>
<jsp:useBean id="hello"
  class="com.taglib.dpsjsp.firststeps.HelloBean"/>
<jsp:setProperty name="hello" property="name"/>
Hello, <jsp:getProperty name="hello" property="name"/>!
</p>
</body>
</html>
```

The first action tag allows the JSP page to use the bean, identified by a particular class name and ID. In this scenario, we use an instance of the HelloBean Class and call "Hello". The <%jsp:setProperty() %> tag causes the request parameter called *name* to be handed as a String parameter to the bean's setName() method. Okay, this example is not complex nor original (everyone writes one of these), but it demonstrates how a JSP calls and uses a JavaBean.

JSP Page Directives

Directives convey processing information about the page to the JSP container. However, note that directives do not produce any output transparent to end users when a page is requested. Instead, they generate various side effects that alter the manner in which the JSP container processes a page.

Table 2-5 displays attributes supported by the *page* directive. By viewing this table, it is clear that JSP permits specifying multiple *page* directives on a single page.

Attribute	Value	Default	Demos
info	Text string	None	info="login form."
language	Scripting language name	"java"	language="java"
contentType	MIME type, char set		contentType="text/html" charset="ISO-8859-1" contentType="text/xml"
pageEncoding	Character set	"ISO-8859-1"	pageEncoding="ISO-8859-1"
extends	Class name	None	extends="com.taglib.dpjsp .MyJspPage"
import	Class and/or package names	None	import="java.net.URL" import="java.util.*, java.text.*"
session	Boolean flag	"true"	session="true"
buffer	Buffer size, or false	"Skb"	buffer ="20kb" buffer="false"
autoFlush	Boolean flag	"true"	autoFlush="false"
isThreadSafe	Boolean flag	"true"	isThreadSafe="true"
errorPage	Local URL	None	errorPage="results/failed.jsp"
isErrorPage	Boolean flag	"false"	isErrorPage="false"

Table 2-5 *Attributes Supported by the* page *Directive*

Table 2-6 presents methods used to convert expression values into strings.
Table 2-7 presents JSP implicit objects and their APIs for the HTTP application.

Value Type	Conversion to String
boolean	java.lang.Boolean.toString(boolean)
byte	java.lang.Byte.toString(byte)
char	java.lang.Character(char).toString()
double	java.lang.Double.toString (double)
int	java.lang.Integer.toString(int)
float	java.lang.Float.toString(float)
long	java.lang.Long.toString(long)
object	toString() method of object's class

Table 2-6 *Methods Used to Convert Expression Values into Strings*

Object	Class or Interface	Description
page	java.servlet.jsp.HttpJspPage	Page's servlet instance
config	javax.servlet.ServletConfig	Servlet configuration data
request	javax.servlet.http .HttpServletRequest	Request data
response	javax.servlet.http .HttpServletResponse	Response data
out	javax.servlet.jsp.JspWriter	Output stream for page content
session	javax.servlet.http.HttpSession	Data shared by all application pages
application	javax.servlet.jsp.PageContext	Context data for page execution
pageContext	javax.servlet.jsp.PageContext	Context data for page execution
exception	java.lang.Throwable	Uncaught error or exception

Table 2-7 *JSP Implicit Objects and APIs for HTTP Applications*

Best Practice for JSP Page Processing

The best practice for designing a JSP page is separating the presentation code from the processing code. Place the presentation code in the JSP program and place all processing code in Enterprise JavaBeans. The JSP program code should call EJBs whenever the JSP program needs to process data. Perhaps the greatest benefit of doing this is that other enterprise applications can share processing code. This is also desirable because processing logic is not present in the JSP program, making the code much easier to read.

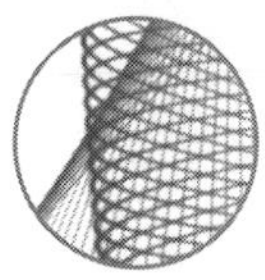

NOTE

I have chosen to present only basic information about JSP pages. For a complete examination of this vast technology, consult the numerous texts that deal exclusively with the entire range of JSP services.

CHAPTER

3

Enterprise JavaBeans, Interfaces, and JDBC Persistence

IN THIS CHAPTER:

Overview of Enterprise JavaBeans

EJB Interfaces

Exploring Implementation Classes

EJBs from a Client's Perspective

Examining How EJB Systems Function

This chapter discusses Enterprise JavaBeans (EJBs) and examines the role they play in the Java 2 J2EE 1.3.1 architecture. Although it is impossible in one chapter to cover the vast number of rules, APIs, and interfaces required to develop Enterprise JavaBeans 2.0, the essential requirements necessary to create EJBs are presented. Simple code fragments accompany many of the topics here. The EJBs examined include both session and entity beans. Their respective categories and individual characteristics and life cycles provided for by a container are discussed in the first part of the chapter, and then some hands-on examples are presented.

Enterprise JavaBeans are designed for flexibility, reusability, and rapid application development. They are built to accommodate every possible type of business model requirement. As long as developers conform to the J2EE specification, the application is portable across multiple platforms and diverse operating systems. The J2EE 1.3 architecture is component and interface based, and therein lies its success. Because it is component based, the J2EE infrastructure makes it easy for developers to create distributed applications for the enterprise.

Listed here are the J2EE application development phases:

- **Application and web component development** During this phase, web developers create web components that encapsulate presentation logic. They represent WAR files. Enterprise JavaBean developers create EJB components that encapsulate business logic. These components compile to class files and are assembled to create an EJB-JAR file.
- **Assembly** The assembler is responsible for selecting the WAR and EJB-JAR files and organizing them into an enterprise archive (EAR) file. Depending on context, the assembler may customize some of the fields in the deployment descriptor file as well as resolve any external dependencies and specify them in the descriptor file.
- **Deployment** The deployer uses the EAR file to examine the deployment descriptor file, resolving any external dependencies and configuring the application to deploy and execute in the intended operational environment. Ultimately, the administrator is responsible for monitoring and managing the application servers.

Overview of Enterprise JavaBeans

Enterprise JavaBeans are server-side components that encapsulate business logic. Typically, a client makes a call to an intermediary, usually a servlet. The servlet intercepts the call and invokes the appropriate EJB to execute and fulfill its task. EJBs are categorized by their communication characteristics: they are either synchronous or asynchronous beans.

- *Synchronous beans* are transient and may not be shared or used by more than one client application at a time. One stipulation for invoking synchronous calls is that both client and Enterprise JavaBean are available at a specified time in order to interact with one another for the duration of a single transaction. The drawback to a synchronous call is the following: a client must wait until the EJB executes and returns the desired result before the client can continue to pursue other tasks. In essence, the communication line is temporarily blocked. Two kinds of EJBs use synchronous communications: session beans and entity beans.
- *Asynchronous beans* are convenient because both caller and EJB need not be available at the same time.
- Message-driven beans (MDBs) use asynchronous communications.

Consider the following scenario: a person orders a new laptop from a vendor. The vendor forwards the client's order immediately to the vendor's fulfillment house for assembling the unit, delivering the product to the consumer, and notifying both billing and customer when the transaction is complete. An asynchronous EJB is perfect for this kind of situation. It would be folly to invoke a synchronous bean and wait until the entire process is finished.

Clients interact with message-driven beans by sending and receiving Java Message Service messages in an asynchronous mode. We'll look at MDBs in more detail later in this chapter. For now, let's see how session beans and entity beans work.

Session Beans

Session beans exist in two categories:

- Stateless session beans
- Stateful session beans

Session beans encapsulate business processes by implementing both business logic and rules. They process credit card approvals, home loans, calculate payrolls, and track deliveries and order fulfillment. Stating it succinctly, session beans are action oriented. For example, a *stateless session bean* exists only for the duration of a single transaction. In case either a system or container event fails, data is not persisted and cannot be recovered. In addition, a stateless session bean is transient and can participate in a single transaction, but is not available for sharing by more than one client.

Stateless session beans are appropriate for occasions when a client request can be accommodated in a short period of time. Conversely, *stateful session beans* are appropriate for spanning multisession interaction between a client and an EJB. Shopping cart applications use stateful session beans for preserving relevant data between calls to the same site.

Entity Beans

Entity beans model data such as Excel spreadsheet data, invoices, and business reports that must be saved to a repository such as a relational database, data warehousing source, or resource planning system. Entity beans provide an in-memory view of persisted data, are transactional, and do survive a container or system failure.

Three kinds of entity beans exist:

- Container-managed persistent (CMP) beans
- Bean-managed persistent (BMP) beans
- Message-driven (MDB) beans

The *container-managed persistent* entity bean absolves the bean developer from responsibility for managing and writing system-level code such as client authentication and authorization, session pooling, the ejbPassivate() method called for use with session beans, and the ejbActivate() method invoked for use with session beans. The container, on behalf of the client, automatically performs these critical tasks.

The developer, responsible for specifying the container-managed persistent fields and container-managed relationship fields, flags data that is saved in the deployment descriptor file.

When a bean is designed to manage its own state, it is called bean-managed persistence.

Message-driven beans are complete enterprise beans. They are stateless, server-side, transaction-aware components used for processing asynchronous Java Message Service messages.

Here is how the EJB components break down so far:

Entity Bean	Session Bean	Message-Driven Bean (MDB)
Synchronous	Synchronous	Asynchronous
Container-managed persistent (CMP)	Stateless	
Bean-managed persistent (BMP)	Stateful	

EJB Interfaces

One of the most important aspects of understanding Enterprise JavaBeans is becoming familiar with a bean's interfaces as well as its life cycle. Let's begin with an exploration of EJB interfaces before discussing each respective bean's life cycle.

EJB component interfaces expose business logic to clients. The session bean class must implement the javax.ejb.SessionBean interface; the entity bean class must implement the javax.ejb.EntityBean interface. Both home and remote interfaces for session and entity beans extend the same parent interfaces.

The bean developer must provide two specialized types of interfaces for accessing remote objects:

- Home interface
- Remote interface (sometimes referred to as the component interface)

The client utilizes the home interface to create, remove, and destroy EJB instances.

The remote interfaces expose methods that offer shopping cart services, such as allowing clients to add selected items to a purchasing list. Once the client has completed the order, the home interface methods remove the shopping cart instance from memory and destroy the EJB instance.

Remote Home Interface

Every bean type contains one home interface, as demonstrated here:

```
public interface javax.ejb.EJBHome extends java.rmi.Remote {
  public EJBMetaData getEJBMetaData() throws RemoteException;
  public HomeHandle getHomeHandle() throws RemoteException;
  public void remove(Handle handle)
  throws RemoteException, RemoveException;
  public void remove(Object primaryKey)
  throws RemoteException, RemoveException;}
```

In order to write EJBs, it is necessary to observe the following methods declared in the home interface:

```
getEJBMetaData();
getHomeHandle();
remove(Object, primaryKey);
remove(Handle handle);
getEJBMetaData();
```

The purpose of these methods is as follows:

- The getEJBMetaData() method returns the Enterprise JavaBean's ejbMetaData interface.
- The getHomeHandle() method returns a home handle. This references a remote home object.
- The remove(Object, primaryKey) method removes an instance of the entity bean associated with a primary key.
- The remove(Handle handle) method removes a bean instance associated with its handle.
- The getEJBMetaData() method necessitates using the PortableRemoteObject.narrow() method to narrow the returned EJBMetaData method. This also applies to the getHomeHandle() method.

Remote Component Interface

The remote component interface executes methods implemented in the bean class. This interface extends the javax.ejb.EJObject interface and throws a RemoteException. Observe the following code:

```
public interface javax.EJB.EJBObject extends java.rmi.Remote{
  public EJBHome getEJBHome() throws RemoteException;
  public Object getPrimaryKey() throws RemoteException;
  public void Remove() throws RemoteException, RemoveException;
  public Handle getHandle() throws RemoteException;
  public Boolean isIdentical(EJBObject obj) throws Remote
  Exception;}
```

Local Component Interfaces

Local component interfaces (exposing business methods) can only be called by local clients residing in the same JVM. See the following code for this interface:

```
public interface EJBLocalObject {
  public EJBLocalHome getEJBLocalHome() throws EJBException;
  public Object getPrimaryKey() throws EJBException;
  public boolean isIdentical() throws EJBException;
  public void remove() throws EJBException, RemoveException;
}
```

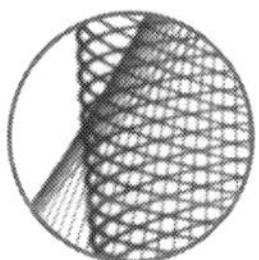

NOTE

The message-driven bean (MDB) has no remote/local home interface or remote/local interface. See "Considering Message-Driven Beans," later in the chapter.

Exploring Implementation Classes

Bean implementation classes expose business logic to clients. They reside within a container such as IBM's WebSphere Application Server, version 5.0. The container intercepts the client's request and delegates it to the appropriate EJB for fulfillment. It is assumed that different types of EJBs contain APIs based on the bean's type, and will therefore behave differently depending on which type of bean is selected.

Container Responsibilities

The EJB container component exists within the J2EE application server's infrastructure. The container provides the Java Runtime Environment (JRE) runtime for all EJB components. The container vendor must implement the services in the J2EE specification, version 1.3.1, which describes the interfaces and their services but never prescribes their implementation. Therein lies the key to J2EE's flexibility and scalability. It represents a contract between the container and the designated EJB.

Life Cycle Management

The following is an overview of an Enterprise JavaBean's life cycle:

- Create an EJB.
- Construct a new enterprise application.

- Generate an enterprise archive (EAR) file.
- Bundle both the entity and session beans into a Java archive (JAR) file.
- Add the JAR file to the new J2EE application.
- Assemble the web components into a WAR file.
- Specify the Java Naming and Directory Interface (JNDI) name and root context.
- Test and verify the application.
- Deploy the application to an operational environment.
- Execute the J2EE application.

The EJB container provides support for low-level tasks such as activating or deactivating objects. In addition, the container manages process, memory allocation, and multithreading.

The container is also responsible for managing the state of an EJB instance. This is desirable because developers can focus on writing business logic, rather than concerning themselves with writing low-level system code.

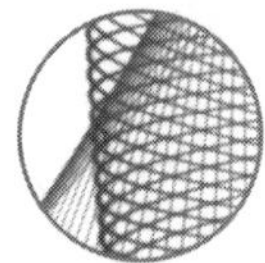

NOTE

The container reads the deployment descriptor file to obtain metadata about the J2EE application in order to provide the appropriate bean's life cycle management. Responsibilities include enforcing security and controlling the bean instance's behavior.

Security

The container manages user authentication and authorization. This functionality is based on security information contained within the deployment descriptor.

Transactions

EJBs provide support for both local and distributed transactions. This is achieved via the Java Transaction API and transaction services. For example, local transactions include interaction with a single relational database such as Oracle9*i*, Sybase, or IBM's DB2 Enterprise Edition. Conversely, distributed transactions involve interaction with several remotely located relational databases spanning more than one server and multiple operating systems.

Developers have the option of implementing EJB transactions programmatically or setting the appropriate fields declaratively in the deployment descriptor file.

Object Persistence

Traditionally, when developers must consider persisting data to a resource, they choose an entity bean for this task. They can then choose between a container-managed persistent (CMP) bean or a bean-managed persistent (BMP) bean.

The CMP is the more desirable of the two types because developers are not responsible for managing persisted transactions; they can depend on container-provided services. The BMP bean requires considerably more attention to facilitating data persistence, managing bean interaction with the repository, and writing low-level code.

EJBs from a Client's Perspective

This part of the chapter presents information from an EJB client's perspective. It explores the technologies necessary for accessing services supported by the EJB container. The following requirements are essential for achieving remote object access:

- Understanding distributed objects and remote services that they support
- Examining the technologies required for accessing remote, distributed objects
- Learning Java Naming and Directory Interface (JNDI) procedures for locating a remote object
- Knowing how to use RMI-IIOP and how it interacts with Enterprise JavaBeans
- Delineating the differences between local and remote interfaces and their APIs
- Exploring techniques for creating a client application

Writing a local nondistributed application that resides on a local machine and interacts with a single relational database does not require a remote interface nor does it present a significant challenge to the developer. However, this type of application has some severe drawbacks, namely, a lack of scalability and flexibility. It cannot process high-volume access to local objects.

In contrast, a distributed application presents numerous challenges. It requires the use of a container to manage system-level tasks; there is a need for managing and preserving state as well as facilitating resource pooling issues and thread management. It must be able to handle multiple requests from a host of client calls. In addition, the programmer must consider the problems involved in interacting with multiplatform operating systems and dealing with transmission protocols in a distributed enterprise environment. The location of remote objects must also be transparent.

What Are Remote Objects?

Remote objects (also called distributed objects) represent units of discrete business logic built into one type of EJB or another. They can reside on more than one application server, and may span multiple platforms and operating systems. The trick is providing seamless accessibility to these remote objects for clients.

Fortunately, the J2EE specification version 1.3.1 offers viable solutions for remote object access, storing and retrieving mission-critical data to both legacy and web service-oriented services. The EJB container, rather than the bean developer, manages low-level transaction and state management details. The success of the interaction and interoperability between remote objects depends on both JNDI and RMI-IIOP technologies. Both technologies provide a standard, consistent methodology for locating and accessing remote objects. See Chapter 4 for a discussion of these two technologies, as well as an examination of the process of assembling EJBs into deployable JAR files. An analysis of the composition of deployment descriptors will reveal their role within the J2EE architecture.

Local and Remote Client View

It is possible for an EJB instance client to function as a servlet, JSP, or another EJB. Here is a typical sequence of events for accessing a remote object:

1. The client calls a business method in a remote component interface.
2. The client passes an object as a parameter.
3. The remote interface stub marshals the parameter before passing it to the EJBObject. This object is the proxy at the container.
4. The EJBObject skeleton must unmarshal the argument.
5. The container performs security, transaction, and life cycle services before the object is passed on to the corresponding business method and is executed on the bean instance.
6. The business method result is returned to the EJBObject.
7. Finally, the EJBObject marshals the result and transmits it back to the remote component interface. Then, the remote component interface unmarshals the object before the client receives the result.

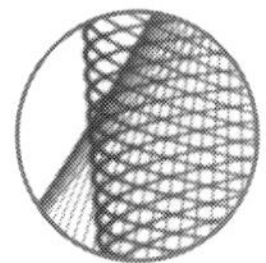

NOTE

With EJB 2.0, when the client session bean instance invokes business methods on an entity bean located in the same JVM, the client can use the local interface rather than the services of a remote object. This makes sense because there is no need for Remote Method Invocation.

Remote and Local Interfaces and Their APIs

Remote interfaces must implement RMI interfaces. This means that parameters and results of methods in remote home and component interfaces must provide support for RMI-IIOP. In this context, all arguments and results are passed by value. In addition, be aware that remote objects implement both remote component and home interfaces that are generated by the container when being deployed. They must throw a RemoteException.

In most cases, developers must use the PortableRemoteObject.narrow() method in order to cast to the desired Java object type. You will see an example of this in the BeanFactory code later in the chapter.

Examining the Local Interface

Local interfaces are available to clients if they reside within the same JVM as the bean instance. This obviates the necessity for providing a remote interface.

Objects that implement local home and component interfaces are not required to support RMI-IIOP. In addition, developers need not use the PortableRemoteObject.narrow() method in order to cast the reference to the desired type.

All parameters and results of local methods are passed by reference rather than by value. In addition, objects implementing the local home and component interfaces are generated by the container at deployment time. They do not need to throw a RemoteException.

Developing Stateful Session Beans

Stateful session beans keep client information between method invocations. It is safe to assume they are appropriate for preserving state in a shopping cart application. Stateful session beans are also used for managing interaction with other EJBs. Frequently, a session bean may interact with several other beans to fulfill a client task. For example, an IFCE stateful session bean that creates a consumer order for purchasing euros will typically call other beans to receive a currency price update from Reuters. The bean will also check with other branches to determine whether they have the amount of currency requested by the client. It will also invoke a bean to check a client's account status, and so on.

Examining a Stateful Session Bean's Life Cycle

Stateful session beans have a complex life cycle. They exist in the following states:

- Does Not Exist
- Method Ready
- Passivated
- Method Ready Transaction

Both client and container affect the state and their transition from one state to another. For example, the initial state is Does Not Exist. When a client invokes the Create <Method>, which is declared in the home interface, the container executes the following steps:

- Create the EJBObject and SessionContextObject
- Create the stateful SessionBean instance
- Call the setSessionContext method followed by a call to its associated matching ejbCreateMethod

Upon completion of the ejbCreate<Method>, the stateful SessionBean instance is now in the Method Ready state. In this state, the stateful SessionBean can execute any nontransactional business methods for the client.

The ejbPassivate() Method

The container is responsible for managing the stateful SessionBean life cycle. In addition to setting the timeout value, the container sets a passivated time for bean instances when they are created. A *passivated time* represents the maximum time that a stateful session bean can reside continuously in memory between repeated client accesses. Both of these values allow the container to provide memory management. When the container is low on memory, it may utilize the ejbPassivation time to choose stateful SessionBean instance candidates, serialize them, and free up memory.

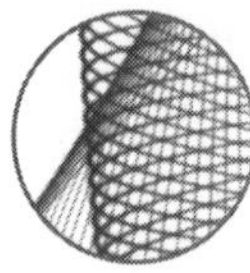

NOTE

A passivated bean instance can transition to a Does Not Exist state if it exceeds the timeout value. *In addition, a container may not interrupt a session bean in the middle of a transaction.*

Examining How EJB Systems Function

This part of the chapter presents some examples using the concepts discussed so far. First, we can add some information to the earlier table showing the basic characteristics of EJBs. Table 3-1 displays the elements of EJBs by type.

Borland's Enterprise server was used to construct the stateless session bean in the example that follows. Table 3-2 provides a list of components within the J2EE architectural blueprint for this server.

The Enterprise JavaBeans component has a well-defined interface. All Enterprise JavaBeans exist and are managed and executed within the container. An EJB component is either an implementation of an interface or extends the EJB class.

The Enterprise container serves as home for all EJB components. It provides the core services for all beans.

Constructing a Session Bean

As you know, stateful session beans represent components dedicated to a single client. They maintain state for a single client only. Inactive bean class instances can be passivated. In contrast, stateless session beans do not maintain state. Therefore, they can be pooled for use by many clients. For example, the sample application in this section retrieves the temperature for a given zip code. Within the IDE, create a new project named SampleSessionBean:

1. Once the default settings are defined (path and class path, etc.), select an EJB module. This module provides an EJB designer within which the developer can create a new Enterprise JavaBean.
2. Implement the following properties:
   - Bean name: beanFactory
   - Interfaces: remote
   - Session type: stateless

EJB Element	Session Bean	Entity Bean	Message-Driven Bean
Interfaces	Yes	Yes	No
EJB classes	Yes	Yes	Yes
Deployment descriptor	Yes	Yes	Yes
Primary key class	No	Yes	No
Helper classes (optional)	Yes	Yes	Yes

Table 3-1 *EJB Elements by Bean Type*

Component	Description
Web server	Its services include a version of Apache.
Messaging service	The SonicMQ Message Broker is a core service.
Web container	Tomcat facilitates running JSPs and servlets.
EJB container	The container hosts EJB components and provides core services for low-level tasks such as memory allocation, pooling, etc.
Transaction services	The server manages transactions both internally and externally.
Session services	The server contains session information stored either within JDataStore or another valid JDBC repository.
Naming service	The JNDI supports lookup services.
RMI-IIOP	Remote Method Invocation supports interaction with remote objects.
JDBC	The Java Database Connectivity interface is used to connect to a relational database or a nonrelational database.
EJB	Enterprise JavaBeans represent a specification for creating enterprise components, as well as managing remote and local Java components.
JMS	JMS is a messaging service supporting both synchronous and asynchronous beans.
JavaMail	JavaMail provides the API for SNMP mail systems.
JCA	Java Connectors represent an interface to connect with disparate systems.

Table 3-2 *Borland Enterprise Server Components*

3. Once these tasks have been fulfilled, right-click on the new session bean and add the following method as defined here:
   - Method name: getCurrentTemp
   - Return type: int
   - Input parameters: Java.lang.String zipcode
   - Interfaces: remote
4. Once these tasks are completed, the following interfaces are generated by the container, a great convenience for bean developers:
   - BeanFactory.java

- BeanFactoryBean.java
- BeanFactory.Home.java

Let's examine the three interfaces before implementing the session bean.

Here is the code for BeanFactory.java:

```
//BeanFactory.java
package com.dps.com.session;

import javax.ejb.*;
import java.util.*;
import java.rmi.*;

public interface BeanFactory extends javax.ejb.EJBHome{
  public BeanFactory create() throws CreateException, RemoteException;
}
```

The BeanFactory.java file contains the contract that will be implemented by the BeanFactoryBean.java file. The interface extends javax.ejb.Home. In addition, the method create() is obligated to throw CreateException and RemoteException.

The BeanFactoryBean.java is the class in which the implementation represents the business logic. Here is code for this class:

```
/**BeanFactoryBean.java - the getCurrentTemp method
 is implemented in this class*/
package com.dps.com.session;

import javax.ejb.*;
import java.util.*;

public class BeanFactoryBean.java implements SessionBean {
  SessionContext sessionContext;
  public void ejbCreate() throws CreateException { }
  public void ejbRemove() { }
    public void ejbActivate() { }
  public void ejbPassivate() { }
  public void setSessionContext(SessionContext sessionContext) {
    this.sessionContext = sessionContext;
  }
  public int getCurrentTemp(java.lang.String zipcode) { }
  }
}
```

Finally, here is the BeanFactoryHome.java interface. This interface is used to create, find, and remove instances for the bean class.

```
//BeanFactoryHome.java interface
package com.dps.com.session;

import javax.ejb.*;
import java.util.*;
import java.rmi.*;
import samplesessionbean.*;

public interface BeanFactoryHome extends javax.ejb.EJBHome {
  public BeanFactory create() throws CreateException, RemoteException;
}
```

The interfaces have been created for the bean implementation. Now, let's write the implementation for the business logic:

```
public int getCurrentTemp(java.lang.String zipcode) {
    int currentTemp;
    Random rnd = new Random(System.currentTimeMillis());
    currentTemp = rnd.nextInt(115);
    return currentTemp;
  }
```

The implementation is complete. The next step involves preparing to deploy the bean. Each created EJB must have a deployment descriptor, which describes the configuration and type to the container. The container subsequently examines the descriptor in order to manage the bean. Here is the deployment descriptor for our interface:

```
<?xml version="1.0" encoding="UTF-8"?>
<!DOCTYPE ejb-jar PUBLIC "-//Sun Microsystems, Inc.
//DTD Enterprise JavaBeans 2.0//EN"
"http://java.sun.com/dtd/ejb-jar_2_0.dtd">
<ejb-jar>
    <enterprise-beans>
        <session>
            <display-name>BeanFactory</display-name>
            <ejb-name>BeanFactory</ejb-name>
            <home>com.dps.com.session.BeanFactoryHome</home>
            <remote>com.dps.com.session.BeanFactory</remote>
```

```
            <ejb-class>com.dps.com.session.beanFactoryBean</ejb-class>
            <session-type>Stateless</session-type>
            <transaction-type>Container</transaction-type>
        </session>
    </enterprise-beans>
    <assembly-descriptor>
        <container-transaction>
            <method>
                <ejb-name>BeanFactory</ejb-name>
                <method-name>*</method-name>
            </method>
            <trans-attribute>Required</trans-attribute>
        </container-transaction>
    </assembly-descriptor>
</ejb-jar>
```

The deployment descriptor contains specific information about the beanFactoryBean. It begins with the XML declaration detailing the version and encoding:

```
<?xml version="1.0" encoding="UTF-8"?>
```

The next line contains the DTD declaration and includes the official organization that defined this DTD:

```
<!DOCTYPE ejb-jar PUBLIC "-//Sun Microsystems, Inc.//
DTD Enterprise JavaBeans 2.0//EN"
"http://java.sun.com/dtd/ejb-jar_2_0.dtd">
```

The <remote> and <home> tags inform the container about the interfaces for BeanFactory. The <ejb-class> tells the container about the implementation class. The final import tag, <session-type>, tells the container that the bean is either stateless or stateful. In our case, the bean is a stateless session bean.

It is easy to test the bean. Simply generate the file based on the framework generated by the container. Here is the code:

```
package samplesessionbean;

import com.dps.com.session.*;
import javax.naming.*;
import javax.rmi.PortableRemoteObject;

public class BeanFactoryTestClient1 extends Object {
```

```
  private static final String
ERROR_NULL_REMOTE = "Remote interface reference is null.
It must be created by calling one of the
Home interface methods first.";
  private static final int MAX_OUTPUT_LINE_LENGTH = 100;
  private boolean logging = true;
  private BeanFactoryHome BeanFactoryHomeObject = null;
  private BeanFactory BeanFactoryObject = null;

  //Construct the EJB test client
  public BeanFactoryTestClient1() {
    initialize();
  }

  public void initialize() {
    long startTime = 0;
    if (logging) {
      log("Initializing bean access.");
      startTime = System.currentTimeMillis();
    }

    try {
      //get naming context

      Context context = new InitialContext();

      //look up jndi name
      Object ref = context.lookup("BeanFactory");
      //look up jndi name and cast to Home interface
      BeanFactoryHomeObject = (beanFactoryHome)
 PortableRemoteObject.narrow
(ref, BeanFactoryHome.class);
      if (logging) {
        long endTime = System.currentTimeMillis();
        log("Succeeded initializing local bean access
 through Local Home interface.");
        log("Execution time: " + (endTime - startTime) + " ms.");
      }
    }
    catch(Exception e) {
      if (logging) {
        log("Failed initializing bean access.");
      }
```

```
      e.printStackTrace();
    }
  }

 /** Methods that use Home interface methods
 to generate a Remote interface reference*/


 public BeanFactory create() {
    long startTime = 0;
    if (logging) {
      log("Calling create()");
      startTime = System.currentTimeMillis();
    }
    try {
      BeanFactoryObject = BeanFactoryHomeObject.create();
      if (logging) {
        long endTime = System.currentTimeMillis();
        log("Succeeded: create()");
        log("Execution time: " + (endTime - startTime) + " ms.");
      }
    }
    catch(Exception e) {
      if (logging) {
        log("Failed: create()");
      }
      e.printStackTrace();
    }


    if (logging) {
      log("Return value from create(): " + BeanFactoryObject + ".");
    }
    return BeanFactoryObject;
  }

// Methods that use Remote interface methods
to access data through the //bean


  public BeanFactory create() {
  BeanFactory returnValue = null;
```

```
    if (BeanFactoryObject == null) {
      System.out.println("Error in create(): " + ERROR_NULL_REMOTE);
      return returnValue;
    }

    long startTime = 0;
    if (logging) {
      log("Calling create()");
      startTime = System.currentTimeMillis();
    }

    try {
      returnValue = BeanFactoryObject.create();
      if (logging) {
        long endTime = System.currentTimeMillis();
        log("Succeeded: create()");
        log("Execution time: " + (endTime - startTime) + " ms.");
      }
    }
    catch(Exception e) {
      if (logging) {
        log("Failed: create()");
      }
      e.printStackTrace();
    }

    if (logging) {
      log("Return value from create(): " + returnValue + ".");
    }
    return returnValue;
  }

  public void executeRemoteCallsWithDefaultArguments() {
    if (BeanFactoryObject == null) {
      System.out.println(
"Error in executeRemoteCallsWithDefaultArguments(): " +
 ERROR_NULL_REMOTE);
      return ;
    }
    create();
  }

  // Utility Methods
```

```
    private void log(String message) {
    if (message == null) {
      System.out.println("-- null");
      return ;
    }
    if (message.length() > MAX_OUTPUT_LINE_LENGTH) {
      System.out.println("-- "
+ message.substring(0, MAX_OUTPUT_LINE_LENGTH) + " ...");
    }
    else {
      System.out.println("-- " + message);
    }
  }
  //Main method

  public static void main(String[] args) {
    beanFactoryTestClient1 client = new BeanFactoryTestClient1();
    // Use the client object to call one of the Home interface wrappers
    // above, to create a Remote interface reference to the bean.
    // If the return value is of the Remote interface type, you can use it
    // to access the remote interface methods.  You can also just use the
    // client object to call the Remote interface wrappers.
  }
}
```

Voila! The session bean works! Now, create an EAR file.

1. Select the EAR icon from the Gallery.
2. Choose File | New, and choose the Enterprise tab.
3. Select the EAR node to add it to the project.
4. Specify the name of the EAR file and node name. Keep the name the same as the project, SessionBean.
5. Use the EAR Wizard's six-step guide to complete the process. Step two is the selection of the SessionBeanSample EJB module included in the project.
6. Step three adds resource adapter archives to the EAR module.
7. Step four adds other archive nodes to the EAR file.
8. Step five adds all web modules to the EAR.
9. Step six adds other resources required for an EAR.

10. Right-click the SessionBean eargrp and select Make. This creates a SessionBean EAR and contains an application.xml descriptor.
11. Start the application server and select Deploy to deploy the bean.

Developing a Stateful Session Bean

When writing a stateful session bean, the client is not required to change code in order to use a stateful bean. The only change is how the developer utilizes the bean. Referring to the getCurrentTemp method, rather than passing in the zip code, it is easy to use a mutator function and subsequently call the method as follows:

```
Package sessionbean;
import java.rmi.*;
import javax.ejb.*;
import javax.naming.*;
class FactoryClient {
public static void main(String([] args) {
  try{
      InitialContext ctx = new InitialContext();
       Object objRef = ctx.lookup("BeanFactory");
      beanFactory factoryHome =
beanFactoryHome(javax.rmi.PortableRemoteObject.narrow(objRef,
       beanFactory Home.class);
       beanFactory factory=factoryHome.create();
       factory.setZipcode("12354");
       System.out.println("Current Temperature is:");
       System.out.println(factory.currentTemp());
      }
       catch (RemoteException ex) {
       System.err.println("Remote Exception:" + ex");
      }catch (CreateException ex) {
      System.err.println("CreateException:" + ex);
      }catch (NamingException ex) {
       System.err.println("NamingException:" + ex);
      }catch (ClassCastException ex) {
       System.err.println("Cast Exception:" + ex);
       }
     }
}
```

The code underscores how easy it is to use a stateful session bean.

Developing Entity Beans

Developing entity beans consists of a specific task: representing an entity of data from a specified data source. Carrying this thought one step further, an entity of data represents a record in a database. How does the entity bean communicate with the relational data store? It is achieved by interacting with data through an interface rather than sending updates, deletes, inserts, or retrieving data directly to the repository. This technique is called *persistence*.

Persistence is managed in the following ways:

- Serialization allows Java objects to suspend the working process of an object from memory, convert it to a byte stream, and persist it to storage.

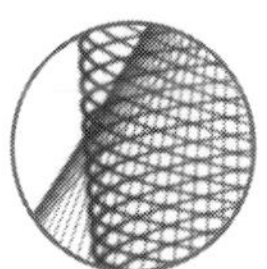

NOTE

Although object serialization is useful for providing data persistence for small individual objects, it is not appropriate for persisting large objects.

- Object/relation mapping represents a fast, efficient way of persisting objects. For example, a customer record usually consists of a first and last name, street address, city, state, zip code, and a contact name. These objects are individually mapped to a relational database. This task is achieved manually through the services of a sophisticated mapping tool.
- An object database management system (ODBMS) stores data directly using the object database API. Utilizing this method eliminates the need for object/relational mapping.

Entity Bean Characteristics

An entity bean represents an in-memory view of persisted data. The following list provides entity bean characteristics:

- Entity beans survive container failures. Both container and entity bean instance work in tandem to synchronize the in-memory data with the database. In essence, entity beans remain in memory until they are explicitly removed.
- Entity beans are ideal for modeling persistent business data such as books, business reports, or employee records.
- Entity beans are identified by primary keys.

- Entity beans are sharable by multiple clients, achieved through a process called *pooling*. Pooling provides efficiency to an entity bean's application.
- Entity beans are *transactional*, meaning transactions are implemented through the use of deployment descriptors.

Entity Bean Types

Recall the two types of entity beans—container-managed persistent beans and bean-managed persistent beans. The CMP entity bean encapsulates the persistent data and business logic. The entity bean *instance* is directly responsible for creating, managing, synchronizing, and removing the state of the persistent data. BMP entity beans require developers to provide the mechanism for managing object persistence. This includes writing the code to provide data access. With CMP, the container bears the responsibility for generating the necessary code for data access and management. The bean developer must specify the container-managed persistence fields and methods in addition to declaring an abstract persistent schema in the deployment descriptor. The container provides a deployment tool that uses the deployment descriptor and CMP bean class to manage persistence and the life cycle for a CMP entity bean instance.

Let's compare the entity bean types. Table 3-3 provides the entity bean characteristics.

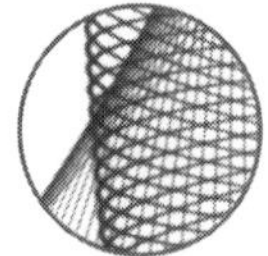

NOTE

The bean developer is responsible for implementing an ejbCreate() method and an ejbPostCreate() method that correspond with each create() method signature within the home interface.

Bean Type	Container Implemented	Developer Implemented
CMP	ejbActivate() ejbPassivate() ejbLoad() ejbStore() Abstract get and set methods	Specify abstract methods and abstract persistence schemas Business logic methods
BMP	None	Business methods ejbActivate() ejbPassivate() ejbLoad() ejbStore() ejbRemove()

Table 3-3 *Comparing CMP and BMP Entity Bean Characteristics*

Four basic operations exist for manipulating data:

- Create
- Read
- Update
- Delete

Create relates to ejbCreate() and ejbPostCreate(). Reading is implemented using ejbLoad(). Update refers to ejbStore(), and delete refers to ejbRemove().

An entity bean uses ejbActivate() as a notification mechanism when the entity bean's instance has been related to a primary key class. ejbPassivate() is called to inform the entity that the primary key is being disassociated from the primary key class and is now available to another entity bean instance.

Creating a CMP Entity Bean

The process of building a CMP bean requires implementing the following steps:

- Defining the home interface
- Declaring the appropriate finder methods
- Implementing the component interface
- Defining the bean implementation class
- Constructing the deployment descriptor
- Deploying the bean

Defining the Home Interface for a CMP Bean

Notice how the home interface is similar to the home interface for a session bean. Its primary tasks are to create an instance, locate existing interfaces, and/or remove an instance. The same is true for the entity bean. Here is the code for building an Employee bean:

```
//Employee CMP bean
import javax.ejb.*;
import java.util.*;

public interface EmployeeHome extends javax.ejb.EJBLocalHome {
  public Employee create(Short empNo) throws CreateException;
  public Employee findByPrimaryKey(long empNo) throws FinderException;
}
```

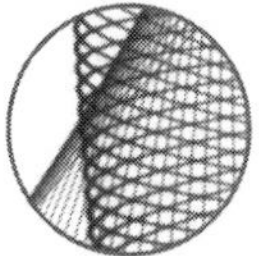

NOTE

The findByPrimaryKey is mandatory for all entity beans. Finder methods perform more than one task. In addition to returning a single instance, they also return a collection of instances.

```
import javax.ejb.*;
import java.util.*;
import java.math.*;

public interface EmployeeHome extends javax.ejb.EJBLocalHome{
  public Employee create(Short empNo) throws CreateException;
  public Collection findSalaryRange(BigDecimal low, BigDecimal high)
  throws FinderException;
  public Employee findByPrimaryKey(long empNo) throws FinderException;
}
```

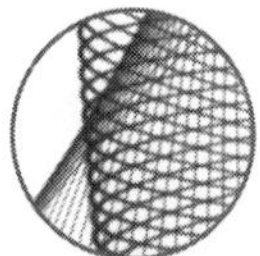

NOTE

The findSalaryRange() returns a java.lang.Collection. This collection represents instances of the primary key only.

Constructing the Component Interface

The component interface defines mutator methods for accessing and manipulating the bean's data.

```
import javax.ejb.*;
import java.util.*;
import java.sql.*;
import java.math.*;
public interface Employee extends javax.ejb.EJBLocalObject{
  public Short getEmpNo();
  public void setFirstName(String firstName);
  public String getFirstName();
  public void setLastName(String lastName);
  public String getLastName();
  public void setPhoneNo(String phoneNo);
  public String getPhoneNo();
  public void setSalary(BigDecimal salary);
  public BigDecimal getSalary();
  public void setFullName(String fullName);
  public String getFullName();
}
```

Implementing the CMP Bean

The CMP EmployeeBean class provides the implementations required for the container to manage the persistence.

```
abstract public class EmployeeBean implements EntityBean {
  EntityContext entityContext;
  public java.lang.Short ejbCreate(java.lang.Short empNo)
throws CreateException {
  setEmpNo(empNo);
  return null;
 public void ejbPostCreate(java.lang.Short empNo) throws CreateException {}
 public void ejbRemove() throws RemoteException{ }
 public abstract void setEmpNo(java.lang.Short empNo);
 public abstract void setFirstName(java.lang.String firstName);
 public abstract void setLastName(java.lang.String lastName);
 public abstract void setPhoneNo(java.lang.String phoneNo);
 public abstract void setSalary(java.math.BigDecimal salary);
 public abstract void setFullName(java.lang.String fullName);
 public abstract java.lang.Short getEmpNo);
 public abstract java.lang.String getFirstName();
 public abstract java.lang.String getLastName();
 public abstract java.lang.String getPhoneNo();
 public abstract java.lang.String BigDecimal getSalary();
 public abstract java.lang.String getFullName();
 public void ejbLoad(){ }
 public void ejbActivate() { }
 public void ejbPassivate() { }
 public void unsetEntityContext() {this.entityContext = null;
 }
 public void setEntityContext (EntityContext) {
  this.entityContext = entityContext;
  }
}
```

The client invokes the create() method of the entity bean's home interface. The anatomy of a descriptor is examined in detail in Chapter 4 along with a discussion on RMI-IIOP and creating JAR files.

Developing a BMP Bean

Bean-managed persistence requires implementing a specific interface. This interface maps to a relational database. Table 3-4 demonstrates how SQL statements relate to bean methods.

Bean Method	SQL Statement
ejbCreate	INSERT
ejbFindByPrimaryKey	SELECT
ejbFindByLastName	SELECT
ejbFindInRange	SELECT
ejbLoad	SELECT
ejbRemove	DELETE
ejbStore	UPDATE

Table 3-4 *SQL Statements Map to Bean Methods*

Defining the Home Interface for a BMP Bean

The home interface is essentially the same as the CMP's Employee home interface. The package is added to the code as follows:

```
package entitybeansample;

import javax.ejb.*;
import java.util.*;
public interface EmployeeBMPHome extends javax.ejbLocalHome {
 public EmployeeBMP create (Short empNo) throws EJBLocalHome {
  public EmployeeBMP findByPrimaryKey(Short empNo) throws FinderException;
}
```

Defining the Remote Interface for a BMP Bean

This interface should also look identical to the CMP bean's remote interface.

```
public interface EmployeeBMPRemote extends javax.ejb.EJBObject{
  public Short getEmpNo()throws RemoteException;
  public void setFirstName(String firstName) throws RemoteException;
  public String getFirstName() throws RemoteException;
  public void setLastName(String lastName) throws RemoteException;
  public String getLastName()throws RemoteException;
  public void setPhoneNo(String phoneNo) throws RemoteException;
  public String getPhoneNo()throws RemoteException;
  public void setSalary(BigDecimal salary) throws RemoteException;
  public BigDecimal getSalary()throws RemoteException;
  public void setFullName(String fullName) throws RemoteException;
  public String getFullName()throws RemoteException;
}
```

Implementing the BMP Bean

This section details the exceptions for the javax.ebj package. It is always important to deal with error-handling in Java, or for that matter, any programming language. Note the following exceptions:

- **ejbCreate throws the CreateException** Invalid input parameter.
- **ejbFindByPrimaryKey throws the ObjectNotFoundException** A database row for the entity cannot be found.
- **ejbRemove throws the RemoveException** The entity bean cannot be deleted from the database.
- **ejbLoad throws the NoSuchEntityException** The database row to be loaded cannot be located.
- **ejbStore throws the NoSuchEntityException** The row to be updated cannot be found.
- **All methods throw the EJBException** A system failure has occurred.

Next, the bean interface generated by the EJB designer wizards needs to be implemented. Here is the example code:

```
package entitybeansample;
import java.sql.*;
import javax.naming.*;
import javax.sql.*;

public class EmployeeBMPBean implements EntityBean {
  EntityContext entityContext;
  java.lang.Short empNo;
  java.lang.String firstName;
  java.lang.String lastName;
  java.lang.String phoneNo;
  java.math.BigDecimal salary;
  java.lang.String fullName;
  public java.lang.Short
ejbCreate(java.lang.Short empNo) throws CreateException {
  setEmpNo(empNo);
  Connection con = null;
try{
  InitialContext initial = new InitialContext();
  Datasource ds = (Datasource)initial.lookup
("java:comp/env/jdbc/EmployeeDate");
  con = ds.getConnection();
```

```
  PreparedStatement ps = con.prepareStatement("INSERT INTO employee (empNo)"
  + "values(?)");
  ps.setShort(1,empNo.shortValue());
  ps.executeUpdate();
  return empNo;
}
catch (SQLException ex) {
  ex.printStackTrace();
 }catch (NamingException ex) {
  ex.printStackTrace();
  throw new CreateException();
 }finally{
  if(con!= null){
    try {
      con.close();
  }
  catch (SQLException ex) {
  ex.printStackTrace();
   }
  }
}
   return null;
}
  public void ejbPostCreate(java.lang.Short empNo) throws CreateException{
}
  public void ejbRemove() throws RemoveException {
  connection con = null;
  try {
    InitialContext initial = new InitialContext();
  DataSource ds = (DataSource)initial.lookup(
  "java:comp/env/jdbc/EmployeeData");
    con = ds.getConnection();
   PreparedStatement ps = con.prepareStatement("DELETE" + "FROM EMPLOYEE
   WHERE empNo = ?");
   ps.setShort(1,getEmpNo().shortValue());
   ps.executeUpdate():
}
   catch(SQLException ex) {
    ex.printStackTrace();
    throw new RemoveException();
} finally{
  if (con !=null){
    try{
       con.close();
    }
     catch (SQLException ex) {
     ex.printStackTrace();
```

```
      }
    }
  }
}
   public void setEmpNo(java.lang.Short empNo){
      this.empNo = empNo;
  }
   public void setFirstName(java.lang.String firstName){
      this.firstName = firstName;
}
   public void setLastName(java.lang.String lastName(){
      this.lastName = lastName();
}
   public void setPhoneNo(java.lang.String phoneNo(){
      this.phoneNo = phoneNo();
}
   public void setSalary(java.math.BigDecimal salary(){
      this.salary = salary();
}
   public void setFullName(java.lang.String fullName(){
      this.fullName = fullName();
}
   public java.lang.Short getEmpNo(){
      return empNo;
}
   public java.lang.String getFirstName(){
      return firstName;
}
   public java.lang.String getLastName(){
      return lastName;
}
   public java.lang.String getPhoneNo(){
      return phoneNo;
}
   public java.math.BigDecimal getSalary(){
       return salary;
}
   public java.lang.String getFullName(){
       return fullName;
}
   public java.lang.Short ejbFindByPrimaryKey(java.lang.Short empNo)
       throws FinderException {
       Connection con = null;
       try {
      connection con = null;
  try {
    InitialContext initial = new InitialContext();
```

```
    DataSource ds = (DataSource)initial.lookup(
  "java:comp/env/jdbc/EmployeeData");
    con = ds.getConnection();
   PreparedStatement ps = con.prepareStatement("SELECT id FROM EMPLOYEE
   WHERE empNo = ?");
   ps.setShort(1,getEmpNo().shortValue());
   ResultSet rs = ps.executeQuery();
     if(rs.next()){
        throw new ObjectNotFoundException();
     }
      return empNo;
   }
   catch(SQLException ex) {
    ex.printStackTrace();
    throw new RemoveException();
} finally{
  if (con !=null){
    try{
       con.close();
    }
     catch (SQLException ex) {
     ex.printStackTrace();
     }
    }
   }
}
   public void ejbLoad(){
   Connection con = null;
   InitialContext = new InitialContext();
   DataSource ds =(DataSource)initial.lookup(
     "java:comp/env/jdbc/EmployeeData");
      con = ds.getConnection();
      PreparedStatement ps = con.prepareStatement(
      "SELECT EmpNo, DeptNo,FirstName," + "FullName,
LastName,PhoneNo,Salary " + "FROM
     EMPLOYEE WHERE empNo = ?");
     ps.setShort(1,getEmpNo.shortValue());
     ResultSet rs = ps.executeQuery();
     if(rs.next()){
      throw new EJBException("Object not located");
}
     setFirstName(rs.getString(3));
     setFullName(rs.getString(4));
     setLastName((rs.getString(5));
     setPhoneNo(rs.getString(6));
     setSalary(rs.getBigDecimal(7));
}
```

```
    catch(SQLException ex) {
    ex.printStackTrace();
    throw new RemoveException();
} finally{
  if (con !=null){
    try{
       con.close();
    }
     catch (SQLException ex) {
     ex.printStackTrace();
     }
    }
   }
}
    public void ejbStore(){
    Connection con = null;
    InitialContext = new InitialContext();
    DataSource ds =(DataSource)initial.lookup(
     "java:comp/env/jdbc/EmployeeData");
      con = ds.getConnection();
  .   PreparedStatement ps = con.prepareStatement(
      "UPDATE employee " + FirstName = ?, FullName = ?,
LastName = ?," + PhoneNo = ?, Salary = ? WHERE empNo = ?");
    ps.setString(2,getFirstName());
    ps.setString(3,getFirstName());
    ps.setString(4,getFullName());
    ps.setString(5,getLastName());
    ps.setString(6,getPhoneNo());
    ps.setBigDecimal(7,getSalary());
    ps.setShort(8,empNo.shortValue());
    ps.executeUpdate());
}
    catch(SQLException ex) {
    ex.printStackTrace();
    } (NamingException ex){
    ex.printStackTrace();
    new RemoveException();
} finally{
  if (con !=null){
    try{
       con.close();
    }
     catch (SQLException ex) {
     ex.printStackTrace();
     }
    }
```

```
   }
}

    public void ejbActivate(){
    }
     public void ejbPassivate(){
     }
      public void unSetEntityContext(){
         this.entityContext = null;
     }
     public void setEntityContext(EntityContext entityContext){
          this.entityContext = entityContext;
   }
}
```

The deployment descriptor is slightly different from the CMP bean. (See the discussion of descriptors in Chapter 4.) Deploying the BMP entity bean is no different from deploying a CMP entity bean. Just as before, the home interface creates, finds, and removes entity instances. The client test would be easy to write. Try one as an exercise.

Considering Message-Driven Beans

Message-driven beans provide a convenient methodology for implementing an onMessage(), which in turn implements an appropriate response to a message received. The container manages the services required to implement and wrap the Java Message Service (JMS). In essence, a client may initiate a message from a web page, or another bean.

An MDB represents a message consumer that implements business logic. Also, an MDB is similar to a stateless session bean. A single instance can be shared by multiple clients. Here is how an MDB functions:

- A message producer writes a message and sends it to a specific topic (more about this in a moment).
- A message consumer subscribes to a specified topic to receive messages.
- The message is delivered from the topic to interested subscribers.

Point-to-Point Compared with Publish/Subscribe

The point-to-point technology is employed when only a single consumer receives a message. The technique used here is as follows:

- A message producer sends a message to a specified queue.
- Each queue has a unique name within the container's naming service.
- Subsequently, the message is received by the queue, and the identified queue forwards the message to a single registered client.

The *publish/subscribe business model* is typically used for general broadcasts. The message server defines a topic. A subject is created for managing messages. Then, a message is created by a producer and sent to a specified topic. The topic receives the message and then delivers the message to all registered subscribers.

Creating MDBs

Here is the basic procedure and some rules for creating MDBs:

- Create a class that implements the javax.ejb.MessageDrivenBean interface.
- Implement the javax.jms.MessageListener interface.
- Create a public constructor with an empty constructor.
- Implement the ejbCreate() method with no arguments.
- Declare the method as public.
- The return type must be void.
- The procedure must declare any application exceptions.

The javax.ejb.MessagedrivenBean has only two methods, and they must be implemented:

- void ejbRemove() throws EJBException
- void setMessageDrivenContext(MessageDrivenContext messageDrivenContext) throws EJBException

The listener interface implements the method for processing incoming messages. See the following code:

```
package javax.jms.*;
public abstract interface MessageListener {
  void onMessage(Message message);
}
```

The message-driven bean's onMessage() method executes all business logic for the EJB. Here is the interface for message-driven beans:

```
package javax.ejb;
public abstract interface MessageDrivenBean extends EnterpriseBean {
 void ejbRemove() throws EJBException;
  void setMessageDrivenContext(MessageDrivenContext messageDrivenContext)
  throws EJBException;
}
```

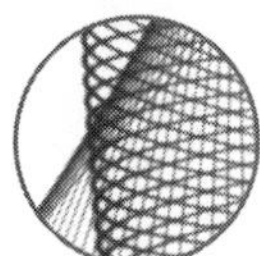

NOTE

Remember that the message-driven bean does not contain either a remote/local home interface or a remote/local interface. MDB developers must ensure that all message processing is asynchronous.

The following code displays the message-driven bean source for implementing EmployeeMDBBean.java:

```
package messagebean;
import java.text.*;
import java.util.*;
import javax.ejb.*;
import javax.jms.*;
import javax.naming.*'

public class EmployeeMDBBean implements MessageDrivenBean, MessageListener {
  private transient MessageDrivenContext mds = null;
  private Context context;
  public EmployeeMDBBean() { }

  public void setMessageDrivenContext(MessageDrivenContext mdc)
  {
    this.mdc = mdc;
  }
  public void ejbCreate() { }
  public void onMessage(Message inMessage) {
  try{
   if(inMessage instanceof MapMessage){
   MapMessage map = (MapMessage)inMessage){
   System.out.Println("Urgent Message");
   System.out.Println("Name: " + map.getString("name"));

   sendNote(map.getstring("Email"));
   }else {
    System.out.println("Incorrect message type");
```

```
    }
  }
    catch Exception ex) {
    ex,printStackTrace();
    }
  }

   private void sendNote(String recipient){
   try{
    Context initial = new InitialContext();
    javax.mail.Session session = (javax.mail.Session)
      initial.lookup("java:comp/env/MailSession");
    javax.mail.Message msg = new javax.mail.internet.MimeMessage(session);
    msg.setRecipients(javax.mail.MessageRecipientType.TO,
      javax.mail.internet.InternetAddress.parse(recipient,false));
      msg.setSubject("Just for your Information");

    DateFormat dateFormatter = DateFormat.getDateTimeInstance
    (DateFormat.LONG, DateFormat.SHORT);
    Date timestamp = new Date();

    String messageText = "This message is urgent" + '\n' + "your friend";
    msg.settext(messageText);
    msg.setSentDate(timestamp);
    javax.mail.Transport.send(msg);
  }
    catch (Exception ex){
         throw new EJBException(ex.getMessage());
    }
  }
    public void ejbRemove() {
      System.out.println("EmployeeMDBBean.ejb.Remove() called.");
    }
  }
```

CHAPTER

4

RMI-IIOP, the JNDI, and Deployment Descriptors

IN THIS CHAPTER:

Understanding Remote Object Access

RMI-IIOP and the Java Naming and Directory Interface

Understanding Deployment Descriptors

Java Remote Method Invocation over the Internet Inter-ORB Protocol represents J2EE's default mechanism for accessing remote objects in a distributed enterprise environment. RMI-IIOP allows developers to create distributed objects and enable them for communication across Java Virtual Machines. Originally, RMI technology was used to execute remote object access by importing the java.rmi package. RMI offers distributed garbage collection and object activation. J2EE uses RMI-IIOP and the Java Naming and Directory Interface (JNDI) for access to remote objects, providing true cross-platform and cross–operating system interoperability.

Developers can also leverage the much simpler lightweight Remote Procedure Call (RPC) request-response technology, provided the client is sending parameters rather than objects to the server. RPCs usually interact with procedural applications, whereas RMI-IIOP provides interoperability with applications written in non-Java languages, the main focus of this book.

This chapter covers some background and specifics of these remote object access technologies along with a detailed discussion on deployment descriptors and how they affect an application's behavior.

Understanding Remote Object Access

All calls invoked on objects residing on a JVM located on a network somewhere in the digital world are remote calls. A Remote Procedure Call represents a procedural invocation from a *process* on a client machine to a *process* on a remote machine. RMI-IIOP facilitates distributed object interaction between the two processes across platforms and operating systems. In essence, RMI-IIOP is protocol and platform agnostic. Clarifying this concept one step further, RMI-IIOP allows developers to invoke methods on *objects* rather than calls on remote *procedures.*

The benefit of using RMI-IIOP is that it conforms to object-oriented programming concepts, including encapsulation, implementation inheritance, and programming to interfaces, rather than using traditional inheritance. Also, the Remote Method Invocation results in the specified object executing in a separate JVM, which enhances performance. As previously stated throughout this text, the J2EE specification defines *what* developers and vendors should adhere to but never *how* they should do it. In this way, RMI-IIOP fits nicely into the scheme.

The following is a list of items that must be considered when invoking remote calls on objects:

- **Marshaling and unmarshaling** When a client calls a remote object, the machine's memory layout is unknown. RMIs and RPCs facilitate passing parameters over the network. Another issue arises when an object reference is sent. In any case, the challenge to developers is that the pointer being sent is not valid on the remote machine because its memory layout is completely different from that of the client machine. The marshaling and unmarshaling process allows developers to manipulate parameters so they are usable on the remote machine.

- **Passing parameters by value and by reference** When values are passed by value, a copy of the data, rather than the original value, is passed. By using this method, any data changes are reflected in the copy rather than in the original. Conversely, a value passed by reference reflects data changes directly in the object. It is important to have flexibility when passing parameters. RMI-IIOP supports both methods.
- **Surviving system failure** Imagine if a distributed application has numerous JVMs collaborating to provide a business solution for a single client. If one machine crashes, the distributed application must survive the system failure. RMI-IIOP provides a standardized methodology for handling such disastrous events.

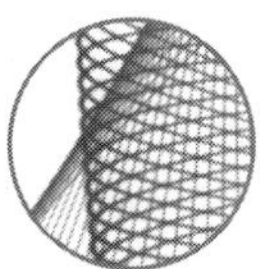

NOTE

J2EE 1.3-compliant servers are mandated to provide RMI-IIOP implementations that enable developers to perform successful networking operations. This represents one piece of the J2EE server's many components and thus fulfills the promise of J2EE, which assures application portability.

Investigating the Interfaces

The remote interface exposes specified information about an object, such as the method names and their parameters. The interface hides the implementation from the client.

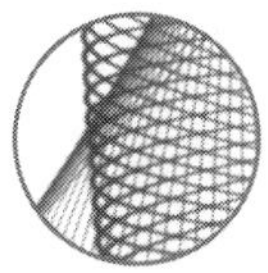

NOTE

The implementation represents business logic, algorithms, and data. Separating the interface from the implementation allows for varying program logic without altering client code. This conforms to the object-oriented principle of allowing object substitutability, a chief benefit provided by programming to interfaces.

RMI-IIOP makes extensive use of this principle. What does this mean to developers? You cannot invoke a remote method directly on an object. The RMI-IIOP invocation must be performed on the remote interface to the object's class. Therefore, you must create a remote interface that extends the interface; this is called java.rmi.Remote. In addition, the custom interface must have within it a copy of each method exposed by the remote interface.

Here is a typical sequence of events for accessing a remote object:

1. The client call invokes a specified business method on a remote component interface. Recall that a client is not allowed to invoke a method on an object directly; it must be invoked on the implementation interface.
2. The client passes an object as a parameter. This can be done by passing the parameters either by value or by reference.
3. The remote interface stub marshals the parameter before passing it to the EJBObject. This object functions as a proxy for the container. The client thinks it is interacting with a local object.
4. The EJBObject skeleton must then take the object parameters and unmarshal them.
5. The container performs the required security, transaction, and life cycle services before the object is passed on to the corresponding business method(s) contained in the remote interface. It is now executed on the bean instance.
6. The business method result is returned to the EJBObject.
7. The EJBObject marshals the result and transmits it back to the remote component interface.
8. Finally, the remote component interface unmarshals the object and presents the result to the client.

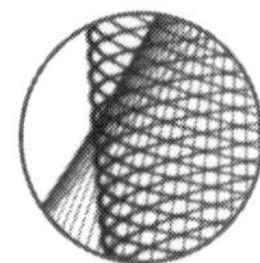

NOTE

With EJB 2.0, when a client bean instance invokes business methods on an entity bean located within the same JVM, the client can use the local interface rather than invoking the services of a remote object.

In the following example, a remote object exposes one method: compute(). It generates a random number each time it is called. The object is an entity bean.

```
import java.rmi.Remote;
import java.rmi.RemoteException;
/**
*This remote interface represents the remote object
*Clients use this interface to execute operations on the remote object.
*/
public interface IFCEObjecGen extends Remote {
 public long compute() throws RemoteException;
}
```

In order to make an object a remote object and provide access for a client, it is necessary to execute one of the following steps:

- Extend class javax.rmi.PortableRemoteObject. This is a base class from which a remote object can be derived. When the client invokes a call on the remote object and the object instance is created, it calls the RemotePortable remote object's constructor. This sequence makes the object available to be called remotely.
- Manually export the object so it is available for invocation by remote hosts as follows: call javax.rmi.PortableRemoteObject.exportObject(). Note that the Java language does not permit multiple implementation inheritance; therefore, it is not possible to extend PortableRemoteObject.

Here is the remote object class:

```
import java.rmi.RemoteException;
import javax.rmi.PortableRemoteObject;

public class RndNumGen()
  extends PortableRemoteObject
  implements IFCEObjecGen
  /*
   *The remote object's constructor
   */
  public RndNumGen() throws Exception, RemoteException {
    super();
}

   /*
    * Generate a unique random number
   */
   public synchronized long compute() throws RemoteException {
      return i++;
  }
 private static long i = System.currentTimeMillis();

}
```

In the remote object constructor, the superclass provides access to remote clients. It makes the object available at a random port number. Once the remote object's constructor is called, the object is always available to anyone.

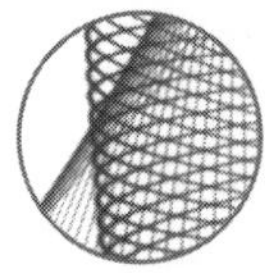

NOTE

RMI-IIOP permits multiple clients to connect to a server at once. Because the remote object implementation may possibly have many threads running at once, you should place a synchronized block around the compute() method to ensure that only one client can generate a unique random number at a time.

Object Serialization

When a client uses RMI-IIOP to invoke a method, all parameters are passed by value. This means all parameters are copied from the client machine to the remote machine. Passing by value presents a problem. When an object is passed over the wire and the object contains references to other objects, how are those external references resolved? Fortunately, the process of *serialization* resolves this issue. Java converts the object into a bit-blob representation of the object. It is possible to send bit-blobs wherever desired over the wire. The Java language takes care of all serialization processing. RMI-IIOP uses object serialization to send bit-blobs over the wire. To inform Java that your object is serializable, you implement the java.lang.Serializable interface.

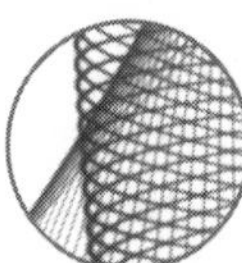

NOTE

The java.lang.Serializable interface defines no methods whatsoever. It therefore serves as a marker interface.

Developers can create a custom serialization by implementing the writeobject() method. It is also possible to provide custom serialization by implementing readObject().

Be aware of the following when using serialization:

- Java objects may be bundled with the serialized bit-blob.
- Any basic type (int, char, etc.) is automatically serialized with the object and is available when deserialized.
- Objects marked *transient* are not serialized with the object and are not available when deserialized.
- Objects that are not marked *transient* must implement java.lang.Serializable. They are converted to bit-blobs along with the original object.

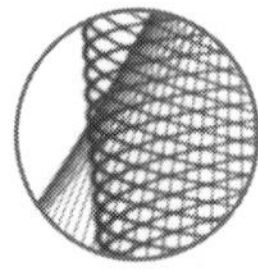

NOTE

If objects are not marked with the transient *keyword and do not implement java.lang.Serializable, a NotSerializable Exception is thrown when writeobject() is called.*

When should a developer mark a member variable as transient? If an object is large, do so because it is not a good candidate for object serialization. If the object represents a resource that cannot be reconstructed on a remote machine—for example, database connections, or if you consider the field data to be sensitive—mark the variable as transient.

RMI-IIOP uses object serialization for passing values via a Remote Method Invocation. When an object is passed as a parameter, the stub is copied via pass-by-reference. Stubs are also serializable and can be passed over the wire as bit-blobs.

In summary, all Java basic primitives are passed by value when invoking methods remotely. If an object is passed over the network by value, the object must implement java.lang.Serializable. If an object is passed by reference, it must be a remote object and must implement java.rmi.Remote. In this case, a stub for the remote object is serialized and passed to the remote host.

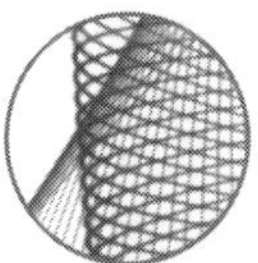

NOTE

Refer back to the Widget application in Chapter 2 for a review of the concepts mentioned here.

RMI-IIOP and the Java Naming and Directory Interface

The JNDI is a J2EE API that provides an interface for locating objects, networks, machines, and so on. For example, JNDI can locate a network printer or connect to a remote database residing in an undefined location somewhere on the Internet.

A naming service relates names to objects. This means binding to an object via a name. An example of naming is the following: when a user wants to locate a machine on a network, the JNDI uses the Domain Name System (DNS) to translate a machine name to an IP address.

A directory service is a naming service extended to provide directory operations. In essence, a directory is a collection of interrelated and connected directory objects. Microsoft's Active Directory is an example of a directory service. Internally, a directory is constructed as a hierarchical treelike structure.

Examining the JNDI Infrastructure

The JNDI consists of the following packages:

- **javax.naming** Contains classes and interfaces for accessing naming services.
- **javax.naming.directory** Extends the core javax.naming package in order to provide functionality for accessing directories as well as naming services.

- **javax.naming.event** Contains classes and interfaces for supporting event notification in naming and directory services.
- **javax.naming.ldap** Contains classes and interfaces for supporting LDAPv3 extended controls and operations.
- **javax.naming.spi** Contains classes and interfaces that permit various naming and directory service providers to be dynamically attached beneath the JNDI.

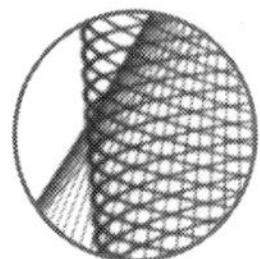

NOTE

The complete details of these classes and interfaces are available for viewing at http://www.java.sun.com.

The JNDI consists of two separate units: the client API and the service provider interface (SPI). Client APIs allow clients to program to a single interface, whereas the SPI allows naming and directory service developers to plug their proprietary protocols into the system. The JNDI requires only a modest learning curve because a single API exists for accessing directory service information.

The JNDI must be used with an LDAP-enabled JNDI provider. It offers the following services:

- Provides a pluggable interface that allows you to talk to any naming service via RMI, LDAP, or DNS.
- Separates the application from implementation details.
- Reads and writes Java objects from directories.
- Makes it possible to link different types of directories, such as an LDAP directory with an NDS directory.
- Retrieves a reference to the Java Transaction API.
- Facilitates connections to JDBC drivers or Java Message Service (JMS) drivers.

The following code demonstrates how to look up an object using the JNDI. The application searches for an object named IFCEObject. The program specifies a service provider to use for the initial context. It places the name of the service provider class in the environment properties, utilizing the services of a Hashtable object. The specified service provider ID calls com.sun.jndi.fscontext.RefFSContextFactory, which is passed as the second argument to the put() method. The Hashtable object, called fpe, is passed as an argument to the InitialContext constructor, subsequently returning the initial context, called ctx. The lookup method for InitialContext is handed the search criteria: the name of the object. Finally, the application displays the object returned by the lookup() method. The context is then closed. Here is the code:

```
import javax.naming.Context;
import javax.naming.InitialContext;
import javax.naming.NamingException;
import java.util.Hashtable;
class MyLookupClass {
  public static void main(String[] args) {
    String MyObject = "MyObject";
    Hashtable fpe = new Hashtable(1);
    fpe.put(Contect.INITIAL_CONTEXT_FACTORY,
       "com.sun.jndi.fscontext.RefFSContextFactory");
    try{
        InitialContext ctx = new InitialContext(fpe);
        Object obj = ctx.lookup(myObject);
         System.out.println("Object: " + obj);
         ctx.close();
   }
   catch (NamingException error) {
    System.err.println("Error: " + error.getMessage());
    }
   }
}
```

Retrieving Attributes

It is possible to retrieve file attributes using directory services. The following example creates a class called MyRetrieveAttributeClass. The small application fetches and presents on-screen attributes related to MyObject. The main() class creates a Hashtable object named fpe. Then the program invokes the put() method twice. The first call places the directory service provider in the hash table, and the second call puts the directory service URL into the same table. Here is the code:

```
fpe.put(Context.SECURITY_CHECK, "userID");
fpe.put(Context.SECURITY_CREDENTIALS, "myPassword");

//MyRetrieveAttributeClass program code
import javax.naming.Context;
import javax.naming.directory.InitialDirContext;
import javax.naming.directory.DirContext;
import javax.naming.directory.Attributes;
```

```
import javax.naming.NamingException;
import java.util.Hashtable;
class MyRetrieveAttributeClass {
  public static void main(String[] args){
     Hashtable fpe = new Hashtable(2);
     fpe.put(Context.INITIAL_CONTEXT_FACTORY,
     "com.sun.jndi.ldap.LdapCtxFactory");
     fpe.put(Context.PROVIDER_URL, "ldap://127.0.0.1:398");
     try{ InitialDirContext ctx = new InitialDirContext(fpe)
     Attributes atr = ctx.getAttributes("MyObject");
     System.out.println(atr.get("MyObject");
     ctx.close();
  }
   catch (NamingException error)
     { System.err.println("Error: " + error.getMessage());
     }
   }
}
```

Using Binding in Your Directory Service

It is possible to bind a name to a specified object in a directory service by using the bind() method of the InitialContext class. The following code demonstrates how to achieve this:

```
//MyAddBinding
import javax.naming.*;
import java.util.Hashtable;
class MyAddBinding {
   public static void main (String[] args) {
      Hashtable fpe = new Hashtable(2);
      fpe.put(Context.INITIAL_CONTEXT_FACTORY,
        "com.sun.jndi.ldap.LDAPCtxFactory");
      fpe.put(Context.PROVIDER_URL, "localhost:1099");
      try {
           InitialContext  ctx = new InitialContext(fpe);
           User newUser = new User("Steve Heim");
           ctx.bind("username", newUser);
           Object obj = ctx.lookup("UserName");
           System.out.println(obj);
            ctx.close();
          }
```

```
          catch (NamingException error) {
           System.out.println("error: " + error.getMessage());
         }
      }
  }
```

It is also possible to replace binding in the directory service. Here is the essential code for replacing binding:

```
//replace binding
import javax.naming.*;
import java.util.Hashtable;

class MyReplaceBinding {
    public static void main (String[] args) {
    Hashtable fpe = new Hashtable(2);
    fpe.put(Context.INITIAL_CONTEXT_FACTORY,
        " com.sun.jndi.ldap.LDAPCtxFactory ");
      fpe.put(Context.PROVIDER_URL, "localhost:1099");
      try {
           InitialContext  ctx = new InitialContext(fpe);
           User newUser = new User("Jonathan Peltzer");
           ctx.rebind("UserName", new user);
           Object obj ctx.lookup("UserName");
           System.out.println(obj);
           ctx.close();
           }catch (NamingException error){
            System.out.println("Error: " + error.getMessage());
       }
    }
}
```

You can remove binding from a directory service. Here is the code for doing so:

```
//Remove binding
import javax.naming.*;
class MyRemoveBinding {
 public static void main (String[] args) {
  Hashtable fpe = new Hashtable(2);

  fpe.put(Context INTITIAL_CONTEXT_FACTORY,
  " com.sun.jndi.ldap.LDAPCtxFactory ");
```

```
    fpe.put(Context.PROVIDER_URL, "localhost:1099");
    try{
       InitialContext ctx = new InitialContext(fpe);
       ctx.unbind("UserName");
       Object obj = null;
    try{
    obj = ctx.lookup("UserName");
    }
    catch (NamingNotFoundException error) {
     System.out.println("Binding Removal failed");
     ctx.close();
    }
    catch (Naming Exception error){
    System.out.println("Error: " + error.getMessage());
     }
    }
}
```

Understanding Deployment Descriptors

As discussed in Chapter 3, bean providers must declare all middleware requirements in a deployment descriptor file; for example, the life cycle for a specified bean, including transactions, persistence, and security services. Entity bean authors indicate how the container should manage the bean. The container should specify whether a bean is a session bean, the type of session bean (stateful or stateless), or one of the two types of entity beans—container-managed persistent bean or bean-managed persistent bean. The deployment descriptor should indicate whether the bean is a message-driven bean. If so, it must indicate that the MDB has no interface.

In EJB 2.0, a deployment descriptor file is an XML file. An EJB container should usually provide a tool to generate the deployment descriptor.

The descriptor file for the bean factory application introduced in Chapter 3 is shown here, and we'll take a close look at the elements in the next section. Here is the file:

```
//An ejb deployment descriptor file for the bean factory application:
<?xml version="1.0" encoding="UTF-8"?>
<!DOCTYPE ejb-jar PUBLIC "-//Sun Microsystems, Inc.
//DTD Enterprise JavaBeans 2.0//EN"
```

```
"http://java.sun.com/dtd/ejb-jar_2_0.dtd">
<ejb-jar>
    <enterprise-beans>
        <session>
            <display-name>beanFactory</display-name>
            <ejb-name>beanFactory</ejb-name>
            <home>com.dps.bean.session.beanFactory</home>
            <remote>com.dps.bean.session.beanFactory</remote>
         <ejb-class>com.dps.bean.session.beanFactoryBean</ejb-class>
            <session-type>Stateless</session-type>
            <transaction-type>Container</transaction-type>
        </session>
    </enterprise-beans>
    <assembly-descriptor>
        <container-transaction>
            <method>
                <ejb-name>beanFactory</ejb-name>
                <method-name>*</method-name>
            </method>
            <trans-attribute>Required</trans-attribute>
        </container-transaction>
    </assembly-descriptor>
</ejb-jar>
```

The bean factory deployment descriptor file begins with the xml declaration, which indicates that the XML file conforms with the XML specification 1.0 and the encoding is UTF-8. The Document Type Definition indicates that the file is an ejb deployment descriptor, and it provides the default namespace declaration as well as the URL for Sun Microsystems, the official body for defining the EJB specification 2.0.

The <ejb-jar> header is the root for the descriptor. Next, the file indicates that the bean type is a session bean. The <display-name> is beanFactory, the <ejb-name> is also beanFactory. The descriptor indicates that the <home> is com.dps.bean.session .beanFactoryHome. The <remote> interface is com.dps.bean.session.beanFactory.

The <ejb-class> is com.dps.bean.session.beanFactoryBean. The descriptor details the <session-type> as stateless. The <transaction-type> is container managed, while the <assembly-descriptor> is a container transaction.

The <method> specified is beanFactory. Finally, the <trans-attribute> indicates that the method is required.

Examining the Deployment Descriptor

The root of every deployment descriptor as displayed here is the <ejb-jar> element. This element contains several subelements, some required, some not. The <enterprise-beans> subelement contains its own set of subelements. They include the following:

- <session>
- <entity>
- <message-driven>

Table 4-1 lists the <ejb-jar> subelements.

Table 4-2 contains a list of <session> and <entity> elements.

Subelement	Required/Optional	Description
<description>	Optional	The subelement.
<display-name>	Optional	The JAR file and other EJB components.
<small-icon>	Optional	A small icon used to represent the JAR file.
<large-icon>	Optional	A large icon used to represent the JAR file.
<enterprise-beans>	Required	Beans residing with the JAR file. Only one such element is permitted within the deployment descriptor.
<ejb-client-jar>	Optional	The path of the client JAR, used by the client to access EJBs listed in the deployment descriptor.
<assembly-descriptor>	Optional	How EJBs are used by the J2EE application.

Table 4-1 *<ejb-jar> Subelements*

Subelement	Required/Optional	Description
<description>	Optional	The session or entity bean.
<display-name>	Optional	The JAR file and EJB components.
<small-icon>	Optional	A small icon used to represent either the session or entity bean.
<large-icon>	Optional	A large icon used to represent either the session or entity bean.
<ejb-name>	Requires one	The name of the session or entity bean.
<home>	EJB 1.1, one required EJB 2.0, optional	The full-qualified class name of the session or entity EJB remote home interface.
<remote>	EJB 1.1, one required EJB 2.0, optional	The full-qualified class name of the session or entity EJB remote interface.
<local-home>	EJB 2.0, optional	The full-qualified class name of the session or entity EJB local home interface.
<local>	EJB 2.0, optional	The full-qualified class name of the session or entity EJB local interface.
<ejb-class>	Requires one	The full-qualified class name of the session or entity EJB class.
<primkey-field>	Entity bean, optional	The entity bean primary key field when the entity bean uses container-managed persistence.
<prim-key-class>	Entity bean, requires one	The primary key class for the entity bean.
<persistence-type>	Entity bean, requires one	Either CMP or BMP beans.

Table 4-2 *<session> and <entity> Elements*

Subelement	Required/Optional	Description
<reentrant>	Entity bean, requires one Values are true or false	Reentrant invocations are either allowed or not allowed.
<cmp-version>	EJB 2.0, optional EJB containers must support both EJB 2.0 and EJB 1.1	The CMP version.
<abstract-schema-name>	EJB 2.0, optional	Identifies entity beans in a JAR file.
<cmp-field>	Entity bean only, zero or more must exist for each cmp field in the entity EJB class. Must contain a <field-name> element	This element is meant for CMP entity beans.
<env-entry>	Optional, zero or more	An environment entry available through JNDI ENC.
<ejb-ref>	Optional, zero or more	A remote EJB reference entry available through JNDI ENC.
<ejb-local-ref>	EJB 2.0, optional, zero or more	A local EJB reference entry available through JNDI ENC.
<resource-ref>	Optional, zero or more	A reference to a connection factory available through JNDI ENC.
<resource-env-ref>	EJB 2.0, optional, zero or more	Required administered objects.
<security-role-ref>	Optional, zero or more	Identifies security roles.
<security-identity>	EJB 2.0, optional	The principal for a method.
<session-type>	Requires one session bean Value: stateless or stateful	Specifies whether a session bean is stateless or stateful.
<transaction-type>	Requires one session bean Value: bean or container	Specifies that a session bean manages transactions or the container manages the transactions.
<query>	EJB 2.0, optional, zero or more	Contains an EJB QL statement bound to a find or select method.

Table 4-2 *<session> and <entity> Elements* (continued)

Table 4-3 presents a list of <message-driven> elements.

Subelement	Required/Optional	Description
<description>	Optional	The session or entity bean.
<display-name>	Optional	The JAR file and EJB components.
<small-icon>	Optional	A small icon used to represent the message-driven bean.
<large-icon>	Optional	A large icon used to represent the message-driven bean.
<ejb-name>	Requires one	The message-driven bean's name.
<ejb-class>	Requires one	The fully qualified class name of the MDB EJB class.
<transaction-type>	Requires one session bean Value: bean or container.	Specifies whether an MDB manages the transaction or the container manages the transaction.
<security-identity>	EJB 2.0, optional	The principal for a method.
<env-entry>	Optional, zero or more	An environment entry available through JNDI ENC.
<ejb-ref>	Optional, zero or more	A remote EJB reference available through JNDI ENC.
<ejb-local-ref>	EJB 2.0, optional, zero or more	A local EJB reference available through JNDI ENC.
<resource-ref>	Optional, zero or more	A reference to a connection factory available through JNDI ENC.
<resource-env-ref>	EJB 2.0, optional, zero or more	Required administered objects.
<message-selector>	Optional	A conditional expression using Boolean logic to select messages received from a topic or queue and subsequently delivered to a client.

Table 4-3 *<message-driven> Elements*

Subelement	Required/Optional	Description
<acknowledge-mode>	Required only if EJB manages transactions.	The type of acknowledgment used when a message is received.
<message-driven-destination>	Required Values: javax.jms.Queue or javax.jms.Topic	The type of destination subscribed or listened to by the MDB.

Table 4-3 *<message-driven> Elements* (continued)

Note that there is one other important piece of information about the <message-selector> subelement. XML files use a special syntax for processing unparsed characters such as the less-than symbol and greater-than symbol.

Here is a method for eliminating this problem:

```
<message-selector>
<![CDATA[ a > 90 and b < 70);]];
```

Understand that the XML parser views the less-than symbol as the beginning of a markup tag. It sees the greater-than symbol as the end of a markup tag. CDATA solves this problem by ignoring both of them. The parser will not try to process them.

Now that you have a complete list of the bean types and their characteristics, the only way to become totally familiar with JNDI is to practice using it. The pursuit is informative and worthwhile.

PART II

Microsoft .NET Internal Interoperability

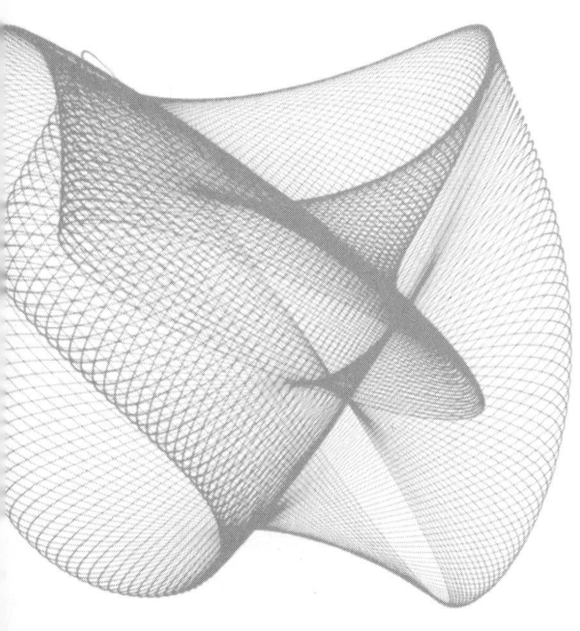

CHAPTER

5

.NET Language Integration Components

IN THIS CHAPTER:

Defining Key .NET Objectives

.NET's Role in the Windows Family

Examining the .NET Framework

What Is Reflection?

Understanding the Common Type Specification (CTS)

Examining the Common Language Specification (CLS)

Creating a Strong Name

How Does .NET Locate an Assembly?

Microsoft .NET facilitates the development of web-enabled applications for any programming language targeting the .NET Framework. The languages include Visual Basic .NET, Visual C# .NET, Visual J# .NET, ASP.NET, and Visual C++ .NET. Microsoft also provides more than 20 interfaces to the Framework for other programming languages such as COBOL, Python, and Perl.

This chapter focuses on the components of the Framework, first taking a macro view of the overall architecture and then a micro view of the Common Language Runtime (CLR) and its tasks. A perusal of the System.Reflection namespace helps to understand how the CLR uses reflection to examine the manifest, which contains metadata about the executable code every Windows application must have. The program executable (PE) file hosts the application's Microsoft Intermediate Language (MSIL) code, the manifest, and an assembly. The latter contains all executable code in binary format.

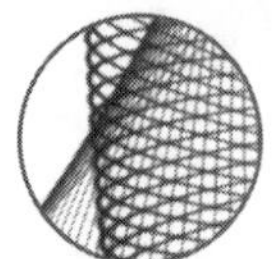

NOTE

Binary formatted code is not native executable code, but it can be executed by the CLR and is MSIL code.

After examining the PE file, we look at a sample application written in Visual Basic .NET for purposes of learning how to create a class library. The last part of the chapter discusses how the Common Type Specification (CTS) and Common Language Specification (CLS) work in conjunction with the CLR. The final section demonstrates how to make an assembly public by creating a strong name.

Before getting into the technical aspects, let's take a look at some of the reasons Microsoft created the Framework.

Defining Key .NET Objectives

The following are several of Microsoft's objectives in creating the Framework:

- **Multilanguage integration** Developers can create applications in any .NET-hosted language and share common data types specified by the Common Type Specification (CTS). They can successfully compile to Microsoft Intermediate Language (MSIL) and then to subsequent application-specific native code.
- **Enterprise services** .NET facilitates scalable, distributed enterprise application development without writing extra code for managing transactions, security, and other related tasks.

- **Modular-based development** COM services enable component integration. However, .NET provides an improved methodology for developing reusable components.
- **Automatic memory management and garbage collection** Traditional C and C++ programmers (pre-.NET languages) were responsible for allocating and deallocating memory as well as providing their own garbage collection. Visual Basic programmers are not accustomed to performing these essential tasks. Now, the CLR and managed code languages provide these services for developers.
- **Distributed application development** Microsoft has entered the Enterprise arena with its release of the .NET Framework. The Framework facilitates Rapid Application Development. In addition, reusable components and interfaces allow for constructing scalable applications.
- **.NET Remote Object Access** Leverages the open Internet standards such as Simple Object Access Protocol (SOAP), Hypertext Transport Protocol (HTTP), and Extensible Markup Language (XML), to access objects residing on remote servers.
- **Enhanced Web Services Development** This is based on the Internet component of the CLR, namely ASP.NET.

.NET's Role in the Windows Family

The Framework is a new member of the family of products based on Windows components. Think of the Framework as a centralized hub with links directed toward other Windows 2000 components, as depicted in Figure 5-1. Each component contains

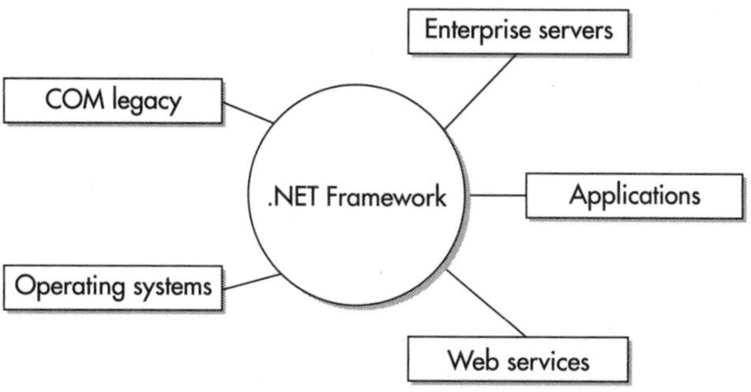

Figure 5-1 *.NET Framework system architecture*

a collection of classes offering specified services and application functionality to clients in a variety of ways. The .NET Framework base classes support both language integration and language independence. Moreover, the Framework is not limited to Windows 2000 and higher. On the server side, ASP.NET, web services, Windows services, and certain other Framework components require Windows 2000 and above. However, the Framework supports client-side applications in Windows 98 and in Windows 98, second edition.

Traditionally, developers view the .NET architecture as multilayered, with the operating system residing on the bottom layer, the Common Language Runtime sitting on top of the OS, and the Framework base classes layered above the CLR. Microsoft .NET is a collection of components that support application integration. Referring to Figure 5-1, the operating systems component includes Windows 2000 Professional, Windows 2000 Server, Windows 2000 Advanced Server, Windows Millennium, Windows CE, Windows XP Home, Windows XP Professional, Windows 2000 Datacenter, and the Windows NT family.

The enterprise servers component hosts the Host Integration Server 2000, Application Server 2000, BizTalk Server, Commerce Server 2000, SQL Server 2000, Internet Information Services, Exchange Server 2000, and Windows Server 2003.

As an example of services offered by individual servers, the Host Integration Server enables legacy system access. It works with a wide variety of network protocols and network service types. The Application Server Center 2000 represents Microsoft's management and deployment tool for web applications.

Microsoft's database technology facilitates direct access to SQL Server 2000 with ADO.NET's native data provider, System.Data.SQLClient. ADO.NET divides the classes supporting database services into two separate namespaces. Clients wishing to connect to SQL Server should use the System.Data.SQLClient namespace, whereas clients desiring to connect to non-SQL Server data resources can utilize the System.Data.Oledb namespace. Classes contained in System.Data (the core class) manage data. Additionally, a number of vendors supply fully enabled ADO.NET providers that allow connections to data sources to be made outside of the Oledb namespace.

Commerce Server 2000 is a completely rebuilt version of Site Server, version 3.0, Commerce edition. It enhances fast construction of an e-commerce shopping cart web site, enabling direct user interaction with the server for purchases and other types of business transactions. In fact, all servers facilitate Rapid Application

Development (RAD) and shorten the length of time required for building scalable, fast-to-market components for large-scale enterprise applications.

The time-tested COM legacy component of the Framework continues to offer its traditional COM services to developers. COM supports language independence but does not allow language interoperability.

The Framework eliminates the need for writing extra code in order to adhere to COM's interface requirements. For example, .NET binaries are reusable without writing extra code to facilitate language integration. A .NET-aware compiler offers a unique approach to application development by generating a program executable file called an *assembly*. The assembly bypasses the need for registering the application binaries in the system registry. It has a *manifest* (metadata about the assembly) containing all application code in binary format, references to external libraries required to execute the application, and program instructions to the Common Language Runtime.

The application component of the .NET Framework contains desktop applications such as the Office integrated suite of applications (Word, Excel, Access, and PowerPoint).

Finally, the web services component contains classes that provide support for web-enabled applications. Three technology classes residing within this component extend the Framework base classes and support web services, Windows forms, and web forms.

Simply put, the .NET Framework hosts components for the next generation of Windows-based applications. In addition, it places a wrapper around *type-safe* code developed with the Framework, thereby shielding the code from operating system–level functionality such as I/O operations, string handling, file services, security, and garbage collection.

The next step in understanding the Framework infrastructure is decomposing the Framework into individual modules (the micro view), thereby allowing us to peek under the hood and enhance our perception of the wide range of services offered. Figure 5-2 illustrates the skeletal structure of the Framework.

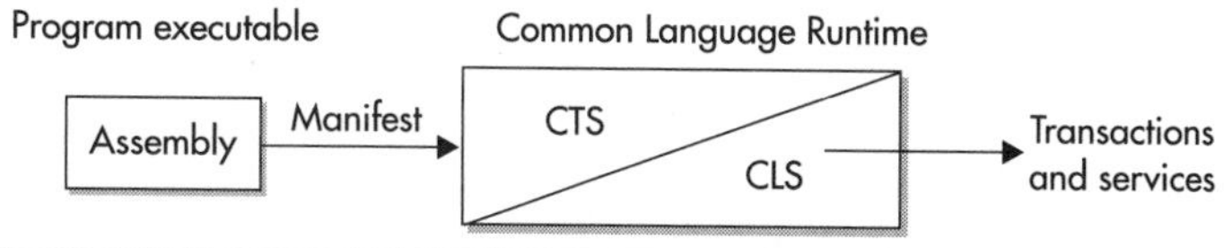

Figure 5-2 *A skeletal view of the Framework*

Examining the .NET Framework

Microsoft divides the Framework's basic components into the Common Language Runtime and the class library.

- The Common Language Runtime provides services for .NET-hosted applications. It also offers security management, error handling, and memory allocation and management.
- The class library contains three essential components: ASP.NET, ADO.NET, and web forms. ASP.NET implements the Internet segment of the Framework by lending support for web services. ADO.NET provides access to Microsoft's flagship database, SQL Server 2000. Web forms enhance smart-client user interface development.

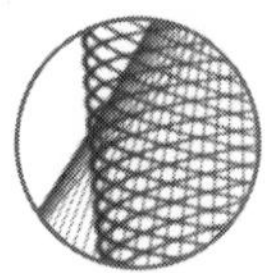

NOTE

ADO.NET is flexible enough that it provides access to any relational database, assuming the availability of an ADO.NET provider.

Defining the Common Language Runtime (CLR)

The *Common Language Runtime* (CLR) manages such services as memory allocation and deallocation, automated garbage collection, loading of components, cross-language debugging, exception handling, type checking, and supporting just-in-time (JIT) compilers for Framework-targeted languages. The Framework base classes offer system-level capabilities for creating a wide range of different type applications, including client-smart applications, enterprise-distributed applications, and web-enabled applications. The base classes also implement I/O, string handling, threading, text, collections, and so forth. The CLR also includes XML and data management for Structured Query Language (SQL). The web services component consists of three user and program interfaces: web services, web forms, and Windows forms.

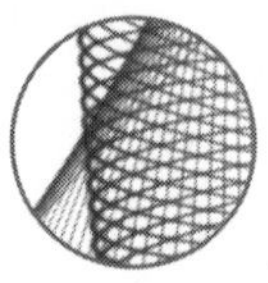

NOTE

Windows forms are part of the various client application constructs. Developers do not need the web services namespace to invoke them.

Web services utilize XML, Simple Object Access Protocol (SOAP), and HyperText Transport Protocol (HTTP) for transmitting documents and mission-critical data between client and server or business trading partners. Web services also contain classes supporting the following:

- Web Services Description Language (WSDL)
- Universal Description, Discovery, and Integration (UDDI)
- DISCO (a Microsoft proprietary XML document format), which allows web sites to advertise formats they expose for locating resources that offer services to interested clients.
- Web forms, which lend support for Rapid Application Development (RAD) and graphical user interface applications.

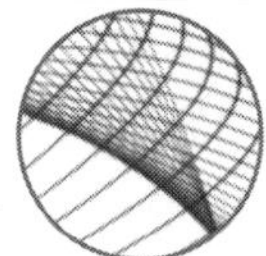

TIP

Apply the same drag-and-drop techniques you use in traditional Visual Basic 6.0 to create GUI applications.

- Windows forms, which contain classes allowing you to develop native Windows UI applications. Within a single Integrated Development Environment, you can utilize the same set of tools and skills for developing wireless device applications, creating distributed server-based applications, and building web services–enabled applications. The Framework lets you develop applications using a consistent interface that all .NET-supported languages share.

The Common Language Runtime itself contains two core entities: the runtime engine mscoree.dl, and the base-class library mscorlib.dll. They contain all essential CLR-related classes offering support for the Framework.

The CLR fulfills many different roles. For example, one essential task is locating an assembly and utilizing classes residing within the System.Reflection namespace to inspect both the manifest *metadata* (information about the data) and all binary data existing within an assembly. The metadata includes type definitions, external assembly references, version information, a description of the assembly's identity (a combination of the assembly name, version, culture, and public key), and other data required by the CLR for program execution. The metadata also describes classes, modules, interfaces, properties, global methods, and so forth. In essence, the assembly contains all required information necessary for .NET to provide application and multilanguage interoperability. It also supplies identity information for security purposes.

Metadata

As just mentioned, metadata is information about data. If you are familiar with XML syntax, you understand that XML is universally accepted as a markup language. It allows you to write your own user-defined markup tags to describe your data. *Tags* are metadata about content. Additionally, XML is nothing but text embedded within markup tags. For example, the following brief XML document uses self-describing markup tags to describe what it is portraying:

```
<?xml version='1.0' encoding='UTF-8'?>
 <message>
  <to>Hamlet</to>
  <from>Francisco</from>
  <messagebody>
   Speak! Where are you? I do not see you.
  </messagebody>
</message>
```

The markup tags portray a particular portion of a scene from *Hamlet*. If you wish to provide further information (metadata) about these actors, you can use attributes to achieve this:

```
<message type="scene" play='Hamlet'/
```

Another component of the Framework, the *just-in-time (JIT) compiler*, reads the metadata to compile Microsoft Intermediate Language (MSIL, or IL) code. IL represents the intermediate state for code and compiles ultimately to an application-specific set of program instructions called *native code*.

In summary, metadata contributes heavily to application and language interoperability by supplying critical information to the CLR, to the JIT compiler, and to all Microsoft .NET tools.

Class Loader

A *class loader* is another essential component of the CLR. Its responsibility is finding and loading .NET classes courtesy of metadata and classes within the System.Reflection namespace. Reflection allows you to examine metadata about the manifest. This file contains all information about the assembly. The CLR determines whether a particular class resides within a local namespace or externally within a dependent assembly located elsewhere. However, before the loader performs its task, it examines a program executable (PE) file for all application information.

What Is Reflection?

Reflection is the process of runtime discovery of data types. It allows you to load an assembly, examine the manifest, and discover all types residing within the assembly. This includes external assembly references, methods, fields, properties, and events defined by a specified type. Reflection also allows you to examine interfaces supported by a given class, a method's parameters, namespaces, and base classes. ILDasm.exe, a tool supplied by the Framework, allows you to inspect an assembly at design time.

To understand reflection, familiarize yourself with the *Type* class defined in the System.Type namespace as well as System.Reflection. (The latter namespace facilitates late binding and permits you to load assemblies at runtime.) Table 5-1 provides a partial listing of the *Type* class.

Type Member	Definition
IsAbstract IsArray IsClass IsCOMObject IsEnum IsInterface IsSealed IsValueType	These properties allow you to discover traits about the *Type*, for example, an array, a nested class, an abstract type, etc.
GetConstructors() GetEvents() GetFields() GetInterfaces() GetMethods() GetMembers() GetProperties()	These methods facilitate access to arrays representing the items, namely, interfaces, methods, properties, etc. Each method returns a specified array. You can retrieve a single item by specifying the name, rather than an array of all items.
FindMembers()	This method returns an array of MemberInfo types.
GetType()	This method returns a *Type* instance.
InvokeMembers()	This method facilitates late binding for a specified item.

Table 5-1 Type *Class (Partial Listing)*

The System.Type Namespace

Let's examine the System.Type namespace. System.Object defines a method called GetType() and returns a valid instance of the *Type* class.

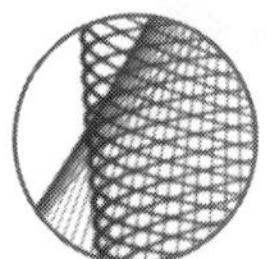

NOTE

Type is an abstract class; therefore, you cannot create an instance using new. *There is, however, a method for achieving this. Observe the following fragments of code.*

```
// Apply a valid Author instance
Author myAuthor = new Author();
Type t = myAuthor.GetType();
```

There is an alternate method:

```
// Use the static Type.GetType()method
Type t = null;
t = Type.GetType('Author');
```

You can employ still another approach:

```
// use the Typeof keyword
Type t = Typeof(Author);
```

Creating a Class Library

Now, as an example, let's build a class library named "Customer." Open Visual Studio .NET and create a project in Visual Basic .NET called Customer.

The class library design begins by creating the project in Visual Studio .NET. Select the class library icon. In VB .NET, the module has a .vb extension and a single source code file. It can contain more than one class. In the code window, change the class definition line to class *Customer*, as shown here:

```
Public Class Class1
to the following:
Public class Customer
```

In the Solution Explorer, right-click on the class1.vb icon and select Rename. Change the name to Customer.vb. Notice that the class does not have a constructor (Public SubNew) or a code designer; there is a way of creating both. Right-click on

Examining Visual Studio .NET

Visual Studio .NET is an Integrated Development Environment (IDE), allowing developers to leverage all .NET tools, profilers, cross-language debugging, and error handling within a single environment. You can also develop *nonmanaged code* (also referred to as native code) and work with traditional COM objects within Visual Studio .NET. This means you write your code with types not supported by the Framework. However, developers are not obligated to develop their code to receive full support from the Framework. Alternatively, you can use your favorite text editor and compile your applications with command line compilers provided by Microsoft for each .NET-hosted language. It is more convenient, however, to develop applications within the IDE because it is user friendly. You can accomplish all programming tasks within the IDE by using the profilers, debuggers, and tools without leaving the IDE.

the project name and choose Add, and then select Add Component. This adds a new file to the class. The *Component* class allows a developer to drag and drop data components to the designer.

It is time to add some code to the *Customer* class. Add a first name property by initially declaring a variable, as shown here:

```
Public Class Customer
    Dim msFirstName As String
    Public Property FirstName() As String
        Get
            Return msFirstName
        End Get
        Set(ByVal Value As String)
            msFirstName = Value
        End Set
    End Property
End Class
```

Compile the Customer project. If everything compiles, build a client and the library's services. From the File menu, select a new project and highlight the Windows application icon. Name the application CustomerClient and select the radio button to add the solution to the current project. Then click OK. In Solution Explorer, right-click the CustomerClient icon and select Set as Startup Project.

The next step is critical because you must have a reference to the Customer DLL. Select the CustomerClient icon and choose Add Reference. In the dialog box that opens, select Project from the tab and browse to the Customer project. The Customer DLL has been placed in the Selected Components box. Select the DLL and click on it to add a reference. Now, proceed to the form and drag a button from the toolbox onto the form. Double-click on the button to access the following code that Visual Studio has generated for you:

```
Private Sub Button1_Click(ByVal sender As System.Object,_
 ByVal e As System.EventArgs) Handles Button1.Click
```

Then, enter the following code and declare the variable first:

```
Dim MyNewCustomer As New Customer.Customer
        MyNewCustomer.FirstName = "Steve"
        MsgBox(MyNewCustomer.FirstName)
    End Sub
End Class
```

Finally, a DLL has been created so it is now possible to examine the PE file that contains the program code. The tool used is dumpbin.exe. The command line format is dumpbin.exe *filename,* and its type, EXE or DLL.

Reading Metadata

The PE file structure and its numerous header segments can be displayed with

```
dumpbin.exe CustomerClient.dll /all
```

Much of the file is left out of the following to highlight only the basic features of its structure:

```
Microsoft <R> COFF/PE Dumper Version 7.10 3077
Copyright <C> Microsoft Corporation. All rights reserved.
 Dump of file Customer.dll
PE signature found
File Type: DLL
File Header values [MS-DOS/COFF HEADERS]
14C machine (x86)
```

```
OPTIONAL HEADER VALUES
 10B magic #(PE32)
 Section Header #1  [SECTION DATA]
     ...
 .text name

  Code  Execute Read
RAW DATA #1
     ...
clr Header
//Section contains the following imports:
 Mscoree.dll
   402000 Import Address Table
   4025F8 Import Name Table
     ...
   0_CorDLLMain
```

The PE file lists the MS-DOS and Common Object File Format (COFF) headers. The overall file structure is the same for all Windows files. Microsoft has extended the PE file by adding headers to accommodate the Framework MSIL binaries.

Continuing through the file, notice that it supports 32-bit Windows programs. The "File Header values" segment indicates there are three sections in this file. "Section Header #1" stores the CLR header and data. The next segment, "Code Execute Read," informs the OS loader that the CLR contains code to be executed by the CLR at runtime. The rest of the PE file holds individual segments for .rdata, .rscr, and .text, as demonstrated before in the header file. When the CLR searches and locates the header, it executes 0_CorDLLMain.

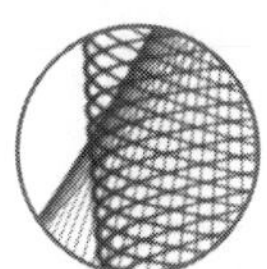

NOTE

The CLR header and data section contain both metadata and IL code. These describe in detail how CustomerClient executes. MSIL code is similar to Java's bytecode. If the file is an executable, it executes 0_CorEXEMain.

The PE file hosts the application code, whereas the manifest (recall that it contains metadata about the assembly) describes all references to external libraries, methods, classes, and types in binary format. Table 5-2 contains a list of manifest tags. As mentioned earlier, Framework provides an external tool, ILDasm.exe, to examine the metadata.

Tag Attribute	Meaning
.assembly	Denotes an assembly declaration.
.file	Indicates files residing within the assembly.
.assembly extern	Informs you that there is an external reference to an assembly residing elsewhere on the Web or other network. This assembly is essential to application execution.
.class extern	Indicates classes exported by the assembly. However, they are declared in another assembly.
.exeloc	Provides information about a location for an executable.
.module	Denotes a .NET module.
.module extern	Indicates that other modules contained within this module have items referenced within the current module.
.publickey	Represents the public key bytes.
.publickeytoken	Contains a token of the public key.

Table 5-2 *Manifest Intermediate Language Tags*

At the Visual Studio command prompt, navigate to the directory where your code lies. Then, type **ildasm.exe** to display the manifest and the assembly. This file references an external assembly, mscorlib. As previously mentioned, this core base-class library represents all classes providing support for the CLR. It identifies the version as 1.0 and a publickeytoken as (B7 7A 5C 56 19 34 E0 89). It also references the System.Windows.Forms. The assembly contains the binaries and offers support for MessageBox.Show. In addition, the manifest lists the current assembly, CustomerClient. Continuing on, mscorlib employs the System.Reflection namespace and its constructors. The manifest also displays a *hash* algorithm value and numerous other properties.

Now, let's examine the assembly itself. The following lists tree icons with their meanings and a description:

Icon	Description
Blue shield	Namespace
Blue rectangle with three outputs	Class
Blue rectangle with three outputs marked 'I'	Interface
Brown rectangle with three outputs	Value class

Icon	Description
Brown rectangle with three outputs marked 'E'	Enum
Magenta rectangle	Method
Magenta rectangle marked 'S'	Static method
Cyan diamond	Field
Cyan diamond marked 'S'	Static field
Green point-down rectangle	Event
Red point-up triangle	Property
Red point-right triangle	Manifest or a class info item

Understanding and Building Dynamic Assemblies

There are two kinds of assemblies, static assemblies and dynamic assemblies. *Static assemblies* are stored somewhere on your hard drive, whereas a *dynamic assembly* is created by System.Reflection.Emit on the fly. System.Reflection.Emit creates a dynamic assembly in memory at runtime. After creating your assembly, store it at runtime on the hard drive. Once the assembly exists, it changes back to its static status. Furthermore, it is possible to add new types dynamically to the runtime assembly. For example, web-enabled languages such as JScript.NET generate raw code, *emit* IL code, and store it dynamically in an assembly. At this point, examine the types defined within the System.Reflection.Emit namespace. Table 5-3 displays several *Types* from this namespace.

System.Reflection.Emit	Namespace Definition
AssemblyBuilder	AssemblyBuilder creates an assembly at runtime. You can use it to create either an executable or DLL binary assembly. Executables should call the ModuleBuilder.SetEntryPoint() method to set the entry point for the module. If no entry point exists, AssemblyBuilder generates a DLL.
ModuleBuilder	Use ModuleBuilder to build a module within the assembly at runtime.
EnumBuilder	EnumBuilder generates a Type, for example, class, interface, etc., within an assembly.
TypeBuilder	TypeBuilder constructs a Type within a module at runtime.

Table 5-3 *System.Reflection.Emit* Types

System.Reflection.Emit	Namespace Definition
MethodBuilder EventBuilder LocalBuilder PropertyBuilder FieldBuilder ConstructorBuilder CustomAttributeBuilder	These items create a defined member of a Type, for example, methods, local variables, properties, attributes, and constructors at runtime.
ILGenerator	ILGenerator generates intermediate language (IL) for a specific member at runtime.

Table 5-3 *System.Reflection.Emit* Types (continued)

International Finance Corporation Exchange: Building a Dynamic Assembly

Using our case study, let's build a dynamic assembly called MyIFCEAssembly, and explore the methods listed in Table 5-3. The application, written in C#, creates a class at runtime named *IFCE.*

```
Public class IFCE
{
  private string Msg;
 //public interface to the class
 IFCE(string s) {Msg = s;}
 Public string GetMsg() {return Msg;}
 Public void  Greeter() {System.Console.WriteLine
("You are now a valid Customer at IFCE!");
 Here is the application followed by comments.
namespace DynamicAssembly
{
using System;
using System.Reflection.Emit;
using System.Reflection;

   //build the assembly dynamically
   public class MyAssemblyBuilder
   {
   public int CreateMyAssembly(AppDomain cAppDomain)

//create assembly name and version
   AssemblyName assemblyName = new AssemblyName();
   assemblyName.Name = "MyIFCEAssembly";
   assemblyName.Version = new Version("1.0.0.0");
```

```
//now create the assembly in memory
 AssemblyBuilder assembly
    = cAppDomain.DefineDynamicAssembly(assemblyName,
  AssemblyBuilderAccess.Save);

ModuleBuilder module =
assembly.DefineDynamicModule
("MyIFCEAssembly", "MyIFCEAssembly.dll");
//Define public class IFCE
TypeBuilder IFCEClass = module.DefineType("MyIFCEAssembly.IFCE",
TypeAttributes.Public);

//Define a private String variable named "Msg"
//private string Msg
 FieldBuilder msgField = IFCEClass.DefineField("Msg",
 Type.GetType("System.String"),
 FieldAttributes.Private);

 //create a constructor
 Type[] constructorArgs = new Type[1];
 constructorArgs[0] = Type.GetType("System.String");
  ConstructorBuilder constructor =

  IFCEClass.DefineConstructor(MethodAttributes.Public,
         CallingConventions.Standard,constructorArgs);

 ILGenerator constructorIL = constructor.GetILGenerator();
 constructorIL.Emit(OpCodes.Ldarg_0);
 Type objectClass = Type.GetType("System.Object");
 ConstructorInfo superConstructor =
 objectClass.GetConstructor(new Type[0]);
  constructorIL.Emit(OpCodes.Call, superConstructor);
  constructorIL.Emit(OpCodes.Ldarg_0);

  constructorIL.Emit(OpCodes.Ldarg_1);
  constructorIL.Emit(OpCodes.Stfld,msgField);
  constructorIL.Emit(OpCodes.Ret);

//create GetMsg() method
MethodBuilder getMsgMethod =

IFCEClass.DefineMethod("GetMsg",MethodAttributes.Public,
Type.GetType("System.String"), null);
```

```
    ILGenerator methodIL = getMsgMethod.GetILGenerator();
    methodIL.Emit(OpCodes.Ldarg_0);
    methodIL.Emit(OpCodes.Ldfld,msgField);
    methodIL.Emit(OpCodes.Ret);

    //create the Customer method
    //public void InformCustomer()
    MethodBuilder GreetingMethod =
    IFCEClass.DefineMethod("InformCustomer",
    MethodAttributes.Public, null, null);
    methodIL = GreetingMethod.GetILGenerator();
    methodIL.EmitWriteLine("Greetings, new Customer");
    methodIL.Emit(OpCodes.Ret);
    IFCEClass.CreateType();
    //save the assembly to your hard drive
      assembly.Save("MyIFCEAssembly.dll");
      return 0;
      }
    }
}
```

Generate a single file assembly called MyIFCEAssembly, and name the class *MyAssemblyBuilder.* Then, build the dynamic assembly in memory and store it on the hard drive. Use AssemblyBuilder.DefineAssembly to create the assembly at runtime and save it with AssemblyBuilderAccess.Save. Next, construct the module bearing the same name as the assembly, MyIFCEAssembly.dll.

Next, TypeBuilder creates the class *IFCEClass* at runtime and declares TypeAttributes as public in scope. The next step requires a private string member variable named “Msg”. For this purpose, apply the FieldBuilder method and declare the variable. Now, write the following constructor

```
(IFCE(String s));
```

then, make use of the IlGenerator to create the underlying intermediate language (IL) for a class member at runtime.

After generating member variable Msg, you must create a method to get the message System.String by applying DefineMethod(“GetMsg”) and make the Method Attributes public.Next, write the InformCustomer method with the IFCE DefineMethod (“InformCustomer”).

When a customer initiates a purchase transaction for foreign currency, IFCE attempts to validate the customer and ascertain whether he or she has an existing account. Depending on the status of the customer (valid or nonvalid), several options exist:

- A valid customer can pay with cash, credit card, or by check.
- A nonvalid customer pays with cash.

The InformCustomer method determines the status and follows the normal procedures for the customer determination.

It is now appropriate to generate the actual class type assembly and save it to the disk. The runtime-generated assembly status is now static.

Next, create a client application and consume the IFCE service by adding a new class to the Dynamic Assembly namespace. Name the public class *AssemblyReader*. Here is the code:

```
namespace DynamicAssembly
{
using System;
using System.Reflection.Emit;
using System.Reflection;
using System.Threading;
public class AssemblyReader
{
      public static int Main(string[] args)
        {
           AppDomain cAppDomain = Thread.GetDomain();
    //create the dynamic assembly
       MyAssemblyBuilder asmb = new MyAssemblyBuilder();
       asmb.CreateMyAssembly(cAppDomain);
     //load the assembly
       Assembly a = null;
            try
            {
            a = Assembly.Load("MyIFCEAssembly");
            }
             catch
            {
              Console.WriteLine(" can't locate the assembly   ");
             }
             //get the Greeter Type
             Type Greeter = a.GetType("MyIFCEAssembly.IFCE");
             //create IFCE object
```

```
            object[]ctorArgs = new object[1];
            ctorArgs[0] = "Welcome, Mr. Hall,
you can now pay by cash,credit card, or by check!";
            object obj = Activator.CreateInstance(Greeter,ctorArgs);
            mi.Invoke(obj, null);
            mi = Greeter.GetMethod("GetMsg");
          Console.WriteLine(mi.Invoke(obj, null));
          Console.ReadLine();
          return 0;
          }
    }
}
```

Declare a new class named *AssemblyReader*. This class consumes the IFCE class services. You can call the appropriate domain utilizing the method Thread.GetDomain(). Then, compile *MyIFCEAssembly*. Now, load the assembly. Next, create the IFCE object and an instance of it. The Activator method invokes GetMessage and displays the message.

Now that a dynamic assembly has been generated at runtime, you can understand how significantly System.Reflection.Emit contributes to creating static assemblies. There can also be multifile static assemblies as well as *shared* assemblies. Before making MyIFCEAssembly a shared, global assembly, you must first create a strong name. It is now important to come to terms with two separate specifications:

- Common Type Specification (CTS)
- Common Language Specification (CLS)

We'll explore the Common Type Specification first.

Understanding the Common Type Specification (CTS)

A *Type* refers to a collection of classes, interfaces, delegates, and structures supported by the Common Language Runtime. Microsoft .NET also allows you to create your own user-defined types. Moreover, you can group the user-defined types into unique namespaces. As previously stated, all objects derive from System.Object. Table 5-4 provides information about the .NET namespaces.

.NET Namespace	Meaning
System	Contains a collection of classes referencing primitive types, math manipulations, garbage collection, debugging, etc.
System.Collections	Defines container objects, for example, ArrayLists, Queues, etc.
System.Data.Oledb System.Data System.Data.Common System.Data.SqlClient	Pertains to all database functionality.
System.IO	Comprises file I/O.
System.Reflection System.Reflection.Emit	Supports IL code and assembly examination at runtime. System.Reflection.Emit allows you to create dynamic assemblies on the fly.
System.Net	Hosts Types relating to network application design.
System.Diagnostics	Facilitates language-agnostic diagnosis.
System.Drawing.System.Drawing2D System.Drawing.Printing	Supports all GDI, bitmaps, icons, and fonts.
System.Runtime.InteropServices System.Runtime.Remoting	Offers interoperability between managed and unmanaged code, for example, COM Servers, Win32 DLLs, etc.
System.Threading	Facilitates multithreading. This includes Types Mutex, Timeout, and Thread.
System.Security	Supports .NET security, for example, CodeAccessPermissions.
System.Windows.Forms	Enables dialog box construction, windows, MessageBox.Show, etc.
System.Web	Provides support for all web services, web application development, and ASP.NET (the presentation layer).
System.XML	Contains a set of classes representing core XML primitives and types, thereby facilitating interaction with XML data.

Table 5-4 *.NET Namespaces*

In Visual Basic .NET, the CTS *Structure* replaces VB *Types*. Whereas VB 6.0 supported the *Type* keyword, thereby enabling developers to create user-defined types, the .NET keyword *Structure* defines numerical types, for example, complex numbers. As observed in our System.Reflection.Emit runtime application, DynamicAssembly, the *Common Type Specification* provides information on all data types supported by the runtime. Simply put, the CTS describes precisely how the disparate data types interact with each other courtesy of the assembly manifest, both at design time and runtime. This demonstrates how .NET reusable binaries can intermingle across all platforms targeting the Framework. *Structures* implement a great number of interfaces.

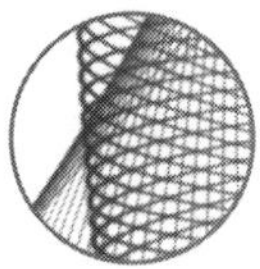

NOTE

The list of tree icons for viewing an assembly, provided in the earlier section "Reading Metadata," displayed a magenta rectangle marked "S." This icon denotes a static method, meaning the method is sealed. Therefore, structures may not derive from other base types.

Before turning our discussion to .NET modules, let's finish this examination of CTS Types. Table 5-5 displays the CTS intrinsic Types. You can see how all languages share the same data type declared and defined in Microsoft .NET class libraries.

Microsoft .NET Types	Visual Basic .NET Type Representation	C# Type Representation	C++ with Managed Extensions Representation
System.Byte	Byte	byte	char
System.SByte	Not supported	sbyte	signed char
System.Int16	Short	short	short
System.Int32	Integer	int	int or long
System.Int64	Long	long	_64
System.UInt16	Not supported	ushort	unsigned short
System.UInt32	Not supported	uint	unsigned int or unsigned long
System.UInt64	Not supported	ulong	unsigned_int64
System.Single	Single	float	float
System.Double	Double	double	double
System.Object	Object	object	Object

Table 5-5 *Microsoft .NET Intrinsic Types and Their Representations in Other Languages*

Microsoft .NET Types	Visual Basic .NET Type Representation	C# Type Representation	C++ with Managed Extensions Representation
System.Char	Char	char	_wchar_t
System.String	String	string	String
System.Decimal	Decimal	decimal	Decimal
System.Boolean	Boolean	bool	bool

Table 5-5 *Microsoft .NET Intrinsic Types and Their Representations in Other Languages (continued)*

.NET Modules

A .NET *module* is a representation of a class type. Public functions, subroutines, and variables defined within module scope are shared members. They are visible to an entire application.

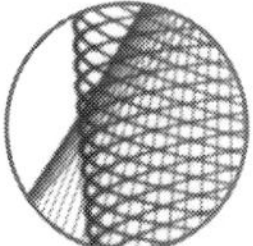

NOTE

You may not create modules. For an example, refer to our IFCE Assembly module:

```
ModuleBuilder module = assembly.DefineDynamicModule
("MyIFCEAssembly", "MyIFCEAssembly.dll");
```

Examining the Common Language Specification (CLS)

The *Common Language Specification* sets forth guidelines that a .NET-aware compiler must follow before it can receive support from the Framework. In other words, adhering to the CLS set of rules guarantees that all .NET-targeted languages can achieve interoperability courtesy of Microsoft's IL code. In order to interact with objects irrespective of their language, objects must expose to callers only features common to all languages. Microsoft has designed the CLS to provide language constructs commonly needed by developers.

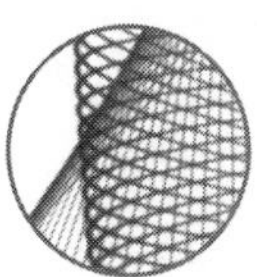

NOTE

Refer to the document that discusses type verification in the Microsoft .NET Framework's Developer Guide.

Here is a brief description of the verification process: Before running MSIL code, you must convert it using the just-in-time compiler. MSIL is CPU-specific code that runs on the same computer as the JIT compiler. The CLR provides a JIT compiler for each CPU-specific architecture.

The JIT compiles only code required for execution rather than loading all existing MSIL in the PE file. Once it has loaded the code, the JIT stores the native code for subsequent calls. The loader creates a stub and attaches it to each of a type's methods. With the initial call, the stub relinquishes control to the JIT compiler. The compiler modifies the stub to provide CPU-specific execution instructions. Subsequent calls go directly to the identified native code rather than repeating the process just described. This substantially reduces the time required to run native code.

Another mode of compilation is called *install-time code generation*. This compilation method converts the MSIL code in the same way as the standard mode just described. However, the JIT converts larger chunks of code at compile time and stores the native code with consideration for what it already knows about other installed assemblies. This file loads and starts more quickly than the standard JIT method.

A verification process validates the code before the JIT compiles the MSIL. It employs reflection to examine both the metadata and MSIL to ensure that the code is type safe. The compiler subsequently accesses only the portions of memory containing the type-safe code. Additionally, the verification process guarantees and enforces security restrictions defined by the CLS.

Let's examine the verification process a little more closely with an example. It is possible to sign an assembly digitally by using a public/private key pair to construct a shared assembly. At build time, the JIT compiler generates hash code for the assembly and then signs the hash with a private key. Subsequently, it stores the signature in a reserved section of the PE file. The public key is also stored in the assembly. Then, the CLR employs the assembly's public key to decrypt and verify the assembly's signature. The original calculated hash is the result of this procedure. Moreover, the CLR applies the information in the manifest to generate the hash dynamically. Next, the hash value is measured against the original hash. If the values are equal, the verification procedure passes and the class loader hands the assembly to the JIT compiler.

The CLR depends on the following items to ensure that it is processing type-safe code:

- Identities must be validated.
- Only type-safe operations are invoked on an object.

If the JIT receives nonverified code, it generates an exception.

Creating a Strong Name

You create a shared assembly by generating a *strong name*. To accomplish this, follow these steps:

1. Use the sn.exe utility located in C:\Program Files\Microsoft Visual Studio .NET 2003.0\SDK\v1.1\Bin. Select sn.exe to place it in the Command window. This utility creates a .snk file. Several flags are provided to generate the strong name. If you select the *-k* flag, it will look like this:

```
sn -k Registration.snk
```

2. The template syntax is <*filename*>.snk. Provide an appropriate name that identifies your class.
3. Select <initial directory> and specify where you want to store your strong name. You will see the strong name being generated. Also, place it in your project directory for easy access.
4. Select OK and you will see your strong name listed on the Tools menu.

Once you have created the strong name, the Framework provides a tool called gacutil.exe, located in the same directory as sn.exe. Type the following from the Visual Studio Command window: **gacutil /i MyIFCEAssembly.dll** to place it in the GlobalAccessCache (GAC). You can use an alternate method by dragging the assembly key to the GAC located in C:\Windows\Assembly. Once you are there, select Properties, and the Strong Name field displays as True.

If your strong name does not appear automatically in the Solutions Explorer window, check to ensure that it has actually been created. If the strong name property displays as False, try selecting AssemblyInfo.cs, and opening the dialog box to see if the following information is present in the assembly:

```
<Assembly: AssemblyTitle("")>
<Assembly: AssemblyDescription("")>
<Assembly: AssemblyCompany("")>
<Assembly: AssemblyProduct("")><Assembly: AssemblyCopyright("")>
<Assembly: AssemblyTradeMark("")>
<Assembly: CLSCompliant(True)>
        ...
Version information for an assembly consists of the following:
'       Major Version
'       Minor Version
'       Build Number Revision
'       Revision
'You can specify all the values or you can default the Build
```

```
'by using the '*' as shown below+
,Assembly:  Assembly Version("1.0">
If you don't see the Assembly key, follow these instructions:
Copy <Assembly: AssemblyVersion("1.0.*")
 Add the following code:
<Assembly: AssemblyKeyFile ("..\\..\\MyIFCEAssembly.snk")
```

Recompile the assembly and check the MyIFCEAssembly property. Then, drag the assembly to the GAC. Voila! Now the assembly is global and can be shared by other applications. It was just that easy to make your assembly public.

How Does .NET Locate an Assembly?

There are three separate procedures for locating an assembly:

- Examining a configuration file
- Probing
- Using a Codebase

The application calls a referenced assembly containing information about the assembly, for example, Name, Version, Culture, and Public Key. First, it examines a configuration file. You can update your assembly by creating a configuration file that looks something like this:

```
<configuration>
<runtime>
<AssemblyBinding xmlns = "urn:schemas-microsoft-com:asm.v1">
<dependentAssembly>
  <AssemblyIdentity name="IFCE"
    <publicKeyToken = "6cf7280fa2c8aa7"/>
 <bindingRedirect oldVersion = "1.0.0.0" new version = "2.0.0.0"/>
 </dependentAssembly>
<publisherPolicy apply="yes"/>
<probing privatePath="C:\Visual Studio Solutions\IFCE"/>
</assemblyBinding>
<gcCurrent enable="true">
</runtime>
</configuration>
```

Another tool, mscoref.msc, manages and configures the assembly. Its location is C:\Visual Solutions\Microsoft.Net\Framework\.

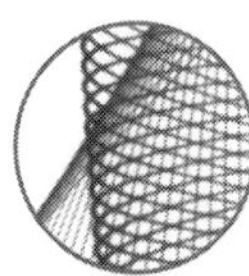

NOTE

You must have a client application before you can employ mscoref.msc.

Probing means the runtime looks for the assembly using the following search criteria: The runtime examines the GAC for the assembly's strong name. If the assembly is private, the runtime searches the application root directory, called the APPBase. If it sees a reference for an assembly, it searches for your DLL. If the assembly is not an APPBase, the runtime alternately searches the configuration file for any specified path. It the assembly is not there, it searches the bin directory.

A <codeBase> element specifies where the CLR can locate your assembly. The runtime uses a configuration file only if the file contains a Redirect Assembly version. After the CLR determines the appropriate version to load, the runtime applies the codebase setting from the file specifying the assembly's version. Here is an example:

```
<configuration>
  <runtime>
     <assemblyBinding = "urn:schemas-Microsoft-com:asm.v1">
            <dependentAssembly name ="IFCE Process"
             PublicKeyToken = "6cf7280fa2c28aa9"
              Culture = "en-us"/>
          <codeBase version="2.0.0.0"
              href="http://www.dps.com/IFCEProcess.dll"/>
          </dependentAssembly>
      </assemblyBinding>
    </.runtime>
<configuration>
```

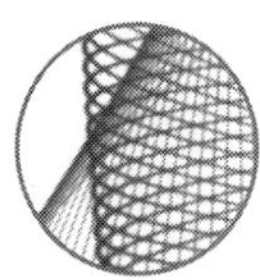

NOTE

Codebase is available for use in an application configuration file, machine configuration file (for example, machine.config), and the publisher policy file.

Conclusion

This chapter began by examining the overall architecture of the .NET Framework, how it fits into the Windows set of operating systems, and the significant role it plays in offering a wide range of services, methods, interfaces, namespaces containing classes and base class libraries that support interoperability. Drilling down from Common Language Runtime tasks and its responsibilities to the JIT compilers, the System.Reflection namespace, the manifest, and assembly, provided an opportunity to learn how .NET provides support for integrated, distributed services for the enterprise. A discussion of the Common Type Specification and Common Language Specification rounded out the chapter. Subsequent chapters examine other CLR-related components such as ASP.NET.

CHAPTER

6

ASP.NET Architecture

IN THIS CHAPTER:

ASP.NET Namespaces

ASP.NET Page Class

Defining Web Form Functionality

Creating User Controls

Error Handling and Security

ASP.NET is not just an upgrade to classic ASP but is completely rebuilt from top to bottom. Yet, many familiar ASP features remain, such as Request and Response objects, Application, and Server. You can use the ubiquitous <script runat = "server"> block or ASP <% %> script delimiters, among other familiar items. Microsoft designed ASP.NET so developers who are accustomed to creating applications with classic ASP can continue to do their work while becoming familiar with ASP.NET. Although you may have much time invested in writing legacy ASP applications, ASP.NET applications can run side by side with classic ASP. This is possible because .NET assemblies are not registered in the system registry. Moreover, if you do need to interact with a COM object from ASP.NET, the CLR allows you to do so by generating a *runtime callable wrapper* (RCW). The RCW functions as a proxy for unmanaged code.

You can also call an ASP.NET object from COM. Again, the runtime generates a *COM callable wrapper* (CCW). This is good news for developers. You need not abandon your legacy code and applications. Interoperability in the .NET environment between COM objects and managed code is provided by the CLR.

The ASP.NET Framework serves as the foundation for creating both web services and browser-based applications and, as mentioned in Chapter 5, has two separate parts, the Common Language Runtime (CLR), which provides support for .NET-hosted applications, and class libraries, which play host to three distinct components:

- ASP.NET implements the Internet segment of the Framework.
- ADO.NET provides access to SQL Server 2000.
- Web forms lend support for smart-client user interfaces.

ASP.NET's features for enhancing web page development, combined with the .NET Framework's support for web services, make it the perfect tool for building web services:

- The *code-behind* model separates HTML (the presentation layer) from program logic (server-side code). This eliminates the dangerous practice of writing spaghetti code that is prone to error.
- An event-driven program model allows you to write your events and create handlers for them.
- Server controls automatically render HTML appropriate for any client browser.

- Server controls manage client state by using ViewState.
- Code is compiled, thereby enhancing performance.
- Application logic can be written in any CLS-compliant programming language, such as Visual Basic .NET, Managed C++ .NET, or C# .NET.
- Web form development is simplified by using Visual Studio .NET as a RAD tool.

Let's look under the hood and see how you benefit by migrating from classic ASP to ASP.NET.

ASP.NET Namespaces

The path to understanding ASP.NET's process lies in examining the underlying infrastructure and observing how ASP.NET interacts with the .NET Framework base-class libraries and namespaces. The Framework supports web services and web forms through namespaces that host classes, such as System.Web.UI and System.Web.UI.WebControls. The System.Web.UI namespace contains classes and interfaces that allow you to create controls and pages that appear in your web applications as user interfaces on a web page. A major advantage offered by ASP.NET is running the controls on the server rather than on the client so you can programmatically control them at runtime.

System.Web.UI Namespace

The System.Web.UI namespace hosts the classes and interfaces especially designed for rendering elements on a web form. You can view all classes in the System.Web.UI namespace as a hierarchical tree beginning with the Control class. This is the mother of all controls. Buttons, text boxes, drop-down list boxes, and so on, derive from the Control class. It encapsulates both functionality and user interface properties for all member controls residing in this namespace. Class properties include Controls, Context, ClientID, EnableViewState, ID, NamingContainer, Parent, Site, TemplateSourceDirectory, UniqueID, Visible, and ViewState.

A collection of classes, interfaces, enumerations, and delegates makes up the namespace and are essential for developers to understand so that they can take full advantage of ASP.NET.

Classes

This table provides a complete list of System.Web.UI classes:

Class	Description
Attribute Collection	Provides all object-model access declared in the opening tag of an ASP.NET server control element. The class cannot be inherited.
BaseParser	Offers a base set of functionality for classes involved in parsing ASP.NET page requests as well as server controls.
ConstructorNeedsTagAttribute	Requires a tag name in the server control constructor.
Control	Defines all properties, methods, and events shared by all ASP.NET server controls.
ControlBuilder	Supports the page parser in constructing a control and its child controls.
ControlBuilderAttribute	Specifies a ControlBuilderClass for constructing a custom control within the parser. The class cannot be inherited.
ControlCollection	Provides a collection container for ASP.NET to maintain a list of its child controls.
CssStyleCollection	Contains the HTML cascading style sheets inline style attributes for a specified HTML server control.
DataBinder	Lends support for RAD developers to generate and parse data-binding expression syntax. This class cannot be inherited.
DataBinding	Contains information about a single data-binding expression in a server control. This feature enhances RAD development and allows developers to create data-binding expressions at design time.
DataBindingCollection	Provides a collection of DataBinding objects for an ASP.NET server control. This class cannot be inherited.
DataBindingHandlerAttribute	Defines a design-time class that performs control data binding within a designer. This class cannot be inherited.
DataBoundLiteralControl	Creates a control for HTML text to enable handling of <% %> data-binding expressions processed by the ASP.NET server. This class cannot be inherited.
EmptyControlCollection	Lends support for an empty control collection.

Class	Description
HTML32TextWriter	Provides a text writer for ASP.NET pages and server controls that render HTML content for HTML 3.2 clients.
HTMLTextWriter	Writes a sequential series of HTML-specific characters and text to a web forms page. The class enables formatting capabilities used by ASP.NET server controls when rendering HTML content to clients.
ImageClickEventArgs	Provides information for events occurring when a client clicks on an image-based server control. This class cannot be inherited.
LiteralControl	Represents HTML elements, text, and other strings on an ASP.NET page not requiring server-side processing.
LosFormatter	Serializes the view state for a web forms page. This class cannot be inherited.
Page	Defines an .aspx file or a web forms page. All other pages derive from the ASP.NET page class in the System.Web.UI namespace.
Pair	Contains two objects that can both be added to an ASP.NET server control's view state.
ParseChildrenAttribute	Defines a metadata attribute that a developer uses when developing ASP.NET server controls. Use this attribute to indicate whether XML elements embedded within the ASP.NET server control's tags should be treated either as properties or as children when the control is used declaratively on a page control. This class cannot be inherited.
PartialCachingAttribute	Represents a class created when a user control (.ascx file) is specified for output caching, using either the @ OutputCache directive or the PartialCachingAttribute, and is added to the page programmatically.
PersistChildrenAttribute	Defines a metadata attribute utilized by ASP.NET server controls. The attribute specifies whether, at design time, the child controls of an ASP.NET server control should be persisted as nested inner controls. This class cannot be inherited.
PersistenceModeAttribute	Defines a metadata attribute that specifies how an ASP.NET server control property or event is persisted to an ASP.NET page. This class cannot be inherited.

Class	Description
PropertyConverter	Contains helper functions to convert property values to and from strings.
StateBag	Manages the view state of ASP.NET server controls, including pages. This class cannot be inherited.
StateItem	Represents an item that is saved in the StateBag class when view state information is persisted between web requests. This class cannot be inherited.
StaticPartialCachingControl	Represents an instance of the UserControl class when it has been specified for output caching and included declaratively in a page or another user control.
TagPrefixAttribute	Defines the tag prefix used in a web page to identify controls. This class cannot be inherited.
TemplateBuilder	Supports the page parser when constructing a template and child controls that it contains.
TemplateContainerAttribute	Declares the type of the INamingContainer that will contain the template once it is created.
TemplateControl	Provides the Page class and the UserControl class with a base set of functionality.
ToolboxDataAttribute	Specifies the default tag generated for a custom control when it is dragged from a toolbox in a tool, for example, Visual Studio.
Triplet	Holds three objects that can all be added to an ASP.NET server control's view state.
UserControl	Represents an .ascx file, requested from a server that hosts an ASP.NET web application. The file must be called from a web forms page, or a parser error will occur.
UserControl ControlBuilder	Supports the page parser when constructing a user control and any child user controls that it contains.
ValidationPropertyAttribute	Defines the metadata attribute used by ASP.NET server controls to identify a validation property. This class cannot be inherited.
ValidationCollection	Exposes an array of IValidator references. This class cannot be inherited.

Interfaces

The following table contains the list of System.Web.UI interfaces:

Interface	Description
IAttributeAccessor	Defines methods used by ASP.NET server controls to provide programmatic access to any attribute declared in the opening tag of a server control.
IDataBindingsAccessor	Permits access to the collection of data-binding expressions on a control at design time.
INamingContainer	Identifies a container control that creates a new ID namespace within a Page object's control hierarchy. This is a marker interface only.
IParserAccessor	Defines the method that ASP.NET server controls must implement to recognize when elements, either XML or HTML, are parsed.
IPostBackDataHandler	Defines methods that ASP.NET server controls must implement to automatically load post-back data.
IStateMapper	Defines properties and methods that any class must implement to support view state management for a server control.
ITemplate	Defines the method to implement for populating an ASP.NET server control with child controls when using a control with inline templates declared in an .aspx file.
IUserControlDesignerAccessor	Defines the properties to implement, and allows designers to access information about a user control at design time.
IValidator	Defines the properties and methods that objects participating in web forms validation must implement.

Enumerations

The following table provides a list of System.Web.UI enumerations used when enumerating more than one item.

Enumeration	Description
HtmlTextWriterAttribute	Specifies the HTML attributes that an HTMLTextWriter or HTML32TextWriter object writes to the opening tag of an HTML element when a web request is processed.
HtmlTextWriterStyle	Specifies the HTML styles available to an HtmlTextWriter or HtmlTextWriter32 object output stream.

Enumeration	Description
HtmlTextWriterTag	Specifies which HTML tags are allowed to be passed to an HtmlTextWriter or HtmlTextWriter32 object output.
OutputCacheLocation	Specifies the valid values for the location of the output cache.
PersistenceMode	Specifies how an ASP.NET server control property or event is persisted declaratively in an .aspx or .ascx file.

Delegates

The final item in the System.Web.UI namespace, *delegates*, contains one item. It describes the method that handles any events raised when a user clicks on an image-based ASP.NET server control. Also, a delegate is a reference type that encapsulates a method that contains a specific signature and return type.

ASP.NET Page Class

ASP.NET pages begin as code in a text file with an .aspx extension. They lie within an Internet Information Service (IIS) virtual directory located somewhere on your LAN or on a remote server. Pages are instantiation classes derived from the parent Page class. For example, you can write your code using any text editor such as Notepad or, preferably, Visual Studio .NET. The text file becomes a valid ASP.NET page only when a client sends a request to the server to render the page to the client browser. The page compiles to a class. It is created at runtime as a Page object and is subsequently cached in memory. It naturally follows that the Page object serves as a naming container for all server controls embedded within the page. The only exception to this is those server controls implementing the INamingContainer interface.

Examining the Page Class

ASP.NET functionality lies primarily with the Page class. Every page derives from the Page class, thereby inheriting all the methods and properties the Page class exposes. The following list describes several members of this class.

- The ASP objects such as Application, Session, Request, Response, Server, and Context are implemented in ASP.NET as class instances, which are exposed as properties of a specified page.

- The Controls collection provides access to the set of controls defined for a specific page. With this collection, you can add or alter controls.
- The IsPostBack property is used to determine whether the current request is a GET request or a POST request.
- The User property provides information about the logged-in user.
- The Cache property enables access to the ASP.NET cache engine. You can use this property to allow data to be cached for later retrieval.
- The FindControl property allows you to locate a control in the Controls collection by specifying the ID attribute property.
- The ViewState property allows you to store a page's state in a hidden form field (key-value pair) between client requests.
- The ClearChildViewState property allows you to delete view state information for any child controls residing on a page.

Two methods exist for inheriting from the Page class: the first is adding the @ Page directive to an .aspx file. By doing so, the directive automatically makes available all page properties and methods for any code written on the page.

```
<%@ Page Language ="vb"%>
```

The second method uses the code-behind feature to inherit from the Page class associated with a particular page by specifying either the Src or Inherits attribute:

```
<%@ Page Language="vb" AutoEventWireup="false"
Codebehind="RegisterForm.aspx.vb"
Inherits="RegisterForm.WebForm1" %>
```

The second method allows ASP.NET to combine the code in the web form's .aspx file with the code in the code-behind class file and compile both files to a single merged file at compile time.

An ASP.NET Page's Life Cycle

Let's examine a page's life cycle to further our knowledge of ASP.NET pages. Figure 6-1 illustrates the page's process from its inception to its destruction.

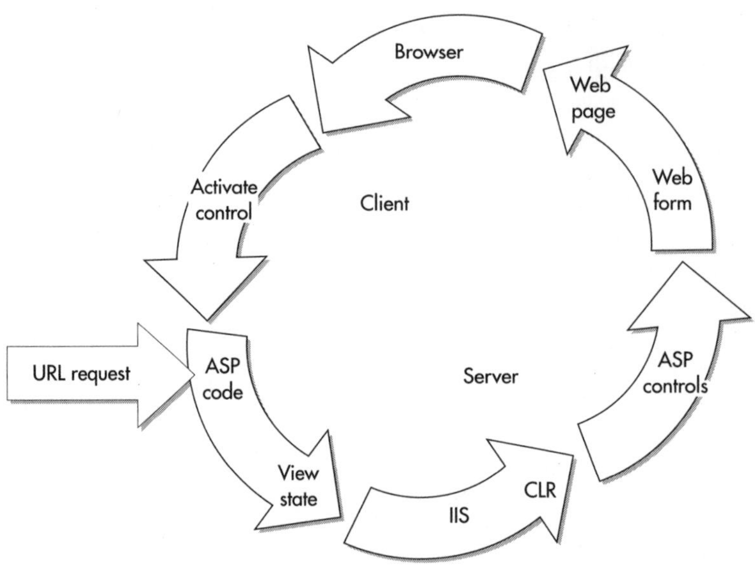

Figure 6-1 *An ASP.NET page's life cycle*

Each ASP.NET page contains a server-side <form> tag. This tag directs the page to post back to itself when a client submits the form. The Form type events include Load, Draw, Render, and Unload.

ASP.NET controls also render JavaScript to the client, enabling actions such as selecting a specified item from a drop-down list, thereby causing a post back to the server. The ASP.NET runtime also renders a hidden form field to the page and allows it to preserve its state between client requests.

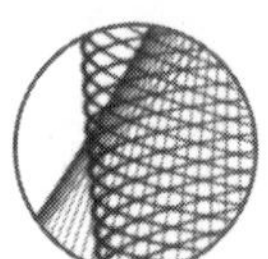

NOTE

The engagement between client and page in the case of hidden form fields occurs on the client side, rather than on the server.

Because ASP.NET is event driven, client and page interaction allows the page to be reconstructed on the server. It also permits code execution in response to events raised by users and any changes occurring in the hidden fields.

The initial event begins with an HTTP URL client request for rendering a specific page to a client's browser. The Load event fires next. Here is where the CLR uses reflection to examine the .aspx page and see if the page is called for the first time, or whether this represents a post back through user interaction with a button or some other page control. If the event is a first-time request, the code is converted to a class. Subsequently, the class compiles to an assembly and is stored in a valid Internet Information Server virtual directory where the page can be located. However, if the page is posted back, ASP.NET restores any data residing in hidden fields (ViewState) and passes the information to the server. The control event triggering the post back then fires. At this point, all control events are initiated. The change events fire first; those events are stored in the browser and execute only when the client sends the page back to the server. After a control event fires, the page is rendered to the browser.

Before Page_Unload() unloads the page from server memory, a final event performs any cleanup tasks before the unload method disposes of the page.

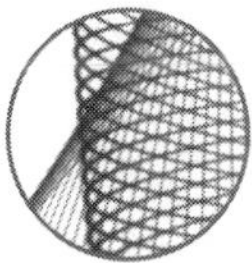

NOTE

A dynamically generated assembly is not static. If you modify any application code in the .aspx page, the DLL is regenerated the next time the page is called before storing it again to the disk. Latency is an issue here. For example, in a network, latency is a delay. Latency could be solved by multithreading. The browser will respond to callbacks and DLL regeneration.

Applying Page Directives

Most likely if you are a classic ASP developer, you have used directives such as @ Include and @ Language. The @ Include directive instructs the ASP runtime to include a particular file inline with the page. The @ Language directive tells the runtime to employ a specific script interpreter located within the <% %> render blocks. Directives provide easy ways for developers to determine declaratively how various aspects of an application will ultimately behave. For example, in addition to the @ Language directive, classic ASP provided only four directives:

- **@ Codepage** Used in globalization to set the code page for an ASP page
- **@ EnableSessionState** Used to disable session state for a specified page
- **@ LCID** Used to set the locale identifier for an ASP page
- **@ Transaction** Used to specify how a page participates in COM+ transactions

ASP.NET has added numerous directives for controlling page behavior, page configuration, and many other tasks. Table 6-1 presents a partial list of new directives included with ASP.NET. Note that in the Values column, T/F stands for true or false.

Attribute	Values	Meaning
@ Page	T/F	Defines page-specific attributes used by ASP.NET compilers and the CLR to determine page behavior.
AutoEventWireup	T/F Default is set in the <pages> segment of the Machine.config or Web.config file	Determines whether handlers are set up automatically. Default is true.
Buffer	T/F	Specifies whether rendered output is buffered before sending it to clients, or sent as it is rendered.
ClassName	Can be any class name	Determines name of page when dynamically compiling the page. This works either with or without CodeBehind.
CodeBehind	File name of CodeBehind class	Visual Studio .NET uses this attribute for locating the CodeBehind class and compiling during a build operation. ASP.NET does not use this attribute.
CodePage	Any code page	The same in both ASP and ASP.NET.
CompilerOptions	A string containing valid compiler options	Allows developers to specify compiler options for a specified page.
ContentType	Any valid MIME type	Sets the MIME type for page output.
Debug	T/F Default is set in the <compilation> section of the Machine.config or Web.config file	Determines whether pages are compiled with debug symbols or not. Default is false.
Description	Any string	Provides a text description of the page. The ASP.NET runtime ignores this attribute.
EnableSessionState	T/F Default is set in the <pages> section of the Machine.config or Web.config file	Determines whether a page request initiates a new session and whether or not the page can access or modify data saved in an existing session. Default is true.

Table 6-1 *ASP.NET Page Directives*

Attribute	Values	Meaning
EnableViewState	T/F Default is set in the <pages> section of the Machine.config or Web.config file	Specifies whether ViewState is enabled for the page. Default is true.
EnableViewStateMac	T/F Default is set in the <pages> section of the Machine.config or Web.config file	Determines whether ASP.NET executes a machine authentication check on the content of a hidden form field that is used to store ViewState and to ensure it is not modified on the client. Default is false.

Table 6-1 *ASP.NET Page Directives* (continued)

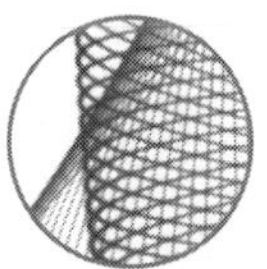

NOTE

The list of directives in Table 6-1 is incomplete. Many other equally important directives exist, such as Inherits, ResponseEncoding, LCID, Strict, and Transaction. You can search for these directives in Visual Studio .NET Help.

Here is a brief example of how you would use the Page directive:

```
<%@ Page debug="true" %>
```

Another example sets the trace directive:

```
<%@ Page trace="true" %>
```

Other directives include the @ Implements directive, employed to implement a defined interface from within an ASP.NET page. In addition, use the @ Register directive to register user controls and custom server controls on an ASP.NET page.

Code-Behind Feature

ASP.NET's code-behind feature separates business logic from the presentation layer. In order to take advantage of this technique, derive from the Page class. Then place your code in an .aspx file and insert a reference to another file containing the business logic, for example:

```
<%@ Page Language="vb"%>
<%@ Register TagPrefix="ASPNETSBtn"
TagName="ClientName" Src="RegisterClient" %>
```

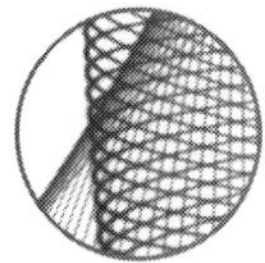

NOTE

Any file rerferenced with the src *attribute of the Page directive is compiled into a separate assembly and added to the list of referenced assemblies when the page is compiled. Additionally, an advantage of using the* src *attribute for the code-behind file is the ease with which the developer can update the code-behind file by replacing the file. Subsequently, the next time a page is requested, ASP.NET recompiles the file.*

The following example contains HTML, text, and several lines of VB .NET code. The web form has two Textbox controls named FirstName and LastName. The form also contains two RequiredFieldValidator controls that prevent you from submitting the form to the server without entering data in the FirstName and LastName Textbox controls.

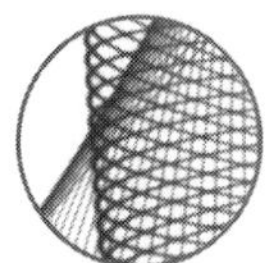

NOTE

The <asp: TextBox> tag informs the compiler that this ASP.NET page contains a text box control for execution on the server.

A typical ASP.NET page looks like this:

```
<%@ Page Language = "vb" AutoEventWireup="false"
 Codebehind = "WebForm1.aspx.vb" Inherits="IFCE.WebForm1"%>
<html><head><title>Registering a new client</title></head>
<body>
<form runat="Server">
<p>FirstName:
<br><asp:TextBox id="firstName" runat="Server"/>
<asp:RequiredFieldValidator ControlToValidate="firstName"
Runat="Server"/>
<p>LastName:
<br><asp:TextBox id="lastname" runat="Server"/>
<asp:RequiredFieldValidator
ControlToValidate="lastname"
Runat="Server"/>
<p>
<asp:button text="Submit Form" Runat="server"/>
</form>
</body>
</html>
```

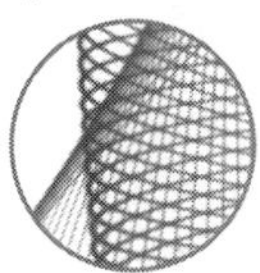

NOTE

If the <form> element is not present on the page, both web controls and HTML controls will not be able to participate in page post backs, nor will they be able to save their state in the page's ViewState. They will continue to function otherwise.

It is unwise to bypass one of the key benefits that ASP.NET offers, namely, preserving state between client page requests. Always add the <form> element to your web forms page. If a post-back event occurs, any state stored in hidden fields rendered to the form is retrieved and sent back to the server for rendering the new page to the browser. The user views the newly rendered .aspx page as though it were the original page. In reality, they are two individually unique pages.

Defining Web Form Functionality

Let's create a new project in Visual Studio .Net. Begin by creating a virtual directory called MyASP.NETPages. Then open Visual Studio .NET and create the new ASP.NET web application project called IFCE. Initially, the location where the application will be stored looks like this: http://localhost/WebApplication1. Rename it to the correct project name, "IFCE." Also, rename public class1 to Register. Notice how public class Register inherits from class System.Web.UI.Page. The next item of interest, Private Sub InitializeComponent(), calls the subroutine InitializeComponent(). Next, Private Sub Page_Init(ByVal sender as System.Object, ByVal e as System.EventArgs) Handles MyBase.Init initializes the page.

```
Public Class Register
    Inherits System.Web.UI.Page
#Region "Web Form Designer Generated Code"
    'This call is required by the Web Form Designer.
    <System.Diagnostics.DebuggerStepThrough()>
    Private Sub InitializeComponent()
    End Sub
    'NOTE: The following placeholder declaration
    is required by the Web Form Designer.
    'Do not delete or move it.
    Private designerPlaceholderDeclaration As System.Object
    Private Sub Page_Init(ByVal sender As System.Object,
    ByVal e As System.EventArgs) Handles MyBase.Init
        'CODEGEN: This method call is required by the Web Form Designer
```

```
        'Do not modify it using the code editor.
        InitializeComponent ()
    End Sub
#End Region
End Class
```

WebForm1.aspx displays the code-behind feature. Inside the ASP.NET script delimiters, the page language is VB; the CodeBehind is Web Form1.aspx.vb. The code indicates that the web form inherits from the IFCE WebForm1. The form ID is Form1; the method is Post, specifying that the page must run on the server.

```
%@ Page Language="vb" AutoEventWireup="false"
Codebehind="WebForm1.aspx.vb" Inherits="IFCE.WebForm1"%>
<html>
  <head>
    <TITLE>WebForm1</TITLE>
    <meta name="GENERATOR" content="Microsoft Visual Studio .NET 7.1">
    <meta name="CODE LANGUAGE" content = "Visual Basic .NET 7.1">
    <meta name="defaultClientScript content="JavaScript">
    <meta name="vc_targetSchema content="http://schemas.Microsoft.com/
intellisense/ie5">
   </head>
</html>
<body MS_POSITIONING="GridLayout">
   <form id="Form1" method="post" runat="server>
   </form>
  </body>
</html>
```

Next, click on the Register icon in the Solution Explorer and select View Designer. Then, click on the Toolbox icon and drag a label onto the web form. Select the label's properties and type **RegisterClient** to the right of the text property. Finally, compile the application, and the label will display in Internet Explorer as follows:

```
Register Client
```

Although this ASP.NET server page does not allow for any user interaction, it does demonstrate browser-based application functionality in its most elementary form.

The Global.aspx.vb file contains information about the sequence of events and when they fire. The file begins by importing System.Web and the System.Web.SessionState. Public Class Global inherits the System.Web.HttpApplication class. After the InitializeComponent() method performs its task and allows for any other initialization, several events fire. The first event is the Application_Start method. The next event, Session_Start, fires, followed by the Application_BeginRequest method, which fires at the beginning of each subsequent request. Then the Application_AuthenticateRequest method fires. Other methods include Application_Authentication, Application_Error, Session_End, and Application_End. Here is the Global.aspx.vb file:

```
Imports System.Web
Imports System.Web.SessionState
Public Class Global
    Inherits System.Web.HttpApplication
#Region " Component Designer Generated Code "
    Public Sub New()
        MyBase.New()
        'This call is required by the Component Designer.
        InitializeComponent()
        'Add any initialization after the InitializeComponent() call
    End Sub

    'Required by the Component Designer
    Private components As System.ComponentModel.IContainer

    'NOTE: The following procedure is required by the Component Designer
    'It can be modified using the Component Designer.
    'Do not modify it using the code editor.
    <System.Diagnostics.DebuggerStepThrough()>
    Private Sub InitializeComponent()
        components = New System.ComponentModel.Container()
    End Sub

#End Region

    Sub Application_Start(ByVal sender As Object, ByVal e As EventArgs)
        'Fires when the application is started
    End Sub
    Sub Session_Start(ByVal sender As Object, ByVal e As EventArgs)
        'Fires when the session is started
    End Sub
    Sub Application_BeginRequest(ByVal sender As Object, ByVal e As EventArgs)
        'Fires at the beginning of each request
    End Sub
    Sub Application_AuthenticateRequest
   (ByVal sender As Object,
    ByVal e As EventArgs)
        'Fires upon attempting to authenticate the user
    End Sub
```

```
    Sub Application_Error(ByVal sender As Object, ByVal e As EventArgs)
        'Fires when an error occurs
    End Sub
    Sub Session_End(ByVal sender As Object, ByVal e As EventArgs)
        'Fires when the session ends
    End Sub

    Sub Application_End(ByVal sender As Object, ByVal e As EventArgs)
        'Fires when the application ends
    End Sub

End Class
```

The lesson learned from examining this file is that the ASP.NET execution works entirely differently from classic ASP pages. Every .aspx page is automatically converted to a class and subsequently compiled to an assembly the first time it is accessed by a client. Expect some latency (delay) from this scenario.

When the user accesses the page, the generated assembly executes and creates an instance of that page. The page object provides a method for each event and generates output that is ultimately sent to the client's browser.

Creating a Web Form

The following ASP.NET browser-based application shows how to enter data and display it back to an ASP.NET label control.

Open Visual Studio .NET and create a new project. Select Visual Basic Projects and click on the Web Application icon. Provide a project name such as RegisterNewClient. Then, select the machine where you wish to create the web site. Click OK to begin the process of creating a new web application. Rename WebForm1 to RegisterNewClient.aspx. Next, select the Toolbox and create the form with the appropriate controls itemized in Table 6-2.

Control Type	Property	Value
Label	Name	Label1
TextBox	Name Text	txtFirst
Label	Name Text	Label2

Table 6-2 *Creating a Web Input Form*

Control Type	Property	Value
TextBox	Name Text	txtLast
Label	Name Text	Label2
Button	Name Text	btnSubmit

Table 6-2 *Creating a Web Input Form* (continued)

Once you verify that this form runs properly, right-click the Register.aspx page and click Set as Start Page. Run the form, and you will be able to enter data in the text fields. Then, click the Register button so the browser will render your page. However, you will not see anything you entered because the page does not contain instructions to do anything yet. Double-click the Register button and enter the following code:

```
Private Sub btnSubmit_Click
(ByVal sender As System.Object,
ByVal e As System.EventArgs)
 Handles btnSubmit.Click
lblName.Text = txtLast.Text & ", " & txtFirst.Text
End Sub
```

Run Register.aspx again, and the result displays in the label as "Peltzer, Dwight." You have retrieved the data you just entered in the Last Name and First Name text boxes and placed the text in the label control.

Creating User Controls

ASP.NET divides the built-in server controls in two groups: HTML controls and web controls. Each is contained within its own namespace. HTML controls map one to one with standard HTML elements, whereas some elements do not map to a specific HTML control. You have the option of changing the functionality of a page at runtime by modifying the control's attributes programmatically. Creating a user control is new to ASP.NET. User controls consist of HTML markup or ASP.NET code that bears the .ascx file extension. You can employ the @ Control directive to specify precisely how a control behaves on the web form. A caveat to employing user controls is that you cannot call them directly. They must reside on an already existing page. In addition, user controls should not contain <html>, <body>, or <form> elements primarily because they are already present on the page where your control is placed. You can strong type the control programmatically by adding the ClassName attribute as follows:

```
<%@ Control ClassName="RegisterClient" %>
```

Let's create a user control and see how easy it is to do.

```
<%@ Control ClassName="RegisterClient" %>
<script language="vb" runat="server" %>
   Private name  As String = ""
   Public Property Name As String
      Get
        Return name
      End Get

      Set
        name = Value
      End Set
   End Property

   Public Sub GreetClient()
     Label1.Text = "Please register to use our services", & name
   End Sub
   </script>
   <asp:Label  id="Label1" runat="server"></asp:Label>
```

The file should be saved as Register.ascx and stored in your Internet Information Services virtual directory.

The code declares a string variable called name; then a property procedure called Name sets and retrieves the value of the variable. Finally, a Sub procedure called GreetClient() sets the Text property of the Label server control.

Adding a User Control Declaratively

Two methods exist for adding the control to a web form page. The first method allows you to place the control declaratively. Create a new web form page called GreetContainer.aspx, and place it in the virtual directory where you saved Register.ascx. Write the following code:

```
<%@ Page Language = "vb" %>
<%@  Register TagPrefix = "ASPNETsbtn" TagName=RegisterClient"
  Src = "Register.ascx" %>
<html>
<head>
  <script runat="server">
    Sub Page_Load(Sender as Object, E As EventArgs)
    MyRegister.Name = "Steve"
    MyRegister.GreetClient
    End Sub
  </script>
</head>
<body>
  <ASPNETsbtn:RegisterClient id= "MyRegister" runat ="server"/>
</body>
</html>
```

The output is as expected:

```
Please register to use our services, Steve
```

Adding a User Control Programmatically

Adding a user control to a web forms page programmatically is similar to the declarative method, but with a few changes. Create a new web forms page named RegisterMoreClients.aspx. Then, save it to the same directory as you did previously:

```
<%@ Page Language = "vb" %>
<%@ Reference Control = "Register.ascx" %>
<html>
<head>
<script runat="server">
    Sub Page_Load(Sender As Object, E as EventArgs)
       Dim MyRegister As Control = LoadControl("Register.ascx")
       RegisterHolder.Controls.Add(MyRegister)
       CType(MyRegister.Register).Name = "Steve"
       CType(MyRegister.Register).GreetClient
     End Sub
   </script>
 </head>
<body>
<asp:placeholder id="Referenceholder" runat="server"/>
```

```
</body>
</html>
```

The @ *Reference* directive tells ASP.NET to compile and link the user control *Register.ascx* with the page when compiled. The Placeholder control allows you to insert a placeholder in the HTML markup so you can add a control to a specific location on the page. Reference the saved page just as you did previously from the Internet Services Manager. Right-click this page, and select Browse to render the page to the browser.

Server Control Types

Server controls can be placed on a web forms page. You can add an HTML control to the page by referencing the System.Web.HTMLControls namespace. Here is how you would add your HTML control to the page:

```
<%@ Page Language = "vb" %>
<html>
<head>
</head>
<body>
      <form runat ="server">
        <input id ="ButtonName" type="submit" runat = "server"/>
      </form>
 </body>
</html>
```

By adding the runat = “server”, you can access the control programmatically on the server side. As you will recall, the server-side <form> causes the page to post back to the server when the user clicks the Submit button.

Web Controls

The syntax for adding a web control is slightly different from syntax for an HTML control. Instead of defining your own tag prefix, use the asp prefix. Here is how you add a web control to the page:

```
<asp: TextBox id = "myTextBox" runat = "server" />
```

Let's add a TextBox control and two web labels to a server-side form. Write the following code to the ServerSideControl.aspx page beginning with the <html> tag:

```
<html>
<head>
 <script runat="Server">
   Sub Page_Load(Sender As Object, E As EventArgs)
      If Is PostBack Then
         GreetingsLabel.Text = "Greetings, " & _
         Server.HTMLEncode(MyNameTextBox.Text)
       End If
    End Sub
  </script>
</head>
<body>
   <form runat="Server">
   <asp:Label id = "MyNameLabel" runat="server">Name: </asp:Label>
   <asp:TextBox id="MyNameTextBox" runat="Server"/>
   <input id="MyNameButton" type="submit" runat="server"/>
   </form>
   <asp:Label id = "GreetingLabel" runat = "server"/>
 </body>
</html>
```

If you run this page, you can enter text in the TextBox control and submit the page. After the post back occurs, provide the proper URL and view the page.

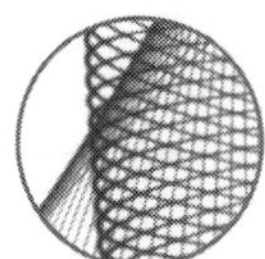

NOTE

Assuming you set the AutoEventWireup to true, if you manually write your code in a text editor such as Notepad, you must set the AutoEventWireup attribute to true. If Visual Studio .Net generates the page, by default this attribute is set to false. This indicates that all event handlers must be manually wired to the events they will handle.

Handling Events in the Server Control

An event handler was provided for the Page_Load event in the previous example. The event handler checks the IsPostBack page property to determine whether a post back occurs because the user has interacted with the Submit button. If this evaluation is true, set the Text property for the label to the appropriate text. In addition, employ the Server.HtmlEncode methodology to encode your text.

Note that when you add an event handler for the Load stage, you should check the IsPostBack page-level property. Handling Control events is slightly different. In this scenario, apply the controlname_eventname instead. Here is an example:

```
Sub NameTextBox_TextChanged
(Sender As Object, E As EventArgs)GreetingLabel.Text
 &=" your name has changed"
End Sub
```

Next, add the following attribute to your NameTextBox server control tag:

```
<asp:TextBox id ="NameTextBox" onTextChanged =
"NameTextBox_TextChanged"
runat="server"/>
```

Error Handling and Security

The Page_Error handler helps manage error handling at the page level. Whenever the page encounters an error, it generates an exception. You can scrutinize the error by applying the Server.GetLastError method. This is invaluable when trying to trace the error to its source.

System.Exception is the base class for all exceptions. When an error occurs, either the system or the executing application throws the exception in a "try, catch" block. Once the exception is thrown, the application handles it by employing the default exception handler.

If you consider how the classic Windows applications handle security, the user has the option of deciding whether to let the executable run or not. For example, if you download some code from the Internet and allow the code to run, you have no control over what the executable actually does. The .NET Framework removes this option and places the application security within the assembly itself.

The assembly defines type scope as well as an assembly's security boundary, so to speak. The CLR implements two distinct types of security:

- Code access security
- Role-based security

The .NET code access security has two criteria: permissions that the code requests and what permissions are based on the security policy in effect when the code executes. An assembly interacts with the CLR in numerous ways. It can request the specific permissions it requires for executing in a given environment. Here are some permissions an assembly can request:

- **UI Permission** Permits access to a specified interface
- **FileIOPermission** Allows access to both files and directories
- **EnvironmentPermission** Enables access to environment variables
- **ReflectionPermission** Provides access to metadata residing within the assembly
- **SecurityPermission** Permits granting access to a group of permissions
- **WebPermission** Manages Internet connections

You have two methods for embedding security permissions within an application: a declarative method and an imperative method. With the declarative method, you can write security code attributes in your code. The attributes become part of the metadata for the assembly. The imperative method lets you insert security permissions dynamically at runtime. The CLR inspects application security requests and compares them with any existing machine security roles. If the security permissions only allow read access to metadata or to specified files or directories, the assembly denies any further access.

An assembly provides several pieces of information about itself:

- The assembly's identity contains a digital signature generated by its publisher.
- The assembly's identity is represented by its strong name.
- The assembly specifies the exact URL from which an assembly was downloaded.
- The assembly identifies the zone defined by Internet Explorer. It reveals the exact source from which the assembly was downloaded.

When the assembly loads, the CLR examines permissions requested by the assembly. Subsequently, the assembly receives permissions specified by the security role in effect for a machine on which the assembly resides.

Role-based security allows the CLR to restrict what permissions are granted based on the assembly's name, its origin, and who published it. Code access security makes no provisions for controlling the behavior of an assembly based on a user's identity. Rather, the Object contains all information concerning the object's identity and roles to which the object is assigned. If you consider the classic Windows method for assigning a role to a user or user group, you can fully understand what role-based security is.

CHAPTER

7

ASP.NET and Web Services

IN THIS CHAPTER:

What Is a Web Service?

Primary Web Services Technologies

Implementing Interfaces

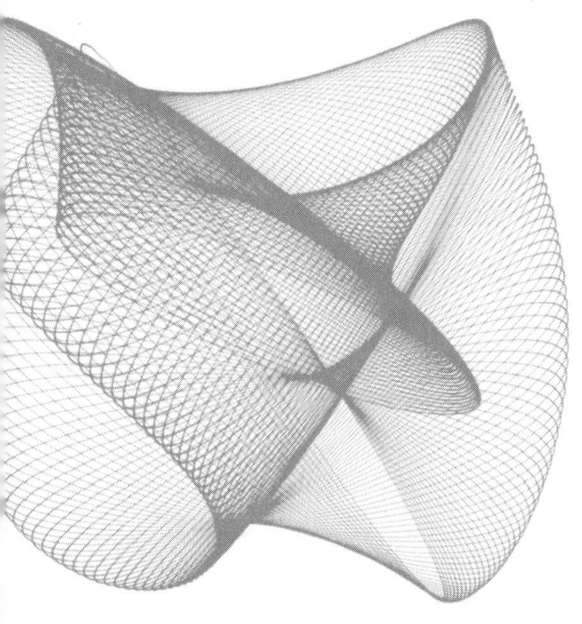

Building an enterprise-distributed web application is becoming increasingly complex. Ever-pressing consumer and business demands necessitate discovering new, more efficient ways of developing improved methods for presenting information through browser-based web applications and personal hand-held devices, and for incorporating legacy systems. Methodologies employed in the past for building applications for the Internet are no longer sufficient for staying competitive. Application aggregation and interoperability is now the norm. Web services have changed business processes forever. There is no doubt that urgent consumer and business demands stretch a company's ability to design, create, and deploy web service–oriented applications. Fortunately, an increasing number of software vendors are assembling systems by defining innovative new business logic that modifies and leverages preexisting repositories of data. It is less common today to construct new applications from the ground up.

The new business model emerging can be thought of as component-based applications supporting reusable component functionality. IBM's WebSphere and Microsoft .NET are representative of component-assembled business solutions. A component-based system must support scalability, flexibility, and security. With the plethora of component collections available, what are the criteria for selecting and differentiating between these components?

- Components must contain no interdependencies with other components.
- A component's functionality must support the object-oriented concept of tight cohesion.
- A collection of component-based functionalities must be assembled into a cohesive whole, thereby facilitating coarse-grained operations on services that encompass more functionality and operate on larger sets of data.
- The integrated components must be designed for distribution across many machines in order to enhance performance and reliability.
- A component exposes one or more services so they can be consumed by other services or clients.

Once the system is built, the component-based infrastructure must describe and expose its services to clients so they can obtain the requisite information necessary for consuming those identifiable web services.

What Is a Web Service?

I'll start by defining a *web service* by describing what a service is not. For example, a web service is not a subscription service but rather represents some kind of business logic processing on a web server. The key word to understanding "process" is "functionality." It defines what process is. "Web," of course, indicates some kind of event that exposes functionality and occurs on a server residing somewhere on the Internet in response to a client's request. The event requires an event handler (a server-side process that manages client requests by forwarding those requests to the appropriate server where a specified web server exposes its services to interested parties). The event (a web service) is invoked at the behest of a client or some application-based invocation. For example, International Foreign Currency Exchange (IFCE) submits requests to a service provider such as Reuters for the most recent stock quote. Reuters, herein now defined as a service provider, resides somewhere on the Web on a wide area network (WAN). Because service providers offer many kinds of services, they must reside on a network so they can expose their services to clients on a large scale.

The term "service" obfuscates the true meaning of a web service because it contains several different meanings, depending on context. Viewing a web service from a developer's perspective is one point of view and differs from a user's point of view, or that of a service provider. For example, in J2EE, the name "component" replaces the term service, whereas in Microsoft .NET, web services use "service."

Web services are accessed by calling a listener (a service provider) capable of providing a contract that describes the particular web service a client seeks. The contract specifies both parameters and data types that the listener anticipates receiving, as well as the return type (if any) it sends back to the client. In addition, the listener facilitates incoming requests, and returns responses to clients. Figure 7-1 is a visual representation of a service provider's functionality.

Creating a Web Service

Microsoft designates ASP.NET as the technology for building web services. Both business logic and presentation layer are bundled together within ASP.NET. The developer begins the web service process by applying attributes that inform the Common Language Runtime (CLR) back to treat a defined class and its methods as a web service. (Refer to Chapter 5 for a complete discussion about the CLR and its functionality.) Web service business logic is stored in an .asmx file. The code can

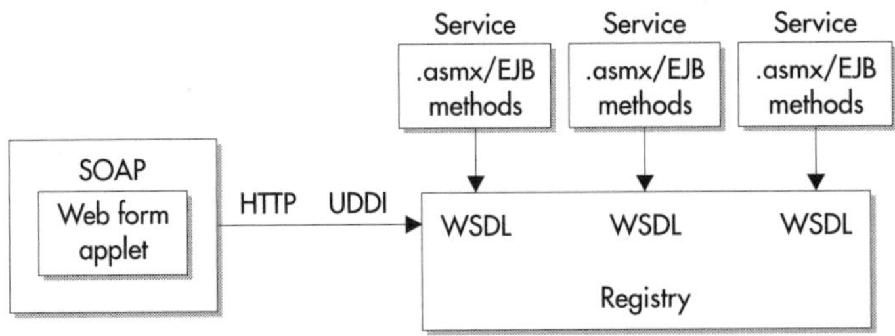

Figure 7-1 *A service provider's functionality*

dwell either within the .asmx file or in a precompiled class. The developer applies the following directive to the file containing the class name and namespace in which the class for the web service resides. It looks like this:

```
<%@ WebService Language = "VB" Class ="IFCE" %>
```

Then, the developer declares a method that includes the number of parameters and its data types, as shown here:

```
<WebMethod()> Public Function ConvertCurrency
(ByVal x As Double, ByVal y as Double) As Double
   //write the code to implement the method
End Function
```

The code is compiled to Microsoft Intermediate Language (MSIL) and to its own specific assembly. Typically, the assembly should be placed in a bin file so others can reference it. Creating a web service class looks like this:

```
Imports System.Web.Services
Public Class IFCE
   Inherits WebService
   'declare the methods here exposed by the Web Service
End Class
```

XML-based web services use the namespace mechanism for defining an end point for the web service, the namespace to whom a client forwards requests. Here is the syntax:

```
<WebService (Namespace="http://www.IFCE.com/Webservices/") _
  Public Class IFCE: WebService {}
```

ASP.NET uses reflection to inspect metadata attributes. Attributes facilitate access to web services by applying the WebMethod metadata attribute to declare methods, as previously demonstrated.

By examining this process, it is clear that the client requests a server-side provider to expose its services. The provider is mandated to issue the client a contract (a WSDL file) that lists the services it exposes. This information informs the client how to communicate with the service provider and utilize its services.

Therefore, it is possible to add to our definition of a web service by describing it as a discrete piece of business logic written in Java, managed C++ .NET, C# .NET, or some other programming language. Depending on the language, a function or method is typically decorated with a web method attribute, thereby designating it as eligible to initiate a call to a web service provider. This process informs the CLR that this call is to be treated as a valid web service invocation.

Defining a Service-Oriented Architecture (SOA)

What is a service-oriented architecture? Web services reside somewhere on the Internet in a *registry*. Registries contain numerous web services, and each individual service exposes its own services to requestors (clients). The services represent publishable and discoverable interfaces.

Let's digress for a moment to define an interface (more about interfaces later in the chapter). An *interface* is an abstract class containing a function or method declaration, which includes a list of parameters, for example:

```
int max( int, int);
```

Every operation declared by an object specifies the following items:

- The operation's name
- The objects it accepts as parameters
- The operation's return values

This is known as the operation's *signature*. By assembling the set of all signatures, we can define them as an interface. However, an interface does not provide an implementation, but only provides the abstract class's method name and a set of signatures.

Perhaps the most important functionality a web service provides is supporting a well-defined business process. Here is a quote describing the benefits SOA offers:

> Service-Oriented Solutions…Applications are constructed as groups of interacting services providing well-defined interfaces to users. (*Java Web Services*, O'Reilly & Associates, 2002.)

SOA is implemented as a discoverable software entity that exists as a single instance. The instance interacts with web applications and represents a loosely coupled message-based communication model.

Conceptually, each individual web service has two parts:

- **Service** This represents the implementation for a web service. The basic requirement is that it must be accessible on a network by a service provider.
- **Service description** Typically, this exists as an XML file containing a complete description of data types, communication protocols, and a URI where the web service implementation resides. This file is called Web Services Description Language (WSDL).

The terminology used to describe SOA elements in web services is specific, as demonstrated in the following.

- **Service provider** A software entity implements the service specification. Any chunk of logic is exposed as a web service residing within the SOA. It could be either a complete mainframe-based business process, such as processing a request to convert a specified currency quote to another type of currency quote, such as the euro equivalent of 100 American dollars, or servicing a mortgage loan request. Providers publish metadata about services they keep in a registry. Typically, these providers are standards-setting organizations like ebXML, W3C.org, WS-1, software vendors, and developers. Several different mechanisms are used to publish service descriptions. Among them:
  - **HTTP Get request** The public repository *http://www.xmethods.com* is where developers can test their own web services.
  - **Dynamic discovery** Perhaps the most used registry is Universal Description, Discovery, and Integration (UDDI).
  - **Direct** A service requestor retrieves the service description from the service provider directly via email, FTP, or other such direct methods.
- **Service requestor** This entity calls a service provider.

- **Service locator** This serves as a registry manager and allows a client to locate registries, service provider interfaces, and service locations.
- **Services broker** This service provider maintains a list of registries and passes on client requests to other service providers.

SOA Web Services

The following items constitute the building blocks for constructing service-oriented architecture web services:

- **Encoding** XML-ized data transmitted between client and server requires encoding. Typically, the decoding is UTF-8. In J2EE it is ISO-8859-1.
- **Description** Web services represent an end point. Once the point is located, the service provider describes metadata about the service and requirements needed by the client in order to leverage its services.
- **DISCO** This is a proprietary Microsoft method for discovery. In order to use DISCO, a URL is required before the document can be located. Use the Disco.exe command-line utility to generate the WSDL contract. Syntax for this is as follows:

```
Disco [options] URL
```

In contrast, UDDI does not require the URL to locate a web service or registry. A registry normally provides a tool for searching by name, location, URL, keyword, and other search criteria. It is possible to search for the keyword *wsdl*. These URLs will always point toward WSDL contracts available for web services.

- **Messaging format** Both client and business partner must agree on a mutual protocol before they can encode, format, and transmit messages to each other via HTTP and SOAP.

Fortunately, Microsoft and Sun Microsystems are assisting developers by releasing software solutions that enable a company to face numerous Internet business challenges.

SOA Best Practices

Service providers not only set forth a description of services but also impose constraints dependent on context. The following list presents some of the primary characteristics for efficient utilization of these services:

- **Interface design** SOA services implement defined interfaces. This is important because multiple web services can implement a commonly shared interface. Conversely, a single service can implement numerous interfaces.

- **Asynchronous calls** Generally speaking, best practices suggest message passing via asynchronous remote calls. This is important because asynchronous calls allow developers to continue working with other development tasks while awaiting a return result from the server. Synchronous calls are less desirable because all other tasks are blocked until the request fulfillment is completed.
- **Coarse-grained services** Object-oriented technologies such as Java expose their services through individual methods. Using an individual method, however, is too fine an operation for processing large quantities of data. It is better to assemble individual methods into a cohesive coarse-grained service and process large amounts of data.
- **Remote Procedure Calls** Web services enable clients to invoke procedures, methods, and functions on remote objects employing an XML-based protocol. RPCs expose both input and output parameters.

Primary Web Services Technologies

The preceding discussion has focused on describing a web service process. It is useful now to explain how the client accesses services by employing the core web technologies—namely, Simple Object Access Protocol (SOAP), HTTP, Web Services Description Language (WSDL), and Universal Description, Discovery, and Integration (UDDI)—to locate the service/services the client specifies. Developers can browse numerous web service repositories (registries) and select appropriate services for implementing their own applications. Figure 7-2 demonstrates how a registry serves as host to a collection of web services.

Simple Object Access Protocol

SOAP provides a standard structure for transmitting XML documents over the wire, which includes SMTP, HTTP, and FTP. SOAP also defines encoding and binding standards for encoding non-XML Remote Procedure Calls. SOAP enhances interoperability between client and server. Clients with .NET can call EJBs through SOAP and vice versa.

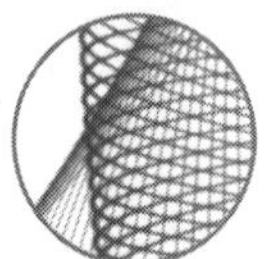

NOTE

Other protocols have been developed, for example, Sun's RPC, Microsoft's DCE, Java's RMI, and CORBA's ORBC.

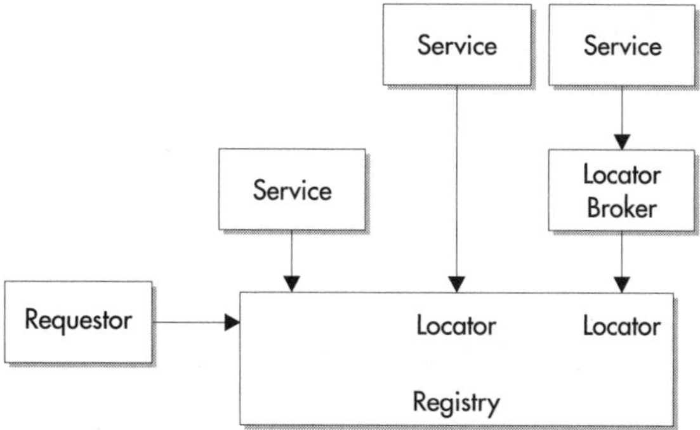

Figure 7-2 *A web service registry*

Why are so many corporations embracing SOAP? It has industry-wide support and is not bound to one programming language. Interestingly, SOAP does not use a specified set of APIs, but rather leaves the implementation up to the programming language (such as Java) and the platform (such as Microsoft .NET). The SOAP specification does not describe how SOAP messages should be bound to HTTP. SOAP is an XML document. Listing 7-1 is representative of a typical SOAP request and response XML file.

Listing 7-1 *SOAP request-response example*

```
POST /MathWebService/Service1.asmx HTTP/1.1
Host: ecom10
Content-Type: text/xml; charset=utf-8
Content-Length: length
SOAPAction: "http://tempuri.org/SelectMaxValue"
<?xml version="1.0" encoding="utf-8"?>
<soap:Envelope
xmlns:xsi="http://www.w3.org/2001/XMLSchema-instance"
xmlns:xsd="http://www.w3.org/2001/XMLSchema"
xmlns:xsd="http://schemas.xmlsoap.org/soap/envelope/">
  <soap:Body>
    <SelectMaxValue xmlns="http://tempuri.org/">
      <x>int</x>
      <y>int</y>
    </SelectMaxValue>
  </soap:Body>
```

```
</soap:Envelope>

HTTP/1.1 200 OK
Content-Type: text/xml; charset=utf-8
Content-Length:  length
<?xml version="1.0" encoding="utf-8"?>
<soap:Envelope
xmlns:xsi="http://www.w3.org/2001/XMLSchema-instance"
xmlns:xsd="http://www.w3.org/2001/XMLSchema"
xmlns:xsd="http://schemas.xmlsoap.org/soap/envelope/">
  <soap:Body>
    <SelectMaxValueResponse xmlns="http://tempura.org/">
     <SelectMaxValueResult>int</SelectMaxValueResult>
    </SelectMaxValueResponse>
   </soap:Body>
</soap:Envelope>
```

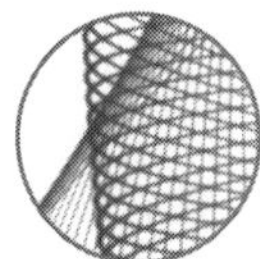

NOTE

In a production environment, change the XML namespace to your own namespace as demonstrated here:

```
<int xmlns="http://www.dp.org/results/>
```

SOAP's Messaging Architecture

Let's step through Listing 7-1. The header indicates this is an HTTP POST request, followed by the name of the method, MathWebService. The .asmx extension is used for files that implement XML web services. Web services can be accessed directly through .asmx files, or this file can redirect the request to a compiled assembly implementing the web service. The root element of the SelectMaxValue document is the Envelope element. The listing has two subelements, the body and header elements.

The next item of interest is the attribute bearing the name of the host machine. The Content-type specifies the file as text/xml, and the encoding is utf-8. The SOAPAction attribute identifies the URI namespace where the method is located and lists the web service name. The XML declaration indicates the SOAP message is XML-based. Next, all SOAP messages have an *envelope*, where the message body is embedded. Both client and recipient must strip the content from the envelope for further processing. Notice the default xmlns namespace declarations. These must precede the SOAP body. Finally, the method is processed where the web service determines whether *int value x* is greater or smaller than *y*. The response is virtually self-explanatory. Beginning with the traditional SOAP header, the SOAP body *result* syntax is similar to the request, with the exception that the Method syntax indicates it is a *response* and returns a *result*.

Before the discussion focuses on other SOAP attributes, here are the key elements discussed so far:

- **The SOAP envelope** This encodes header information about the message and body of the message.
- **SOAP encoding** This allows for a standardized method of serializing data into the body of a SOAP message.
- **RPC-style messages** This entails the type of protocol a developer can employ to facilitate procedure-oriented communications via a request-response message.
- **HTTP binding** This is the industry-wide method of binding SOAP messages to the HTTP messaging protocol.

Other SOAP Attributes

A SOAP message defines a *SOAP actor*, which is divided in two parts:

- A *default actor* is the intended final recipient of a SOAP message.
- An *intermediary actor* can act on the content of a SOAP message by modifying the content in some way.

The intermediary actor may manipulate the message content in an unspecified way before forwarding the message to its final destination. Although the message is altered, it is still considered the same message as the one originally sent.

An optional header element will transmit data that might not be appropriate to encode in the envelope body. For example, if a default actor receives an encoded, compressed message, it would need to know what type of algorithm is used to compress the code before it could decode the message. Other types of optional headers include the all-important authentication method, routing information, transactions, and security information. A default actor may require the sender to provide authentication information before the recipient can process the message. A message may require specific routing to more than one destination. In addition, the recipient may require security information to determine whether a message is modified before arriving at its destination. For example, it is important for a stock quote to remain in its original state before a brokerage firm can sell the stock to clients. The header element can be added to the SOAP envelope as a child element. Listing 7-2 demonstrates this.

Listing 7-2 *Defining a child node within the SOAP envelope*

```
<?xml version="1.0" encoding="utf-8" ?>
<soap:Envelope xmlns:soap="http://schemas.xmlsoap.org/soap/envelope/">
  <soap:Header>
    <Manifest>BH784Fg23559></Manifest>
  </soap:Header>
<soap:Body>
    <StockReport>
      <StockSymbol>JANS</StockSymbol>
      <Price>29.13</Price>
      <!--Ouch, a huge financial loss- ->
     </StockReport>
  </soap:Body>
</soap:Envelope>
```

The mustUnderstand Attribute

Use the mustUnderstand attribute when information embedded within the header should not be ignored. Therefore, mustUnderstand provides a method for differentiating between noncritical information and mission-critical data that requires attention. By specifying a value of 1 in the header's root element, the identified data cannot be ignored. Listing 7-3 demonstrates how to use this attribute.

Listing 7-3 *Using the mustUnderstand attribute*

```
<?xml version="1.0" encoding="utf-8"?>
<soap:Envelope xmlns:soap="http://schemas.xmlsoap.org/soap/envelope/">
  <soap:Header>
     <TransactionID soap:mustUnderstand="1">19.92</TransactionID>
      </soap:Header>
    <soap:Body>
      <UpdateStockQuote>
        <email>DPeltzer@IFCE.com</email>
          <f_Name>Dwight</f_Name>
          <l_Name>Peltzer</l_Name>
      </UpdateStockQuote>
     </soap:Body>
  </soap:Envelope>
```

This example shows how the recipient must update the specified stock quote within scope of the client's transaction. In the event the transaction is going awry in some way, the application must roll back any changes made to the client's account. The mechanism used for this is the mustUnderstand attribute, and is achieved by setting the attribute to 1.

The Actor Attribute

The Actor attribute provides a mechanism for annotating SOAP headers. For example, a document can be routed to an intermediary that will create a transaction, specifying the URI for the intermediary for which a portion of the message is intended.

If the header is destined for processing by the *next* recipient of a SOAP message, set both the mustUnderstand attribute and the Actor attribute. Listing 7-4 demonstrates how to do this.

Listing 7-4 *Setting the next recipient*

```
<?xml version="1.0" encoding="utf-8"?>
<soap:Envelope xmlns:soap="http:////schemas.xmlsoap.org/soap/envelope/">
  <soap:Header>
    <TransactionID soap:mustUnderstand="1"
      actor="urn:TransactionCoordinator>19.90</TransactionID>
       </soapHeader>
       <soap:Body>
       <UpdateStockQuote>
      <Source>102420484096</Source>
      <Destination>102420484096</Destination>
        <Price>12.95></Price>
        </AddNewClient>
      </soap:Body>
  </soap:Envelope>
```

If the TransactionCoordinator does not know how to interpret this message, it raises an error. The </AddNewClient> directive does not belong in this message. This is evidenced by lack of a corresponding opening tag. Before the message is passed on, all foreign elements must be removed. However, the intermediary can add header elements before forwarding the message to the next intermediary or final recipient.

The Body Element

All SOAP messages must have exactly one <soap:Body> element. The body element contains the payload. There are some constraints on how the body is encoded. The payload can consist of a string of ASCII characters, a byte array, or XML text. However, the contents may not contain any characters that would invalidate the embedded XML document.

XML messages can be placed in two categories: document-oriented messages and procedure-oriented messages. For example, a document that provides a stock quote to a client can be encoded within the body of a SOAP message and specify a particular routing for an intended recipient. The procedure-oriented messages offer two-way communications and are frequently referred to as RPC messages.

The Fault Element

SOAP messages fail for a number of reasons. It is important to use the Fault attribute and generate an error message back to a client. SOAP specifies a format for handling errors. Listing 7-5 demonstrates this.

Listing 7-5 *Web services error handling*

```
<?xml version="1.0" encoding="utf-8"?>
<soap:Envelope xmlns:soap="http:////schemas.xmlsoap.org/soap/envelope/">
<soap:Body>
  <soap:Fault>
     <soap:FaultCode>Client.Security</soap:faultcode>
     <soap:faultstring>Access denied</soap:faultstring>
     <soap:faultactor>http://dps.com</soap:faultactor>
     <soap:detail>
       <myError>
         <Originator>File System></Originator>
         <Resource>My File.txt></Resource>
       </myError>
     </soap:detail>
   </soap:Fault>
  </soap:Body>
</soap:Envelope>
```

The Faultcode contains a value to determine the kind of error it encounters. Several fault codes are available for use:

- **Version Mismatch** This specifies an invalid namespace declared for the SOAP envelope.
- **MustUnderstand** A child element residing within the SOAP header contains a mustUnderstand attribute. If the attribute is set to 1, it indicates the attribute was not understood.
- **Client** Content located within the message body was found to be faulty.
- **Server** The server determines that the error lies with the inability to obtain resources or the inability to process the message.

The SOAP features presented here must be adhered to when processing SOAP messages. The next major web services technology, Web Services Description Language (WSDL), describes what a SOAP payload contains.

Web Services Description Language

WSDL documents contain metadata about a client's input and output parameters from an invocation externally. This means a user is invoking a method externally. In addition, the WSDL file describes the service's functionality. In essence, the file facilitates interaction between disparate clients by providing the requisite information on how to achieve interoperability between them.

Let's create a small web service in ASP.NET and then inspect the WSDL file. The first task required for building a web service in the .NET world is creating a virtual directory in Internet Information Services.

1. Create a folder on the server, and name it "MySOAPExamples."
2. In Windows 2000 or Windows XP, select Start | Control Panel | Administrative Tools | Internet Information Services. Open IIS, right-click the default web site, select New, and then select Virtual Directory. A dialog box will appear on your screen. Select Next, and enter **MySOAPExamples** in the Alias dialog box. Make sure the subdirectory is already created somewhere on the hard drive. Finally, proceed to Finish to generate the virtual directory.
3. Create a new project in Visual Studio .NET called "IFCEBrokerage."
4. Rename Webservice1.asmx to IFCEBrokerageFirm.asmx. The extension .asmx represents an ASP.NET web service extension.
5. The namespace should be named "namespace IFCEBrokerage."
6. Enter the code shown in Listing 7-6.

Listing 7-6 *IFCEBrokerageFirm web service code*

```
using System;
using System.Web;
using System.Web.Services;
namespace IFCEBrokerage
{
		public class SecuritiesExchange : System.Web.Services.WebService
	{
		[WebMethod]
		public double StockQuote(string symbol)
		{
			double quotePrice= 0;
			switch(symbol)
			{
				case "JANS":
					quotePrice = 29.95;
					break;
				case "MSFT":
					quotePrice = 49.97;
					break;
				case "ORCL":
					quotePrice = 37.72;
					break;
			}
			return quotePrice;
		}
	}
}
```

Several IFCEBrokerageFirm items require clarification. An excellent place to begin learning about them is in web service namespaces. Table 7-1 displays them with comments.

These namespaces enable developers to create XML web services using ASP.NET and XML web service clients. XML web services represent applications that enhance the ability to exchange messages in a loosely coupled environment using protocols such as HTTP, XML, XSD, SOAP, and WSDL. They facilitate constructing modular applications in a heterogeneous environment that promotes interoperability between applications, smart client devices, and implementations.

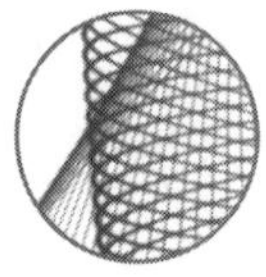

NOTE

The WebMethodAttribute class must be applied to any method where a developer wants to expose it programmatically.

Class	Description
WebMethodAttribute	Adding this attribute to a method when defining a web service created in ASP.NET makes the method callable from remote web clients.
Web Service	This class defines the optional class for XML web services, thereby providing access to common ASP.NET objects, for example, application and session state.
WebServiceAttribute	This class is used to append additional information to an XML web service, such as a string explaining its functionality.
WebServiceBindingAttribute	Declares binding for one or more XML web service methods implemented within the class that is implementing the web service.

Table 7-1 *System.Web.Services Namespace Descriptions*

Because the implementation of a web service is encapsulated within a class, it is important to define an end point for the web service. The .asmx file serves as the end point for the web service. When a client calls the .asmx file, the ASP.NET runtime processes the file.

Usually, each .asmx page has a language directive at the top of the page, as displayed here:

```
<%@ WebService Language="C#" Class= "IFCEBrokerage.SecuritiesExchange" %>
```

The first time the web service is called, the ASP.NET runtime uses the Language directive to compile the code first to MSIL and subsequently to the language specified by the directive. In this case, the directive specifies the C# .NET programming language. This means the IFCEBrokerage class code shares the CLR runtime services and data types defined in the CTS with all other .NET programming languages.

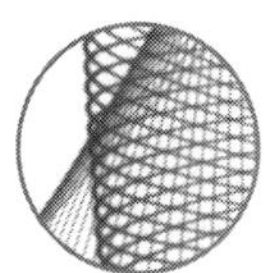

NOTE

The Class attribute bears the fully qualified name of the class that implements the web service. Because the default language in the machine.config file is set to "vb," the IFCEBrokerageFirm.asmx language should be set to C# .NET.
Here is the machine.config file segment:

```
<compilation debug="false" explicit="true" defaultLanguage="vb">
```

It is also wise to place the web service's implementation in its own assembly. By convention, the assembly is placed within the web application's bin directory because this directory is placed within the search path.

The SecuritiesExchange web service client can access this web service only through HTTP for the simple reason that ASP.NET supports only this transmission protocol. However, the web service supports three kinds of protocol bindings:

- SOAP
- HTTP Get
- HTTP POST

All ASP.NET web services support SOAP because the SOAP body content is strongly typed and is XML based through the XSD Schema.

Web Services Documentation

ASP.NET's runtime includes services such as documentation. This is a major benefit because the CLR uses System.Reflection to generate two kinds of documentation:

- Documentation utilized by clients so they can interact with web services
- Documents referenced by people

HTML-based documents are accessible by entering the URL in a browser. Both the WebMethod and its companion attribute WebService expose the Description property. Listing 7-7 demonstrates how to include documentation in the IFCEBrokerage.asmx file.

Listing 7-7 *Adding the Description attribute*

```
using System;
using System.Web;
using System.Web.Services;
namespace IFCEBrokerage
{
      [WebService(Description ="This demonstrates how to use the Description
 attribute")]
      public class SecuritiesExchange : System.Web.Services.WebService
      {
            [WebMethod]
            public double StockQuote(string symbol)
            {
                  double quotePrice= 0;
```

```
                switch(symbol)
                {
                    case "JANS":
                        quotePrice = 29.95;
                        break;
                    case "MSFT":
                        quotePrice = 49.97;
                        break;
                    case "ORCL":
                        quotePrice = 37.72;
                        break;
                }

                return quotePrice;
            }
        }
}
```

The documentation automatically generated for the IFCEBrokerageFirm is shown in Listing 7-8:

Listing 7-8 *Sample documentation for IFCEBrokerageFirm*

```
SecuritiesExchange
This demonstrates how to use the Description attribute
The following operations are supported.
For a formal definition, please review the Service Description.
StockQuote
This web service is using http://tempuri.org/ as its default namespace.
Recommendation: Change the default namespace
before the XML Web service is made public.
```

Examining Namespaces

Each XML web service needs a unique namespace in order for client applications to distinguish it from other services on the Web. The http://tempuri.org/ namespace is available for XML web services that are under development, but published XML web services should use a more permanent namespace.

Your XML web service should be identified by a namespace that you control. For example, you can use your company's Internet domain name as part of the namespace. Although many XML web service namespaces look like URLs, they need not point to actual resources on the Web. (XML web service namespaces are URIs.)

For XML web services created using ASP.NET, the default namespace can be changed using the WebService attribute's Namespace property. The WebService attribute is an attribute applied to the class that contains the XML web service methods. Listing 7-9 shows an example that sets the namespace to http://microsoft.com/webservices/.

Listing 7-9 *HTML-based documentation*

```
C#
[WebService(Namespace="http://microsoft.com/webservices/")]
public class MyWebService {
    // implementation
}
Visual Basic.NET
<WebService(Namespace:="http://microsoft.com/
webservices/")> Public Class MyWebService
    ' implementation
End Class
For more details on XML namespaces,
see the W3C recommendation on Namespaces in XML.
For more details on WSDL, see the WSDL Specification.
For more details on URIs, see RFC 2396.
```

This web page shows the method exposed by the web service StockQuote. It also provides the following recommendation:

```
Recommendation: Change the default namespace
 before the XML web service is made public.
```

And it lists some examples for changing the namespace.

Listing 7-10 displays the web service WSDL file that strong-types the web service.

Listing 7-10 *IFCEBrokerageFirm WSDL file*

```
<?xml version="1.0" encoding="utf-8" ?>
<definitions xmlns:http="http://
schemas.xmlsoap.org/wsdl/http/" xmlns:soap="http://
schemas.xmlsoap.org/wsdl/soap/" xmlns:s=
"http://www.w3.org/2001/XMLSchema" xmlns:s0="http://tempuri.org/"
xmlns:soapenc="http://schemas.xmlsoap.org/soap/encoding/"
xmlns:tm="http://microsoft.com/wsdl/mime/textMatching/"
xmlns:mime="http://schemas.xmlsoap.org/wsdl/mime/"
```

```
targetNamespace="http://tempuri.org/" xmlns=
"http://schemas.xmlsoap.org/wsdl/">
<types>
<s:schema elementFormDefault="qualified"
 targetNamespace="http://tempuri.org/">
<s:element name="StockQuote">
<s:complexType>
<s:sequence>
  <s:element minOccurs="0" maxOccurs="1" name="symbol" type="s:string" />
  </s:sequence>
  </s:complexType>
  </s:element>
<s:element name="StockQuoteResponse">
<s:complexType>
<s:sequence>
  <s:element minOccurs="1" maxOccurs="1"
 name="StockQuoteResult" type="s:double" />
  </s:sequence>
  </s:complexType>
  </s:element>
  </s:schema>
  </types>
<message name="StockQuoteSoapIn">
  <part name="parameters" element="s0:StockQuote" />
  </message>
<message name="StockQuoteSoapOut">
  <part name="parameters" element="s0:StockQuoteResponse" />
  </message>
<portType name="SecuritiesExchangeSoap">
<operation name="StockQuote">
  <input message="s0:StockQuoteSoapIn" />
  <output message="s0:StockQuoteSoapOut" />
  </operation>
  </portType>
<binding name="SecuritiesExchangeSoap" type="s0:SecuritiesExchangeSoap">
  <soap:binding transport="http://
schemas.xmlsoap.org/soap/http" style="document" />
<operation name="StockQuote">
  <soap:operation soapAction="http://
tempuri.org/StockQuote" style="document" />
<input>
  <soap:body use="literal" />
  </input>
<output>
```

```
  <soap:body use="literal" />
  </output>
  </operation>
  </binding>
<service name="SecuritiesExchange">
  <documentation>This demonstrates how to use the Description
 attribute</documentation>
<port name="SecuritiesExchangeSoap" binding="s0:SecuritiesExchangeSoap">
  <soap:address location="http://
localhost/IFCEBrokerage/IFCEBrokerageFirm.asmx" />
  </port>
  </service>
  </definitions>
```

The WSDL file has several interesting characteristics, described shortly in some detail. But first, Listing 7-11 demonstrates the standard form that every WSDL file takes.

Listing 7-11 *IFCEBrokerageFirm.asmx WSDL file*

```
<?xml version="1.0" encoding="utf-8" ?>
<definitions xmlns:http="http://
schemas.xmlsoap.org/wsdl/http//
" xmlns:soap="http://schemas.xmlsoap.org/wsdl/soap/"
xmlns:s="http://www.w3.org/2001/XMLSchema
" xmlns:s0="http://tempuri.org/" xmlns:soapenc=
"http://schemas.xmlsoap.org/
soap/encoding/" xmlns:tm="http://microsoft.com/wsdl/
mime/textMatching/" xmlns:mime="http://
schemas.xmlsoap.org/wsdl/mime/"
 targetNamespace="http://tempuri.org/"
xmlns="http://schemas.xmlsoap.org/wsdl/">
<types>
<s:schema elementFormDefault="qualified"
targetNamespace="http://tempuri.org/">
<s:element name="StockQuote">
  <s:element minOccurs="0" maxOccurs="1" name="symbol" type="s:string" />
<s:element name="StockQuoteResponse">
<s:complexType>  <s:element minOccurs="1"
 maxOccurs="1" name="StockQuoteResult"
type="s:double" />
  </s:sequence> </types>
<message name="StockQuoteSoapIn">
```

```
  <part name="parameters" element="s0:StockQuote" />
  </message>
<message name="StockQuoteSoapOut">
  <part name="parameters" element="s0:StockQuoteResponse" />
  </message>
<portType name="SecuritiesExchangeSoap">
<operation name="StockQuote">
  <input message="s0:StockQuoteSoapIn" />
  <output message="s0:StockQuoteSoapOut" />
  </operation>
  </portType>
<binding name="SecuritiesExchangeSoap" type="s0:SecuritiesExchangeSoap">
  <soap:binding transport="http://
schemas.xmlsoap.org/soap/http" style="document" />
<operation name="StockQuote">
  <soap:operation soapAction="http://
tempuri.org/StockQuote" style="document" />
<input>  <soap:body use="literal" />
  </input>
<output>  <soap:body use="literal" />
<service name="SecuritiesExchange">
<port name="SecuritiesExchangeSoap" binding="s0:SecuritiesExchangeSoap">
  <soap:address location="http://localhost/
IFCEBrokerage/IFCEBrokerageFirm.asmx" />
  </port>  </definitions>
```

The WSDL file defines its own namespace. WSDL adds a targetNamespace attribute to the <definitions> element. The targetNamespace attribute may not use a relative URI. Conversely, it must use the fully qualified URL. The namespace allows the author to qualify references to entities contained within the WSDL document.

By doing this, the WSDL file assigns the prefix wsdlns to reference the namespace. This prefix fully qualifies all references to entities combined within the document. In addition, it sets prefixes for the <types> element as well as the XSD Schema. The <definitions> element sets boundaries for a specified name. All elements declared within the WSDL file define entities for messages and ports. Assign entities utilizing the Name attribute.

In a production environment, it is imperative to change the target namespace to your own. The temporary namespace displayed in the WSDL document, for example,

```
targetNamespace="http://tempuri.org/"
 xmlns="http://schemas.xmlsoap.org/wsdl/"
```

specifies the http://tempuri.org namespace. It is better to do the following:

```
targetNamespace="http://IFCEBrokerageFirm.com/"
 xmlns="http://schemas.xmlsoap.org">
```

Returning to Listing 7-10, the <types> element contains XSD Schema information contained within the WSDL file. For example, examine the following document segment, and observe how the schema element appears as an immediate child of <types>. In addition, <types> functions as a container for XSD Schema complex types.

```
<s:element name="StockQuote">
  <s:complexType>
    <s:sequence>
     <s:element minOccurs="0" maxOccurs="1" name="symbol"
       type="s:string"/>
    </s:sequence>
  </s:complexType>
</s:element>
```

The same is true for StockQuoteResponse. Its type is s:double.

The <message> element contains two parts, the message name and the part name. The message name is StockQuoteSOAPIn. The part name is parameters, and the element is s0:StockQuote. Notice that the message segment contains both a

```
<message name="StockQuoteSoapIn">
```

and a

```
  <part name="parameters" element="s0:StockQuote" />
  </message>
  <message name="StockQuoteSoapOut">
```

The <message> element contains descriptions for logical elements of messages. The <part> represents a parameter passed to the method.

The <portType> element defines a list of operations, each individually assigned to a specified <operation> child element. In this case, SecuritiesExchange SOAP is the portType name. The <operation> name is StockQuote. The input and output messages are

```
s0:StockQuoteIn
```

and

```
s0:StockQuoteOut
```

Implementing Interfaces

Recall that an interface is made up of a set of signatures, which in turn are made up of an operation's name, the objects that it accepts as parameters, and its return values. The interface represents the entire set of requests that are sent to the interface. For example, by *typing* an interface, that is, Type IFCE, the interface accepts all requests for operations defined in that interface. Two objects representing the type can share individual parts of an interface. In addition, interfaces can contain other interfaces, referred to as subsets. Frequently, we can refer to a subtype as inheriting from its supertype interface.

Interfaces are fundamental to object-oriented programming. An interface represents an abstract concept by declaring its intentions, but never reveals the *how.* In essence, the interface says nothing about its implementation. This is a win-win situation for developers. They can mutually share the same interface and write totally unique implementations without conflict, as long as they adhere to the interface's signature.

Dynamic Binding

Interfaces support dynamic binding for disparate objects sharing the same signature. For example, developers can submit a request to an object with confidence, knowing it will accept the request because it supports object substitutability. One object containing the same interface is interchangeable with another object at runtime, courtesy of a mechanism called polymorphism. As long as the object's signature is adhered to, the object will process any request with equanimity.

During component-based development, you construct the interface so a client invocation on a specified service will never know *how* the request is implemented. Encapsulation shields the implementation from the client. Therefore, you can think of an interface as having two parts:

- **Interface** Defines a set of public method signatures but provides no implementations
- **Published interface** A uniquely identifiable interface made available through a registry to clients for dynamic discovery

Interfaces declared in Java or managed C++ typically provide only method signatures. Therefore, they describe *why* but not *how* the interface should be implemented. This allows for multiple implementations and allows services or components to enhance both flexibility and scalability. However, the stateless Internet environment does not guarantee that the interface's implementation is always secure and compliant with any behavioral specification. Despite this limitation, businesses are gravitating toward more service-oriented systems. Perhaps it is possible to adhere to the safe practice of defining a behavioral interface.

Objects are created by instantiating a class. This process allocates storage for the object's internal data consisting of instance variables. This in turn binds the object with its variable types. By employing a methodology called class inheritance, the subclass inherits all parent data type definitions and its behavioral characteristics. This means objects will perform operations defined in both the parent and child classes.

The sole purpose of an abstract class is to define a common interface for its child subclasses. However, an instance of this class can never be instantiated. Operations defined by an abstract class are called abstract operations, whereas classes that are not declared as abstract are called concrete classes. *Abstract classes* describe general behavioral characteristics, whereas *concrete classes* define more specific operations on an interface's signature.

Class Inheritance vs. Interface Inheritance

It is important to distinguish between an object's class and its type. A class defines an object's internal state and provides information on how to implement it. For example, superclass Employer is inheritable by several subclass employee types. A salaried employee defines its implementation in reference to class Employer. An employee retained on commission defines its behavior in reference to class Employer, and so on. In essence, class inheritance is just a mechanism for implementing and extending a specified class's functionality. To be a bit banal, a child inherits all genetic characteristics from his/her parents, but extends the parents' genetic and social inclinations by building on them and becoming an individual person. Interface inheritance reduces implementation dependencies between subsystems and components. Therefore, it is safe to assume that programming to an interface is better than programming to an implementation. Best practices suggest it is better to declare variables that are instances of an abstract class rather than instances of a concrete class.

In conclusion, perhaps one of the most important concepts is learning how to design reusable components. In addition, knowing how to implement abstract interfaces is essential to designing web-based applications in ASP.NET. Remember, the .NET Framework and the ASP.NET runtime are composed of reusable components and interfaces. Therein lies the key to understanding .NET and ASP.NET.

PART

Cross-Platform Interoperability

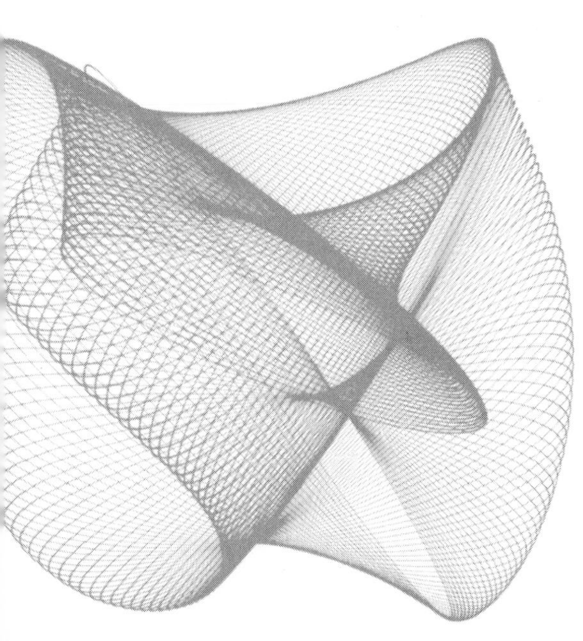

CHAPTER

8

Interoperability Solutions from Third-Party Vendors

IN THIS CHAPTER:

Writing and Deploying Applications for Any Platform

Ja.NET and J-Integra

JNBridgePro: Infrastructure and Features

Overview of Installation

A Working Example: JNBridgePro and WebSphere 5.0

In today's rapidly developing digital economy, businesses must reevaluate their methods of doing business in a distributed environment, preserving their heavy investment in legacy code while merging with the new technologies offered by Sun's Java platform and Microsoft's .NET Framework. J2EE and .NET provide numerous technologies to achieve interoperability, both internally and externally. For example, J2EE offers support for the constantly improving new technologies such as connectors and web services, whereas .NET provides multilanguage interoperability. Considering the success of the two diverse platforms and their unique approach to building distributed applications, how is it possible to take advantage of both technologies and build cross-platform applications?

Writing and Deploying Applications for Any Platform

Developing distributed applications in either J2EE or .NET presents a problem for the programmer: selecting a platform before writing the application. Which approach will solve a particular need? Java's philosophy is to write an application and deploy it on any platform containing a JVM. Only one caveat exists: the application *must* be written in the Java language.

Conversely, .NET offers developers multilanguage interoperability. A .NET application can run on any platform that has the .NET Framework on it. This is similar to a JVM, where Java bytecode can run on any platform where a copy of the JVM exists. However, currently only the Windows platforms have the Framework on them.

Enter third-party vendors. JNBridge LLC and Intrinsyc Software are two major vendors of cross-platform technologies for J2EE and .NET. Both have recognized the predicament developers face when attempting to make their choice between J2EE and .NET technologies, and they offer interoperability solutions that share much in common:

- Support for enterprise application servers, including WebSphere, BEA WebLogic, Oracle9*i*, Borland Enterprise Server, and JBoss
- Support for HTTP and TCP/IP protocols
- Support for SOAP
- Support for binary messages

- Client-activated and server-activated objects
- Invocation of methods on Java objects from the CLR
- Invocation of methods on CLR objects from Java
- Support for passing Java/CLR objects by reference and by value as parameters/return values
- Marshaling objects by value or by reference
- Callbacks

It is no longer necessary for developers to make a critical choice. JNBridge LLC's product, JNBridgePro, and Intrinsyc's Ja.NET bridge the gap between Java and .NET.

JNBridge's cross-platform technology is available in two versions: SE (Standard Edition) and EE (Enterprise Edition). The Enterprise Edition is covered in this chapter. But before going into the details of JNBridgePro, we'll take a brief look at Intrinsyc's solutions.

Ja.NET and J-Integra

Ja.NET makes it possible to write clients for Enterprise JavaBeans in a .NET language targeting the .NET Framework. Using any language hosted by the Framework in conjunction with Ja.NET facilitates interoperability between Java objects or entity JavaBeans. Additional features permit reusing components written in Java within the .NET environment or vice versa. In essence, Ja.NET Java components act as though they are Microsoft .NET, and vice versa, because Ja.NET leverages .NET remoting.

Ja.NET provides a tool called GenJava to generate a Java proxy for .NET components. For example, access to an Internet Information Server (IIS) component from Java is easy. The Janetor tool configures the Ja.NET runtime. Then, Java clients can use the proxies to access a remote CLR component as though it were a local Java component. The tool can also generate a .NET component bearing proxies for Enterprise JavaBeans client-side classes. Then, Janetor generates a web application archive (WAR) file containing all web server–deployable files. Another beneficial feature permits the CLR client written in any language to access Enterprise JavaBeans as though they were local CLR components.

Intrinsyc Software has another interop tool called J-Integra. It is a COM-Java tool employed for accessing ActiveX components as though they are Java objects. Conversely, accessing Java objects as though they are Microsoft .NET components is allowed. J-Integra works seamlessly with any Java Virtual Machine on any platform and requires no native code. Additionally, J-Integra speaks native DCOM and is layered over Remote Procedure Calls. J-Integra requires no JVM or additional software installs on the COM platform.

Ja.Net and J-Integra technologies are worth pursuing. You can freely download these solutions. Because URLs change frequently, I recommend that you search for them through your favorite search engine. Although this chapter does not examine Intrinsyc Software's solutions, this does not reflect on the quality of their products. Check them out. They offer an excellent alternative to JNBridgePro.

JNBridgePro: Infrastructure and Features

JNBridgePro supports the creation of scalable and flexible distributed applications. Developers can access Enterprise JavaBeans, JMS, JNDI, and other services from .NET clients (Enterprise Edition only). JNBridgePro provides support for transactions via thread-true classes. The classes ensure they are managed by the same .NET-Java thread and guarantee data integrity. With JNBridgePro version 1.3.4 EE, developers can employ Java code in the .NET Framework as though Java is a .NET language. Fields, methods, and Java classes can be called from .NET classes without the caller being aware that the accessed classes are actually written in Java.

Microsoft .NET programmers can derive classes from Java. This feature allows the inherited classes to be written in a .NET language of choice, such as Visual Basic .NET, C#, J#, or managed C++ to name a few. The inheritance will be reflected on the Java side. Therefore, method calls overridden by derived .NET classes are redirected back to the .NET assembly. Subsequently, the Java classes can be linked to directly, or accessed over the network. This methodology supports a wide variety of platform architectures and communication mechanisms. An additional JNBridgePro benefit permits .NET classes to be implicitly accessed from Java code through the familiar Java callback listener method. (Java callbacks are discussed later in this chapter.)

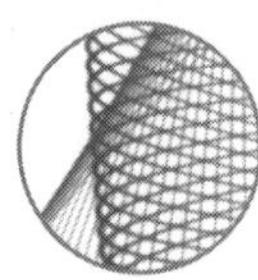

NOTE

In order to work along with this chapter, an evaluation copy of JNBridgePro can be downloaded from the JNBridge web site. Because web site URLs can change quite frequently, simply type JNBridge into a search engine.

The JNBridgePro Infrastructure

Before examining the features that JNBridgePro offers developers, let's examine the infrastructure. The architectural details for the .NET-side are as follows:

- **.NET management** This is performed by the CLR.
- **Proxy generator** The JNB Proxy Generator creates the class proxies.
- **.NET classes** All .NET classes call the generated proxies. The proxy acts as the intermediary. In fact, this action is mandatory.
- **Generated proxies** The .NET assembly consists of generated proxy binary information.
- **Runtime component** This consists of a set of core proxies and classes to manage Java-.NET communications and references to Java objects. This can be a standalone application, an ASP.NET web application, or web service.

Details of the Java-side are as follows:

- **JVM** A standalone JVM or application server containing a J2EE servlet container
- **Java runtime component** SOAP or Fast Binary Protocol based on .NET remoting
- **Object reference table** Points to individual Java classes

JNBridgePro includes JNBProxy, a graphical user interface and proxy generator, and JNBCore, the interface that manages communications between .NET and the JVM. The JNBridgePro runtime architecture consists of a set of Java binaries (JAR or class files) containing the legacy Java code that runs on a JVM and Java Platform (J2SE) or (J2EE). This is the environment in which the Java code executes.

The JNBCore module manages communications between native-side proxies and the JVM. The JNBCore represents a uniform interface to either the .NET remoting framework that includes SOAP, the XML-based mechanism for invoking methods remotely on objects, or the faster binary protocol.

Residing on top of the JNBCore module is a set of native-side proxy classes that make up a .NET assembly, through which the .NET code accesses Java binaries. There must be *one proxy class for each Java class* accessed by .NET code. The proxy's invocation interface matches the corresponding Java class. In order to create a corresponding Java object, the .NET code invokes the appropriate constructors on the proxy class and procures a reference to the new proxy object. To access a member field or method in a Java class, the .NET code invokes the corresponding field accessor or method in its associated proxy class.

Primitive values or references to proxy objects can be passed as parameters or returned as values. Exceptions thrown by Java objects are thrown back to the .NET code that invokes the proxies.

JNBProxy can be instructed to generate proxies for Java classes accessed by .NET code. This includes superclasses, exceptions, interfaces, return values, and parameters, or for that matter, any subset of them in between. Generating proxies for the maximum set of classes provides fine-grained granularity and maximum flexibility.

JNBridgePro Features

The key features offered by JNBridgePro include the following:

- Cross-platform and cross-language support and portability
- Class-level interoperability
- Large-scale distributed application support

Cross-Platform and Cross-Language Portability

The ability to integrate Microsoft .NET with Java classes enables Java classes to function as though they are in reality a .NET-supported language. This technology requires no change to the Java code base. In fact, JNBridge LLC suggests developers can even make use of third-party libraries to achieve class integration. Despite Java and .NET class intermingling, the Java code remains cross-platform portable and conforms to existing J2EE standards.

Java code can run on a .NET machine or, for that matter, any machine supporting the JVM or a J2EE-compliant application server. An additional benefit is the ability to call Java classes and methods from any .NET-targeted Framework language.

Class-Level Interoperability

Class-level interoperability provides access to Java objects and classes from .NET via proxies generated by the proxy generation tool JNBProxy. This tool lets developers explore the interfaces and functionality of the available Java classes, allowing them to determine through a visual interface which classes should be exposed to .NET. Once the decision is made, JNBProxy generates the required proxies and writes them to a .NET assembly DLL file. Therein lies the key to understanding how JNBridge Pro functions.

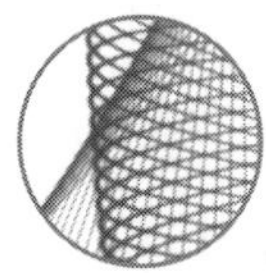

NOTE

Once the proxy is generated, .NET invokes all Java classes, methods, and fields on the proxy interface.

As you may recall from Chapter 5, the .NET assembly is made up of two essential components: the manifest and the assembly itself. The manifest contains the metadata about the assembly. The assembly contains version information and the name of the assembly as well as the application binaries.

The first portion of the assembly references all external assemblies required by the current assembly to execute the application successfully. The second segment of the assembly enumerates each module contained within the assembly. It is possible to load the assembly at runtime and procure a list of all types contained within a module. This includes both .NET and Java methods, events, fields, and properties. This is achieved by means of reflection.

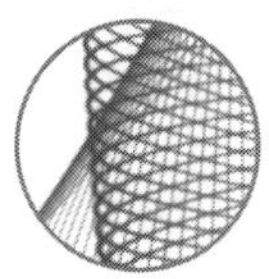

NOTE

Each class whose functionality is exposed causes a proxy of the same name to be generated. Generated proxy members (constructors, methods, and fields) correspond to the members of the Java class underlying the proxy. Microsoft .NET interacts directly with the proxies rather than with the actual underlying Java classes.

Developers can call methods, access fields, create objects, access static and instance members of Java classes, and catch exceptions thrown by Java classes through the proxies.

Passing by Reference vs. Passing by Value

Beginning with version 1.3, JNBridgePro supports both reference and value objects. Passing by reference is faster than passing by value. A JNBridgePro reference is always smaller than the corresponding object. Moreover, repeated access to members of a reference object requires frequent trips between .NET and Java. In contrast, passing an object by value may take longer because the value object is larger. However, subsequent member accesses are much quicker because the data resides locally. Therefore, round-trips between Java and .NET are avoided. This enhances performance. It is always important to evaluate and determine which method offers increased performance. It always depends on application requirements.

Class-Level Interoperability Facilitates Using Java Callback Methods

Class-level interoperability allows developers to use Java's event listener methods. The .NET code can be called from Java via the standard Java callback mechanism, allowing the Java code to remain portable. For example, EJB containers are responsible for managing entity beans. Containers interact with entity beans by calling a bean's management or life cycle methods as necessary. These methods represent the bean's callback methods that only the container invokes, not the caller. These methods allow the container to alert a bean when middleware events occur, such as when an entity bean is going to be persisted to storage.

Java Data Types Are Automatically Converted to .NET Data Types

Java primitive types, strings, and arrays are automatically converted to corresponding .NET primitives, strings, and arrays. In contrast, the .NET primitives, strings, and arrays can be passed as parameters to Java classes and are subsequently converted to their Java counterparts.

With version 1.3, JNBridgePro automatically maps between native Java and .NET collection objects. Java ArrayLists, LinkedLists, Vectors, and HashSets are converted to .NET ArrayLists when they are returned from a .NET call to a specified Java method. Conversely, ArrayLists are converted from .NET to Java when they are passed as parameters in a call from .NET to a Java method. JNBridgePro maps between Java Hashtables, HashMaps, and .Net Hashtables as well.

Inheritance, Implementation, and Class Proxies

.NET classes can inherit from Java classes by inheriting from the Java classes' proxies. Calls to any methods that the new class does not override are directed to the underlying Java class. Additionally, .NET classes may implement Java interfaces by implementing their proxies.

Java-.NET Class Integration

Once a proxy DLL is generated, the developer adds it to the current project. This allows the developer to access Java classes from .NET, a technique of considerable significance. Remember, the proxy DLL is written to the .NET assembly, the place where all information about Java classes, methods, and fields reside.

How is it possible to construct a Java object from .NET code? Simply call a constructor that corresponds to the Java constructor bearing the same name signature of the associated proxy class. In order to invoke an instance method on a Java object, the .NET code invokes the appropriate method or accesses the specified field *on the corresponding proxy object.*

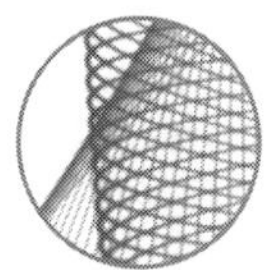

NOTE

All .NET interaction with Java occurs through the generated proxy for a specified Java class. Every Java class contains a corresponding proxy.

Invoking a static method or field on a Java class calls the corresponding proxy class. Finally, if a Java method throws an exception, the .NET method catches the exception. Additionally, if the proxy method is no longer referenced, it is garbage collected, providing there are no further references to the object.

Overview of Installation

JNBridgePro includes a comprehensive set of evaluation and installation guides. This includes a PDF readme file as well as documentation for installations of the following containers:

- JNBridgePro with Borland Enterprise Server 5.0
- JNBridgePro with JBoss - Tomcat
- JNBridgePro with JRun
- JNBridgePro with Oracle9*i*AS
- JNBridgePro with Sybase EAserver 4.*x*
- JNBridgePro with WebLogic 6.1
- JNBridgePro with WebLogic 7.0
- JNBridgePro with WebSphere 4.0
- JNBridgePro with WebSphere 5.0

A little later in the chapter, we will look at an example using WebSphere's 5.0 server edition.

The general procedure for installing JNBridgePro is as follows:

1. Run the installer jnbSetup1_1ee.msi or jnbSetup1_1se.msi on the development machines where proxies are generated.
2. Configure the communications on the appropriate .NET and Java machine(s).
3. Copy the appropriate component and configuration files to the respective .NET-side and Java-side machines, and modify the configuration files as directed for runtime proxy-use deployment.

For an understanding of the specifics involved in installation, let's review the related topics as they are presented in the JNBridge guide.

Architectural Elements

When JNBridgePro is used to interoperate .NET and Java code, the .NET code runs on a .NET Common Language Runtime (CLR) and Java code runs on a Java Virtual Machine (JVM). Every application using JNBridgePro consists of one or more instances of the CLR and one or more JVM instances.

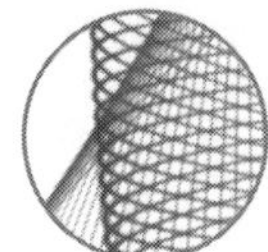

NOTE

Here, the set of all .NET CLRs in an application are collectively referred to as the ".NET-side," while the set of all instances of the JVM are referred to as the "Java-side."

The .NET-side and the Java-side can run on the same machine or on different machines connected by a network. The .NET-side must reside on a Microsoft .NET supported machine; the Java-side can reside on any machine with a standards-compliant JVM.

Configuring the .NET-Side

A copy of the .NET Framework must reside on the .NET-side. In addition, the .NET classes using JNBridgePro require the .NET-side to have a copy of jnbshare.dll, as well as a copy of the DLL file containing the generated proxies. These two DLL files must reside in the same folder as the application using them.

The configuration file jnbproxy.config must reside in the same folder as jnbshare.dll. If HTTP/SOAP is used for communications between .NET and Java, jnbproxy.config must contain a copy of jnbproxy_http.config. Conversely, if the binary protocol is used, jnbproxy.config must contain a copy of jnbproxy_tcp.config supplied with the JNBridgePro software distribution. Additionally, the configuration file must be edited to indicate the name or IP address of the host on which the Java classes reside, as well as the port number on which the Java-side listens for messages. If both the .NET-side and the Java-side reside on the same machine, the host name "localhost" may be used.

Since the .NET Framework supports distributed computing, the .NET-side can reside on several different machines, where classes communicate with each other through .NET remoting. If this scenario exists, each .NET-side machine communicating with the Java-side must contain a local copy of the generated proxy DLL file, jnbshare.dll, and jnbproxy.config.

Configuring the Java-Side

A copy of the Java Runtime Environment (JRE) must reside on the Java-side. If the Java-side resides on more than one machine, each respective machine must contain a JRE copy. The Java-side must also include any Java classes being accessed and must therefore have a copy of jnbcore.jar on each machine where the Java-side resides. The locations of the Java classes and jnbcore.jar must be in either the CLASSPATH environment variable or must be supplied to the Java runtime when invoked. Moreover, the Java-side must contain a copy of jnbcore.properties. Depending on whether communication is via HTTP/SOAP or binary protocol, jnbcore.properties should have a copy of one of the prototype properties files, jnbcore_http.properties or jnbcore_tcp.properties. Edit the Ports field in the properties file to indicate the port on which the Java-side should listen to messages from the .NET-side.

The Java-side for an application can reside on more than one machine, with the restriction that .NET classes sitting on one machine may only communicate with the Java classes on a single machine.

About Communications Protocols

JNBridgePro supports communication between .NET and Java code using two communications protocols:

- Proprietary binary protocol
- HTTP/SOAP communications protocol

The binary protocol is fast and efficient but may not penetrate corporate firewalls; the HTTP/SOAP protocol is slower, but will pass through firewalls. JNBridgePro recommends using the faster proprietary binary protocol.

If communications between .NET and Java employ HTTP/SOAP, a copy of a JAXP-compliant XML package must reside on the Java-side. Any such package may be used; one such package is located on Sun's JAXP site (http://java.sun.com/xml/jaxp/index.html). Installation details vary for each package. Programmers should consult instructions included with the selected package. To use HTTP/SOAP communications, the locations of the files in the JAXP package must either appear in the CLASSPATH environment variable, or they must be supplied to the Java runtime when invoked.

Table 8-1 lists JNBridgePro components and related configuration files.

Component	File Name	Description
JNBProxy GUI version	jnbproxygui.exe	Generates .NET proxies enabling .NET classes to communicate with Java classes.
JNBProxy command-line version	jnbproxy.exe	Represents the command-line version of the proxy generation tool.
JNPBCommon	jnbpcommon.dll	Contains functionality shared by the GUI and command-line versions of JNBProxy.
Generated proxies	*.dll	A .NET assembly contains the generated proxies built especially for the application.
JNBShare	jnbshare.dll	A .NET assembly contains core functionality used by generated .NET proxies.
JNBCore	jnbcore.jar	A Java JAR file that manages communications for both Java and .NET classes, as well as the object's life cycle—that is, creation, use, and object destruction of Java objects created by calls from .NET objects.
Registration tool	registrationTool.exe	Registers and licenses JNBShare on additional machines where the proxy generation tool has not been installed.
.NET-side proxy configuration file	jbnproxy.config	Specifies on the .NET-side, the protocol, host, and port used to communicate between .NET classes and Java classes.
Java-side configuration file	jnbcore.properties	Specifies on the Java side, the protocol and port number to communicate between the user's .NET classes and the Java classes.

Table 8-1 *JNBridgePro Development Components*

Executing the Installer

To install the JNBridgePro development components for proxy generation, double-click on the installer file jnbSetup1_1ee.msi or jnbSetup1_1se.msi, and follow the instructions, selecting one of the following options:

- Development configuration (proxy generation tools, plus Java and .NET runtime components)
- Deployment configuration (Java and .NET runtime components only)

In either case, the installer installs the files jnbshare.dll, jnbcore.jar, and registrationTool.exe, as well as sample configuration files and additional documentation. If the programmer selects the development configuration, the files jnbproxy.exe, jnbproxygui.exe, and jnbpcommon.dll are installed as well.

Configuring the Communications Protocol

As you already know, JNBridgePro supports communications between .NET classes running in a CLR and Java classes running in a JVM. The CLR and the JVM can reside on the same machine or on different machines. The JNBProxy proxy generation tool is simply a .NET application communicating with Java classes like any other .NET application utilizing JNBridgePro. Therefore, JNBProxy also requires a CLR and a JVM, existing on either the same or different machines.

1. Navigate to the folder in which jnbproxy.exe and jnbproxygui.exe were installed (for example, C:\Program Files\JNBridge\JNBridgePro).
2. Generate a new configuration file, jnbproxy.config, specifying the protocol (HTTP/SOAP or binary) used to communicate between .NET and Java classes.
    - For HTTP/SOAP, copy jnbproxy_http.config to jnbproxy.config.
    - For binary protocol, copy jnbproxy_tcp.config to jnbproxy.config.
3. Modify the new jnbproxy.config file in order to reflect the proper host name and port number for the Java runtime component.
    - Open jnbproxy.config using a text editor and locate the URL, which will either be http://localhost:8085/JNBDispatcher, for HTTP/SOAP, or jtcp://localhost:8085/JNBDispatcher, for the binary protocol.

- Edit the host name (currently "localhost") and port number (currently "8085") to indicate the host on which the Java classes and the JNBCore component will reside and the port on which JNBCore will be listening for messages. If JNBCore resides on the same machine as the .NET classes, leave the host as "localhost."

The default JNBCore is residing on the same machine as the .NET classes; JNBCore listens on port 8085. If this is acceptable, do not change the configuration file. Save it, and close the text editor.

4. Copy the jnbcore directory into a location of choice on the machine where the Java environment resides. This directory contains the Java runtime component jnbcore.jar and two properties files, jnbcore_http.properties and jnbcore_tcp.properties. This directory must be on the same machine as the Java classes accessed from .NET code. Add the JAR's full path to the CLASSPATH environment variable.
5. Generate a new properties file, jnbcore.properties, corresponding to the protocol used to communicate between .NET classes and Java classes.
   - For HTTP/SOAP, copy jnbcore_http.properties to jnbcore.properties.
   - For binary protocol, copy jnbcore_tcp.properties to jnbcore.properties.
6. On the Java machine, open jnbcore.properties using a text editor. Edit the value of the port to agree with the value chosen in jnbproxy.config. Save the file, and close the text editor. The resultant file should look like the following:

```
serverType=tcp
workers=5
timeout=10000
port=8085
```

If using HTTP/SOAP for communications between the .NET classes and Java classes, and a JAXP-compliant XML package is not installed, install one. If using the binary protocol, skip this step.

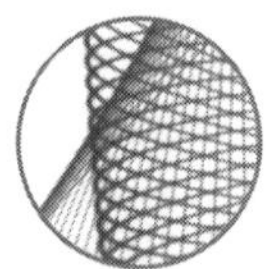

NOTE

Any JAXP-compliant XML package can be installed. Follow the installation instructions for the selected package. Following installation, add the JAR file's full path to the CLASSPATH environment variable.

Improving Network Performance

By default, JNBridgePro sends out network packets between the .NET and Java sides as soon as they are created. In most cases, this leads to improved performance. However, this behavior means that typical JNBridgePro-generated network packets are small, and in some cases this could lead to network congestion and degraded performance. If network performance degradation occurs, turn off the NoDelay option so packets are aggregated before they are sent out. This may improve network performance. Typically, if calls or returns contain a large amount of data, turning NoDelay off may improve performance. The NoDelay option can also be controlled independently in the .NET-to-Java and Java-to-.NET directions. To turn the NoDelay option off in the .NET-to-Java direction, add the following to the .NET application's configuration file. For example, if the application is x.exe, create or open the file x.exe.config in the same folder as x.exe and add the following to the file:

```
<configuration>
<appSettings>
<add key="JNBridge_TCP_NoDelay" value="false"/>
</appSettings>
</configuration>
```

To turn the NoDelay option off in the Java-to-.NET direction, add the following line to the jnbcore.properties file: **nodelay=false**.

Starting Java for Proxy Generation

JNBProxy uses the Java reflection API to discover information about Java classes for which it is generating proxies. To do this, a JVM must be running that contains the JNBCore component and the Java classes for generating proxies.

JNBProxy users (both the GUI and command-line versions) may choose to have the Java-side started automatically or manually. If the Java-side resides on some other machine, JNBProxy will be unable to start; therefore, a manual start is required. To manually start the Java-side, issue the following command from the command-line:

```
java -cp classpath com.jnbridge.jnbcore.JNBMain /props propFilePath
```

where classpath must include the following:

- The Java classes for which proxies are generated (and their supporting classes).
- jnbcore.jar.
- The JAR files for the XML package (if using HTTP/SOAP communication).
- The –cp classpath option can be omitted, in which case the required information must be present in the CLASSPATH environment variable: propFilePath is the full file path of the file jnbcore.properties.

The folder containing the java.exe executable must be in the system's search path (typically described in the PATH environment variable). If not, specify the full path of java.exe on the command line.

When starting the Java-side manually, you will see the following output if using the binary protocol:

```
JNBCore v1.2
Copyright 2002, JNBridge
creating binary server
```

Or the following output will be seen if HTTP/SOAP is used:

```
JNBCore v1.2
Copyright 2002, JNBridge
creating http server
```

Configuring the System for Proxy Use

To deploy JNBridgePro runtime components for proxy use (that is, on machines other than ones containing the proxy generator), copy and run the installer on those machines, and select Deployment Configuration when requested by the installer. Also create versions of the configuration files jnbproxy.config and jnbcore.properties as described in the earlier section "Configuring the Communications Protocol." JNBridgePro searches for the configuration file jnbproxy.config in the following folders:

- It looks first in the folder where jnbshare.dll is located.
- If not located there, it looks in the folder <System-drive>:\Inetpub\wwwroot, where <System-drive> is the drive on which the running system is installed (typically C, but not always). If the proxies are called from ASP.NET, place jnbproxy.config in this folder.

If jnbshare.dll is not found there, JNBridgePro looks in the folder <System-drive>:\ (the root folder of the drive on which the system is installed, typically C, but not always). Any user accessing proxies generated by JNBridgePro must specify Read and Write access to the folder <System-drive>:\Documents and Settings\AllUsers\Application Data\Microsoft\Crypto\RSA\MachineKeys.

If the user does not have access to this folder, the proxies cannot be used. This is only an issue on systems running the NTFS file system. On systems running other file systems, users should automatically have this access.

Configuring Proxies for Use with ASP.NET

If the developer is calling the generated proxies from ASP.NET, place the configuration file jnbproxy.config in the folder <System-drive>:\Inetpub\wwwroot, where <Systemdrive> is the drive on which the running system is installed (typically C). If the ASP.NET machine is running on an NTFS file system, make sure the user account has Read and Write access to the folder <System-drive>:\Documents and Settings\All Users\ApplicationData\Microsoft\Crypto\RSA\MachineKeys.

If the required access permission is not assigned, the ASP.NET program will not be able to use the proxies.

Starting a Standalone JVM for Proxy Use

JNBridgePro applications accessing Java classes and objects from .NET must have an installed and running Java-side. This can be either a standalone JVM, or a J2EE application server. You will find information on configuring a J2EE application server to work with JNBridgePro in the *Users' Guide*. A standalone JVM must contain the JNBCore component and Java classes before generating the proxies.

To start the Java-side manually in a standalone JVM, specify the following command-line command:

```
java -cp classpath com.jnbridge.jnbcore.JNBMain /props propFilePath
```

where classpath must include the following:

- Java classes and their supporting classes for generating proxies
- jnbcore.jar
- JAR files for the XML package (if using HTTP/SOAP communication)

If the –cp classpath option is omitted, include the following information required in the CLASSPATH environment variable: propFilePath, the full file path for jnbcore .properties. The folder containing the java.exe executable must be in the system's search path (typically described in the PATH environment variable). If not, specify the full path of java.exe on the command line.

When starting the Java-side manually, you will see the following when using the binary protocol:

```
JNBCore v1.2
Copyright 2002, JNBridge
creating binary server
```

or the following if using HTTP/SOAP:

```
JNBCore v1.2
Copyright 2002, JNBridge
creating http server
```

Running the Java-Side Under Nondefault Security Managers

The Java-side will work under the default security manager (that is, the one used if no security manager is explicitly set). If a security manager is set, permissions may need to be granted explicitly to allow jnbcore.jar to run. In the appropriate copy of the file java.policy, add the following lines:

```
grant codebase "file://location_of_jnbcore.jar_goes_here"
{
permission java.lang.RuntimePermission "*", "accessDeclaredMembers";
permission java.net.SocketPermission "*", "accept,resolve";
}
```

jnbcore will now run with all required permissions. If a security manager has been set, you may also need to grant permissions for your Java classes running on the Java-side.

A Working Example: JNBridgePro and WebSphere 5.0

Let's observe an example provided by JNBridgePro called BasicCalculatorEJB. It demonstrates how to access Enterprise JavaBeans from C#. The EJBs will be running on IBM WebSphere Application Server 5.0. Assume that JNBridgePro 1.3

or later and a .NET framework are installed on a Windows machine. Also assume that WebSphere 5.0, along with the accompanying examples, exists on a compatible machine, which may be either the same machine as the .NET machine or a different machine reachable on the network.

Creating jnbcore.war

Create the jnbcore.war file as follows:

1. Create a blank folder to hold the WAR file components. Call this folder <warroot>.
2. Create folders <war-root>/WEB-INF and <war-root>/WEB-INF/lib.
3. In <war-root>/WEB-INF/lib, place a copy of jnbcore.jar (copied from the JNBridgePro installation folder) and a copy of the BasicCalculatorEJB.jar file found in the Demos/J2EE-Examples/WebSpere5.0 folder in the installation.
4. In <war-root>/WEB-INF, place copies of the files jnbcore.properties and web.xml found in the Demos/J2EE-Examples/WebSphere5.0 folder in the installation. Open a command-line window and navigate to <war-root>.
5. Run the command **jar cf jnbcore.war WEB-INF**.
6. Install jnbcore.war by starting the WebSphere Application Server and opening the Administration console. Install jnbcore.war in the usual way, using the supplied default values. There are two places where you must supply data:
   - When prompted for the context root, enter **/jnbcore**.
   - When asked for the JNDI name for the EJB-reference, enter **WSsamples/BasicCalculator**.
7. Make sure the box asking whether the EJBs should be deployed remains unchecked. The BasicCalculator EJB has already been deployed.
8. Once jnbcore.war is deployed, save it to the master configuration and start it.
9. Exit the Administration console. Shut down WebSphere Application Server for the moment so that its jnbcore does not interfere with the jnbcore used by JNBProxy.

Building the Proxy DLL

Build the proxy assembly DLL as follows:

1. Start a copy of the JNBProxy GUI-based tool.
2. Select the menu item Project.Java options. Verify that the box Start Java Automatically is checked, and the Java configuration data is correct.

3. Close the dialog box.
4. Select the menu item Project.Edit Classpath and add the following files to the classpath:
   - <JNBridgePro-WebSphere5-demo-folder>/BasicCalculatorEJB.jar (it contains the classes BasicCalculator and BasicCalculatorHome, used in the C# code).
   - j2ee.jar in <was-server-root>/lib (it contains the classes EJBHome, EJBObject, and other EJB-related and JNDI-related support classes, including classes Context, InitialContext, and CreateException, used in the C# code). Close the dialog box. Create a proxy for RemoteException. The Java class is found in the local J2SDK file; no additional JAR file is needed.
5. Select the menu item Project.Add Classes from Classpath and add the following classes. Make sure the box Include Supporting Classes is checked for each class added.
   - com.ibm.websphere.samples.technologysamples.ejb.stateless .basiccalculatorejb.BasicCalculator
   - com.ibm.websphere.samples.technologysamples.ejb.stateless .basiccalculatorejb.BasicCalculatorHome
   - javax.naming.Context
   - javax.naming.InitialContext
   - javax.naming.NamingException
   - javax.rmi.PortableRemoteObject
   - java.rmi.RemoteException
   - javax.ejb.CreateException
6. Click OK to add the classes and all supporting classes to the Environment pane. This will take a few minutes. Check all the items in the environment (use the menu item Edit.Check All in Environment), and click on the Add button to move them all to the Exposed Proxies pane. Select the menu item Project.Build to build the proxy assembly. Choose an assembly name and click OK. The assembly will be written to a DLL file.

Building and Running the Client Application

These tasks can be similarly accomplished using the .NET Framework SDK:

1. In Visual Studio .NET, create a new C# console application.

2. Replace the generated file Class1.cs with the file Class1.cs located in the Demos/J2EE-Examples/WebSphere5.0 folder. You may wish to examine this file to see how the Java classes and EJBs are accessed from .NET.
3. Add references to the previously generated proxy assembly DLL and to the assembly jnbshare.dll found in the JNBridgePro installation folder.
4. Build the project.
5. Find the file jnbproxy_tcp.config in the JNBridgePro installation folder and make a copy of it in the current project build directory. Rename the file jnbproxy.config.
6. Restart WebSphere Application Server and verify that jnbcore.war has been deployed by looking in the standard output log or by opening the Administration console. Then run the .NET application. Output showing the results of calculations will be displayed.

The BasicCalculatorEJB Sample Files

Let's look at some of the files for this example. First, the C# file. Here is the code:

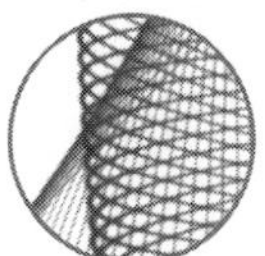

NOTE

JNBridge LLC has given permission to quote the following code examples, which you can use as templates for developing your applications.

```
using System;
using java.lang;
using java.rmi;
using javax.ejb;
using javax.naming;
using javax.rmi;
using com.ibm.websphere.samples.technologysamples._
ejb.stateless.basiccalculatorejb;
/*
In C#, using imports the class libraries
*/

// JNBridgePro example C# code for WebSphere 5.0.
// Copyright 2003, JNBridge, LLC

namespace ws5Demo
{
      /// <summary>
      /// Summary description for Class1.
```

```
        /// </summary>
        class Class1
        {
                /// <summary>
                /// The main entry point for the application.
                /// </summary>
                [STAThread]
                static void Main(string[] args)
                {
                        BasicCalculatorHome basicCalculatorHome = null;

                        // get the context
                        // get the calculator home interface
                        try
                        {
                                System.Console.WriteLine("JNDI stuff...");
                                Context ctx = new InitialContext();
                                System.Console.WriteLine("Got context");
                                java.lang.Object homeObject =
ctx.lookup("WSsamples/BasicCalculator");
                                System.Console.WriteLine("Got home object");

                                basicCalculatorHome =
                                (BasicCalculatorHome) homeObject;
System.Console.WriteLine("Got calculator home interface");
                        }
                        catch( NamingException e )
                        {
                                System.Console.WriteLine("NamingException: " + e);
                                return;
                        }
                        catch( java.lang.Exception e2 )
                        {
                                System.Console.WriteLine("Generic exception: " + e2);
                                return;
                        }

                        // create the remote interface
                        BasicCalculator basicCalculator = null;
                        try
                        {
                                basicCalculator = basicCalculatorHome.create();
                                Console.WriteLine("got remote interface");
                        }
                        catch ( javax.ejb.CreateException e1)
                        {
                                Console.WriteLine("CreateException: " + e1);
```

```
                    return;
                }
                catch( java.lang.Exception e2 )
                {
                    Console.WriteLine("Generic exception: " + e2);
                    return;
                }

                // do some calculations
                try
                {
                    double arg1 = 2.5;
                    double arg2 = 3.9;
                    double result;
// In C# we box the parameter into an object using {}, one for each argument
                    result = basicCalculator.makeSum(arg1, arg2)
                    Console.WriteLine("{0} + {1} = {2}", arg1, arg2, result);
                    result = basicCalculator.makeDifference(arg1, arg2);
                    Console.WriteLine("{0} - {1} = {2}", arg1, arg2, result);
                    result = basicCalculator.makeProduct(arg1, arg2);
                    Console.WriteLine("{0} * {1} = {2}", arg1, arg2, result);
                    result = basicCalculator.makeQuotient(arg1, arg2);
                    Console.WriteLine("{0} / {1} = {2}", arg1, arg2, result);
                }
                catch(java.lang.Exception ex)
                {
                    Console.WriteLine("Generic exception
                    in calculation: " + ex);
                    return;
                }
            }
        }
}
```

Next, here is the Web-app file:

```
<?xml version="1.0" encoding="UTF-8"?>
<!DOCTYPE web-app PUBLIC"-//Sun Microsystems,Inc.//
DTD Web Application 2.2//EN" "http://java.sun.com
/j2ee/dtds/web-app_2_2.dtd">
<web-app>
      <display-name>JNBridgePro Servlet</display-name>
```

```
      <servlet>
            <servlet-name>JNBServlet</servlet-name>
        <servlet-class>com.jnbridge.jnbcore.JNBServlet</servlet-class>
            <load-on-startup>1</load-on-startup>
      </servlet>
      <ejb-ref>
            <ejb-ref-name>WSsamples/BasicCalculator</ejb-ref-name>
            <ejb-ref-type>Session</ejb-ref-type>
            <home>com.ibm.websphere.samples.technologysamples.
ejb.session.basiccalculatorejb.BasicCalculatorHome</home>
            <remote>com.ibm.websphere.samples.technologysamples.
ejb.session.basiccalculatorejb.BasicCalculator</remote>
            <ejb-link>BasicCalculator</ejb-link>
      </ejb-ref>
</web-app>
```

JNBridgePro has included a Demo package with source code for you to use as a template for your own cross-platform applications. Here are the three classes: Book.Java, Author.Java, and DemoDBConnection.Java, in that order:

```
//Book.Java
package Demo2;
// Copyright 2002, JNBridge LLC
import java.sql.*;
import java.util.*;

public class Book
{
      public String title;
      public String publisher;
      public String year;

      public Book(String title, String publisher, String year)
      {
            this.title = title;
            this.publisher = publisher;
            this.year = year;
      }

      public static Book[] getBooks()
      {
            try
            {
                  Connection conn = DemoDBConnection.getConnection();
```

```
                Statement stmt = conn.createStatement();
                ResultSet titles = stmt.executeQuery
               ("SELECT Title, Publisher, Year FROM Titles
                 ORDER BY Title");

                Vector v = new Vector();
                while (titles.next())
                {
                      v.add(new Book(titles.getString("Title"),
titles.getString("Publisher"), titles.getString("Year")));
                }

                Book[] results = new Book[v.size()];
                for (int i = 0; i < v.size(); i++)
                {
                      results[i] = (Book) v.get(i);
                }

                return results;       // for now
          }
          catch(Exception e)
          {
                e.printStackTrace();
                System.out.println(e);
                return null;
          }
    }

    public static Book[] getBooks(String firstName, String lastName)
    {
          try
          {
                Connection conn = DemoDBConnection.getConnection();
                Statement stmt = conn.createStatement();
                String query = "SELECT Title,
 Publisher, Year FROM Titles, Authors " +

 "WHERE FirstName = \'" + firstName + "\' AND " +

 "LastName = \'" + lastName + "\' AND Authors.ID =
 Titles.AuthorID ORDER BY Title";
```

```
                    ResultSet titles = stmt.executeQuery(query);

                    Vector v = new Vector();
                    while (titles.next())
                    {
                   v.add(new Book(titles.getString("Title"),
 titles.getString("Publisher"),
 titles.getString("Year")));
                    }

                    Book[] results = new Book[v.size()];
                    for (int i = 0; i < v.size(); i++)
                    {
                          results[i] = (Book) v.get(i);
                    }

                    return results;       // for now
             }
             catch(Exception e)
             {
                    e.printStackTrace();
                    System.out.println(e);
                    return null;
             }
      }
}
```

Here is Author.Java:

```
//Author.Java
package Demo2;
// Copyright 2002, JNBridge LLC
import java.sql.*;
import java.util.*;

public class Author
{
      public String firstName;
      public String lastName;

      public Author(String firstName, String lastName)
      {
            this.firstName = firstName;
```

```
            this.lastName = lastName;
      }

      public static Author[] getAuthors()
      {
            try
            {
                  Connection conn = DemoDBConnection.getConnection();
                  Statement stmt = conn.createStatement();
                  ResultSet authorNames =
stmt.executeQuery("SELECT LastName, FirstName
 FROM Authors ORDER BY LastName");

                  Vector v = new Vector();
                  while (authorNames.next())
                  {
                   v.add(new Author
(authorNames.getString("FirstName"),
authorNames.getString("LastName")));
                  }

                  Author[] results = new Author[v.size()];
                  for (int i = 0; i < v.size(); i++)
                  {
                        results[i] = (Author) v.get(i);
                  }

                  return results;       // for now
            }
            catch(Exception e)
            {
                  e.printStackTrace();
                  System.out.println(e);
                  return null;
            }
      }
}
```

DemoDBConnection.Java follows:

```
//DemoDBConnection.Java
package Demo2;
// Copyright 2002, JNBridge LLC
```

```
import java.sql.*;

public class DemoDBConnection
{
      private static DemoDBConnection theDBConnection
      = new DemoDBConnection();
      private Connection theConnection;

      public static Connection getConnection()
      {
            return theDBConnection.theConnection;
      }

      private DemoDBConnection()
      {
            try
            {
                  // load the database driver
                  Class.forName("sun.jdbc.odbc.JdbcOdbcDriver");


                  // allocate a connection object
                  theConnection = DriverManager.getConnection
                  ("jdbc:odbc:BookDemo");
            }
            catch(Exception e)
            {
                  System.out.println(e);
            }
      }
}
```

Next, the three stubs are presented. First, the Book stub:

```
//public class Book
package Demo2;
public class Book {
  // Fields
  public String title;
  public String publisher;
  public String year;

  // Constructors
```

```
  public Book(String string, String string1, String string2) { }

  // Methods
  public static Book[] getBooks() { return null;}
  public static Book[] getBooks
  (String string, String string1) { return null;}
}
```

Next, the following code is the Author stub:

```
package Demo2;
public class Author {
  // Fields
  public String firstName;
  public String lastName;

  // Constructors
  public Author(String string, String string1) { }

  // Methods
  public static Author[] getAuthors() { return null;}
}
```

The following code represents the DemoDBConnection stub:

```
//This stub is DemoDBConnection
package Demo2;

// Imports
import java.sql.Connection;

public class DemoDBConnection {

  // Fields
  private static DemoDBConnection theDBConnection;
  private Connection theConnection;

  // Constructors
  private DemoDBConnection() { }

  // Methods
  public static Connection getConnection() { return null;}
}
```

Next, we present the WebForm1.cs file:

```
using System;
using System.Collections;
using System.ComponentModel;
using System.Data;
using System.Drawing;
using System.Web;
using System.Web.SessionState;
using System.Web.UI;
using System.Web.UI.WebControls;
using System.Web.UI.HtmlControls;
using Demo2;

// Copyright 2002, JNBridge LLC

namespace Demo3
{
      /// <summary>
      /// Summary description for WebForm1.
      /// </summary>
      public class WebForm1 : System.Web.UI.Page
      {
            protected System.Web.UI.WebControls.Label Label1;
            protected System.Web.UI.WebControls.ListBox ListBox1;
            protected System.Web.UI.WebControls.Label Label2;
            protected System.Web.UI.WebControls.ListBox ListBox2;

            private void Page_Load(object sender, System.EventArgs e)
            {
                  // Put user code to initialize the page here
            }

            #region Web Form Designer generated code
            override protected void OnInit(EventArgs e)
            {
                  //
                  // CODEGEN: This call is required
 by the ASP.NET Web Form Designer.
                  //
                  InitializeComponent();
                  base.OnInit(e);
            }

            /// <summary>
            /// Required method for Designer support - do not modify
```

```
        /// the contents of this method with the code editor.
        /// </summary>
        private void InitializeComponent()
        {
              this.ListBox1.Load +=
newSystem.EventHandler(this.ListBox1_Load);
this.ListBox1.SelectedIndexChanged += new
System.EventHandler(this.ListBox1_SelectedIndexChanged);
              this.Load += new System.EventHandler(this.Page_Load);

        }
        #endregion

        private void ListBox1_Load(object sender, System.EventArgs e)
        {
              if (ListBox1.Items.Count > 0)
              {
                    return;      // don't add anything more
              }

              // load the authors
              Author[] authors = Author.getAuthors();
              for (int i = 0; i < authors.Length; i++)
              {
                    ListItem li = new ListItem();
                    li.Text = authors[i].lastName + ", " +
                    authors[i].firstName;
                    ListBox1.Items.Add(li);
              }
        }

        private void ListBox1_SelectedIndexChanged
        (object sender, System.EventArgs e)
        {
              // clear listBox2
              ListBox2.Items.Clear();

              // if nothing selected, return
              ListItem li = ListBox1.SelectedItem;

              if (li == null)
              {
                    return;
              }

              // last, first names
              string name = li.Text;
```

```
                    int separator = name.IndexOf(",");
                    string lastName = name.Substring(0, separator);
                    string firstName = name.Substring(separator+2);

                    // look up books
                    Book[] titles = Book.getBooks(firstName, lastName);

                    // write out books
                    for (int i = 0; i < titles.Length; i++)
                    {
                      ListItem li2 = new ListItem();
                      string theBook = titles[i].title + "
                          (" + titles[i].publisher + ", "
                          + titles[i].year + ")";
                          li2.Text = theBook;
                          ListBox2.Items.Add(li2);
                    }
            }
      }
}
```

A copy of the Access database including the Author and Book may be found in the Demo2 folder included with the JNBridgePro installation package.

In summary, JNBridgePro and Intrinsyc offer viable cross-platform business solutions for every business scenario. Finally, developers have a tool to facilitate true interoperability between J2EE version 1.3.1 and Microsoft .NET.

CHAPTER

9

Best Practices, Design Patterns, Security, and Business Solutions

IN THIS CHAPTER:

Applying Best Practices

Examining the Container's Role

Securing an Enterprise Application

Providing an IFCE Business Solution in Visual Basic .NET

As defined in the J2EE Blueprints, the Java 2 Enterprise Edition platform provides a component-based approach to building a scalable, multi-tiered architecture. This architecture offers developers the building blocks with which to model complex business infrastructures. The components are dispersed across disparate operating systems and frequently require software solutions allowing clients and Enterprise JavaBeans to communicate with each other in a multi-tiered environment. One method of invoking remote procedure calls uses RMI-IIOP and JNDI to locate an object and leverage its services. Another option available to developers is employing third-party solutions such as JNBridgePro to generate proxies that allow clients in a JVM environment to call functionality defined within the Microsoft .NET Framework and vice versa. Yet a third method available to developers creating applications in either the J2EE or .NET platform is using XML SOAP-based calls via HTTP to invoke web services. Interoperability, the central theme of this book, is essential for success in today's digital economy and requires flexibility in both architectural design and business model implementation.

Applying Best Practices

This chapter focuses on best practices, design patterns, and security for both the J2EE platform and .NET Framework. It closes with an example business solution written in VB.NET to demonstrate how a .NET solution can be written in any language hosted by the .NET Framework.

Examining the Container's Role

The components making up the J2EE architecture are executed in runtime environments called containers. The containers provide essential key infrastructure services such as an object's life cycle management, distribution, and security. In a web-based, thin-client application, the software resides within two containers running inside an application server. J2EE servers provide both an Enterprise JavaBean container and a web container. These two individual environments serve as the foundation for constructing multi-tiered transactional business applications.

The J2EE application architecture consists of three tiers:

- Client tier
- Middle tier
- Enterprise Information System (EIS) tier

The client tier contains either a web-enabled browser such as Microsoft's Internet Explorer or a Java application client. The middle tier consists of both a web container and an Enterprise JavaBean (EJB) container. This tier hosts the application's business logic and performs services for the client. The EIS tier consists of databases, other types of resources such as flat files, ISAM format repositories, and legacy applications.

Interaction between client and business service–oriented components requires careful application planning. The developer has several responsibilities when designing client-side software. They include the following items:

- Presenting the application's user interface to the client. The browser is written in either HyperText Markup Language (HTML) or the Extensible Markup Language (XML) and runs on the client machine.
- Gathering and processing mission-critical information from an HTML form.
- Controlling client access to resources.
- Preventing duplicate client submissions.

An enterprise application uses the thin-client model in which functionality occurs on the server tier rather than on the client tier. In a thin-client business model layer, user interaction between client components and business layer components consists of submitting HTML forms, managing state within a user session, processing client requests, generating dynamic web pages, and returning results to the client.

The thin-client model does have some disadvantages. First, the developer has little control over presentation to clients. Each solution must be tested for browser reliability. The user agent (browser) attempts to interpret and output everything submitted to it. Consequently, the results vary and the renderings are frequently incorrect. For example, Netscape Communicator will output run-on sentences with no line breaks and not interpret the data correctly, whereas Internet Explorer version 5 and above has a sophisticated transformation engine built into it and will "pretty-print" the data. It detects syntax errors and will inform the user where errors occur by placing a caret in the offending position. In addition, the presentation is limited to interactions that can be implemented using a markup language such as XML, or a plug-in. Otherwise, the data cannot be implemented within the application. Finally, the presentation is server-side dependent. This means client access to the server is far more frequent than when using a rich-client solution, in which an applet or application has a graphical user interface programmatically built in. The rich-client methodology enables the developer to trap events, which means that the client accesses the server only when needed, rather than responding to each event that occurs in the presentation.

Best Practice: Separating Business Logic from Presentation in J2EE Applications and .NET

As discussed in Chapter 2, the design pattern Model, View, Controller (MVC) provides developers with a business model to create user interfaces. Recall that MVC consists of three types of objects: the model is the application object; view is the screen presentation; and the controller mediates between model and view by defining the way the user's interface reacts to client input. Leveraging the MVC model conforms to object-oriented programming principles by decoupling the three objects—meaning the components are reusable, thereby eliminating object dependencies.

MVC uses a subscribe-notify protocol, meaning a view must guarantee that its appearance accurately reflects the state of the model. For example, when the model's data is modified, the model is obligated to notify a view of any changes so it can respond accordingly, reflecting all data modifications. The MVC approach allows developers to attach multiple views to a model and provide many different presentations. This business paradigm facilitates creating new views without the necessity of subsequent rewrites.

Best Practice: Use ASP.NET's Code-Behind Feature

The MVC model is applicable to both J2EE and the .NET Framework. The code-behind feature, new in ASP.NET, allows developers to separate the presentation interface code from business logic code in Visual Basic .NET, C# .NET, and several other languages targeting the .NET Framework. Numerous ASP.NET features add value:

- **Clean separation of HTML and code** Code-behind allows HTML page designers and developers to focus on what they do best, while eliminating the possibility of mixing presentation logic with business logic and messing up each other's code.
- **Code reuse** Code bearing the .aspx extension and not interspersed with HTML is reusable in other applications.
- **Easy maintenance** Separating HTML and business logic makes ASP.NET pages easier to read and maintain.
- **Deployment without source code** Visual Studio .NET projects that contain code-behind modules can be deployed as compiled code. This makes it easy for developers to protect their source code.

Best Practice: Maximize Benefits from Both Thin-Client and Rich-Client Applications Where Applicable

Best practices suggest using a rich-client solution where complex user presentations cannot be handled by browser-based applications. Numerous client round-trips to the server severely impact performance.

User Input Validation

All user data is subject to validation. This process occurs on either the client or server side. Let's assume that IFCE financial services receive periodic stock quote updates throughout the day from Bloomberg and Reuters. Three types of validation are required for validating the quotes: syntactical, lexical, and semantic. *Syntactic* information is determined by checking a stock quote for proper formatting. For example, Microsoft's stock quote may look like this: 47.5, in which the fraction is separated by a decimal point from the whole number 47. *Lexical* validation examines a value's data type to ensure that the data type entered corresponds to the data type anticipated by the application. *Semantic* validation may check to ensure that the stock price does not exceed a limit imposed by a business rule or the SEC. A wide price swing in either direction raises a warning flag requiring manual inspection to make sure the quote has not been tampered with, or is incorrect for some other reason, before returning the stock quote to the pool for selling to clients.

Preventing Duplicate Client Requests

Submitting duplicate client requests requires validation and special treatment. The developer must ensure that a request is single threaded. Duplication occurs when several instances of client software are instantiated. Many different reasons exist for duplicate calls by multiple clients, including several clients attempting to access the same object. Applying best practices in this context means compiling a pattern such as the Pattern class in JDK 1.4 and using it with many different processes. Simply declare the Pattern as a static member of the validation class, thereby guaranteeing that only one copy is compiled. An alternative is using the Singleton pattern. It ensures that a class has only one instance and provides multiple-client access.

It is imperative for some classes to have only one instance. How does the developer ensure that a class has only one instance, accessible to all users? The solution is to make the class responsible for tracking its sole instance. A method of doing this is to intercept requests to create new objects.

The Singleton class provides this functionality. A best practice is using the Singleton class when the following situations occur:

- There is only one instance of a class.
- The instance is accessible to all client requests.
- The single instance is made extensible through subclassing, and clients are able to use an extended instance without any code modification.

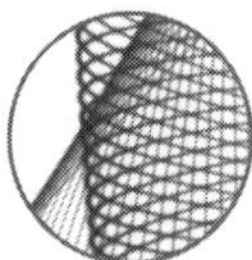

NOTE

An instance is a static member function in C++.

The following code demonstrates how to define a class implementation in C++:

```
class Singleton {
public:
  static Singleton* Instance();
protected:
     Singleton():
private:
     static Singleton* _instance;
};
```

Here is the implementation for the Singleton class:

```
Singleton* Singleton::_instance = 0;
Singleton* Singleton::Instance (){
    if (_instance == 0) {
       _instance = new Singleton;
       }
       return _instance;
}
```

Limiting a User's Input Choices

Another best practice method for reducing user input error is limiting a user's choices for input. This can occur, for example, in the .NET Framework by using ASP.NET web form controls. Radio buttons, check boxes, list boxes, and combo drop-down boxes do not need to be validated. They already provide valid choices. The only errors that can occur here are human-judgment errors.

A viable alternative to using ASP.NET web forms and controls is BEA's Web Logic Integration (WLI) tools. They work in collaboration with the company's WebLogic Application Server. The WLI environment allows developers to drag and drop controls onto a form. WLI tools provide similar controls limiting the user's input to valid choices provided by the controls.

Managing Session State in a Distributed Environment

How does a developer manage session state in a web-based enterprise application? Typically, a client initiates a session with the web tier. The client request contains a beginning point and an end point. The beginning occurs when a client starts sending requests; an end is defined when a client stops sending requests. During a session, clients and web components exchange information. This information can consist of something as small as a user ID, or information submitted via a form. The component retains the information until a client request is fulfilled. The results are returned to the client, and the information is destroyed.

Unfortunately, components lack persistence. Therefore, it is up to the developer to find a way to preserve state. State can be preserved on either the client side or on the server side on the J2EE Enterprise JavaBeans tier.

ASP.NET applications make it simple to manage session state. The session is created automatically. Furthermore, a SessionID is assigned to the session. This enhances the ability to identify multiple client visits to the web site via the SessionID. It is also possible to store session state in an offline mode. This feature demonstrates a distinct advantage over preserving state in J2EE.

Best Practices: Client-Side Session State

Two kinds of session beans exist: stateless and stateful. Stateless session beans have no capability of preserving state, and developers must use one of the following methods to preserve state on the client tier. Stateful session beans preserve state between multiple visits by a single client by using one of these methods:

- Hidden fields in an HTML form
- Rewriting URLs
- Using cookies

Usually, enterprise applications use an HTML form to collect information and store it in a hidden field:

```
<INPUT TYPE="TEXT" NAME="LASTNAME" SIZE = "50">
<INPUT TYPE = "SUBMIT" VALUE = "SUBMIT">
<INPUT TYPE = "RESET" VALUE="CLEAR">
```

When a user clicks on the Submit button, the browser takes the information from the fields and places it in a query string. The browser then calls a specified component on the web tier, typically a JSP or servlet, and passes the field data as parameters to the component. Once the component processes the information, it generates a dynamic web page containing another form and returns the results embedded within that form to the client. It could look something like the following:

```
www.dpsoftware.com/jsp/myjsp.jsp?LASTNAME=Peltzer
```

Best Practice: Using Hidden Fields

Components can make use of a hidden field within an HTML form to store information between multiple sessions by a single client. This field is not displayed on the form but is hidden. This field is similar to other form fields but provides a valuable mechanism for holding the submitted information. The component, rather than the user, assigns the data to this field. Just as before, the browser gathers all form field information and passes this data to the component for processing. Let's see what a hidden field looks like:

```
<INTPUT TYPE="HIDDEN" NAME="CLIENTID" VALUE="12345">
<INPUT TYPE="TEXT" NAME="LASTNAME" VALUE="PELTZER">
<INPUT TYPE = "SUBMIT" VALUE="SUBMIT">
<INTPUT TYPE="RESET" VALUE="CLEAR">
```

The best practice when using a hidden field to maintain state is including a hidden field only when processing small units of information, such as a client ID. Performance degradation occurs when large amounts of information require extensive processing. Along with this process, passing session state to the browser with each page will also impact performance. This is true even if session state does not relate to this particular session. Additionally, hidden fields may only contain string values rather than other data types such as dates. If, for example, a date is passed, the component will need to convert the data to a string data type.

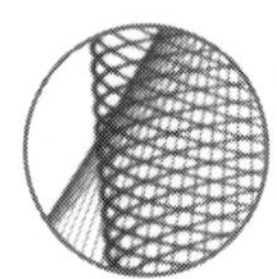

NOTE

In .NET, the HttpSessionState class provides similar functionality to that of Java.

Best Practice: Rewriting URLs

Rewriting URLs is another method available to developers for preserving session state. What is URL rewriting? The URL is a web page element that identifies a component used by the browser to request a web service. The browser can associate with the URL field names and values that are passed to the component if the component needs this information to process the client's request. This always occurs when a user submits an HTML form. The developer places field names and values into a query string as an integral component of the URL. Subsequently, when the user selects the hyperlink associated with the URL statement, the browser calls the component specified by the URL and passes the component field names and values contained within the URL statement.

The best practice when using URL rewriting to preserve session state is using it only when a client does not use an HTML form.

URL rewriting is not always a good idea because it is always dependent on the client machine. Any OS failure or machine problem will cause the session to lose state. Keep in mind that server-side session management is more efficient.

Best Practice: Using Cookies

A cookie is frequently used in an enterprise application to store a small unit of data on a client's machine. A developer can create a JSP program to generate a page dynamically that writes and reads a cookie. This mechanism preserves session state between pages.

It is prudent to use a client-side cookie to preserve state only when storing a client ID. A developer must have a contingency strategy should a client decide to disallow cookies or delete them.

Preserving Server-Side State in J2EE and .NET

A preferable alternative to preserving state on the client is storing information between sessions on the server. Recall that preserving session state on the client side has serious implications, mainly because preserving state is dependent on the client machine. In contrast, corporations go out of their way to make sure that networks and servers are functional 24 hours a day, seven days a week. This is an IT top-priority item.

Best Practice: Using the HttpSession Interface in J2EE

The best practice is to preserve session state on the Enterprise JavaBeans tier by employing the services of an Enterprise JavaBean, or on the web tier by using the HttpSession interface. Each session is assigned a unique session ID associated with a particular client session.

It is always a best practice to assign a specific server to a client, making sure the client always uses that server during a session. Additionally, check to ensure that session state is always stored on the same server.

Most applications use pieces of data, or variables, that need to be maintained across a series of requests or shared among multiple users. As previously stated, in a rich-client application it is easy to maintain state by allocating space on the client machine. However, web applications present significant challenges because HTTP is inherently stateless. ASP.NET presents a solution to this.

Defining Application State in .NET

Application state refers to any data a developer wishes to share with multiple users. This can include connection information for a DBMS, although this information is better restricted to the business tier of an application, which includes cached datasets.

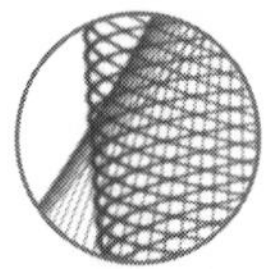

NOTE

ASP.NET provides a cache engine for storing datasets.

Best Practice: Using the HttpApplicationState Class

ASP.NET provides a collection of key-value attributes that enable developers to store data values and object instances. A best practice is to store application state using the .NET HttpApplicationState class, an instance exposed as the application property of the Page class. The collection can be accessed in the following manner:

```
'VB.NET
Application("MyApplicationVar") = "MyValue"
MyLocalVar = Application("MyApplicationVar")
```

Here is the same code written in C#:

```
Application["MyApplicationVar"] = "MyValue";
MyLocalVar = Application["MyApplicationVar"]
```

Best practices make it possible to add new items to the Application collection using the Add method exposed by the Application object. In addition, use the Remove method exposed by the Application.Contents collection as follows:

```
'VB.NET
Application.Add("MyApplicationVar", "MyValue")
Application.Remove("MyOtherApplicationVars")
//In C#
Application.Add["MyApplicationVar", "MyValue"];
Application.Remove["MyOtherApplicationVars"];
```

It is also possible to clear the contents of the Application collection by using the Clear method exposed by the Application object. The following code demonstrates this:

```
'VB.NET
Application.Clear()
ApplicationRemoveall()
```

Best Practice: Synchronizing Access to Application State

ASP.NET's Application object provides Lock and Unlock methods that developers can use to guarantee that only a single consumer can update application state data at any given time. Developers should call Application.lock() before modifying any data stored in the application collection. Once the modification is completed, the developer can call Application.Unlock().

Many times it is not appropriate to store Application state for DBMS connections and other application configuration settings. The best practice for storing infrequently accessed settings is to place these settings in a Web.config file and retrieve them with the GetConfig() method of the Context object.

Another best practice is caching frequently read datasets using the ASP.NET cache engine to cache expensive (large) or frequently accessed data.

Yet another best practice is storing shared application flags in a database. This method provides fine-grained control over the reading and updating of individual units of data. Additionally, consider storing references to an object instance and ensuring that the class from which the class is created is thread safe.

Using Session State in ASP.NET

Session state in classic ASP posed several challenges for developers. They included

- **Web farms** Session state could not be scaled across multiple servers in a web farm.

- **Endurance** Session state could be destroyed by a server crash or restart. In this context, shopping cart applications were difficult to develop and/or maintain.
- **Cookie reliance** Classic ASP provided no solutions for preserving state with browsers that would not accept cookies, or users who chose to reject cookies.

Best Practice: Using ASP.NET Session State

ASP.NET's Session object is exposed as a property of the Page class. This allows access to the Session object using the *Session* keyword, as demonstrated here:

```
'VB.NET
Session("MySessionVar") = "MyValue"
MyLocalVar = Session("MySessionVar")
//C#
Session["MySessionVar"]= "MyValue";
MyLocalVar = Session["MySessionVar"]
```

Session functionality is provided by the HttpSessionState class.

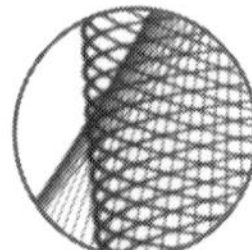

NOTE

The Session collection stores references or object instances, utilizing similar syntax to store object references at the application level. Note the following code:

```
'Global.asax
<object runat="server" id="MyClassInstance" class="MyClassName"
  scope="Session">
</object>
'Web Forms page
Response.Write("Value =" & MyClassInstance.Myvalue)
```

Best Practice: Enabling Session State

A best practice to preserve state is *enabling* session state before using it. The default configuration file at the server level automatically enables session state in Machine.config.

In the event developers wish to delay the creation of a session until necessary, a best practice allows them to add the following code to the @Page directive:

```
<%@ Page EnableSessionState="False" %>
```

It is also possible to set the session state to read-only for a specified page by setting the EnableSessionState to ReadOnly.

Configuring Session State Storage

ASP.NET provides several methods for storing session state. They include the following:

- **In-process (InProc)** InProc is the default setting. This is also true for classic ASP.
- **Out-of-process (StateServer)** StateServer indicates that a server executing the ASP.NET state service will store session state.
- **SQLServer (SQLServer)** This setting specifies that session state will be stored in an SQL Server database.
- **Cookieless session** This setting allows the developer to maintain session state for users whose browsers do not support cookies.

Best Practice: Storing Session State In-Process and Out-of-Process

The best practice for storing session state in-process requires no changes to the application configuration file. However, the best practice for storing session state out-of-process is as follows:

1. Open the Web.config file for your application and locate the sessionState configuration session.
2. Change the mode attribute from "InProc" to "StateServer".
3. Modify the stateConnectionString attribute to represent the server name or IP address of the state server and the port that the ASP.NET state service is monitoring (by default this is 42424).
4. The complete sessionState configuration file will typically look like the following code:

```
<sessionState
   mode="stateserver"
   stateConnectionString = "tcip=127.0.0.1:42424"/>
```

5. Start the Services MMC snap-in by selecting Start | Programs | Administrative Tools | Services.

6. Start the ASP.NET state service on the desired server from the Services MMC snap-in. ASP.NET will automatically connect to the specified state server and store session state for your application.

Preserving State in SQL Server

Preserving state in SQL Server has numerous advantages. Storing session out-of-process means that a specified SQL Server database can receive requests from multiple servers. It is particularly significant that storing session out-of-proc can provide scalable session state across a web farm. Session state is stored in SQL Server and survives any crashes of web servers or web application processes. The best practice for storing session SQL Server is as follows:

1. Execute the installSqlState.sql batch file (located in the .NET Framework installation directory %windir%\Microsoft.NET\Framework\%version%) against the SQL Server specified for use.
2. Locate the Web.config file and navigate to the sessionState configuration section.
3. Change the mode attribute from "InProc" to "SQLServer".
4. Modify the sqlConnectionString attribute so it identifies the IP address of the designated SQL Server, and include the user ID and password used to gain access to SQL Server.
5. The sessionState configuration section will look like the following:

```
<sessionState
mode="SQLServer"
sqlConnectionString="data source  127.0.0.1:user id=sa:password="/>
```

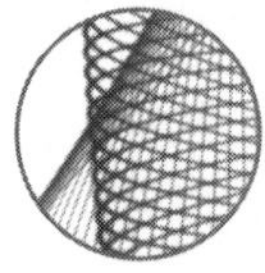

NOTE

A best practice uses a trusted connection in SQL Server rather than placing the SQLServer user ID and password in the connection string in the Web.config file.

Cookieless Sessions

ASP.NET provides a simple way to store session state for users whose browser will not accept cookies. The best practice for storing session state in this context is to take the following steps:

1. Locate the sessionState configuration section in the Web.config file.
2. Modify the Cookieless attribute so it reads "true" rather than "false".
3. The complete sessionState configuration section will look like the following (note that the stateConnectionString, sqlConnectionString, and timeout have been omitted):

   ```
   <sessionState
      Cookieless="true"/>
   ```

When the Cookieless attribute is set to "true", ASP.NET automatically embeds the SessionID in the URL for all user requests. A best practice is always to use a relative URL for internal links within the application. Relative URLs contain only path and file information for the requested resource but not protocol and domain information.

Using Client-Side Cookies for Storing State

A best practice for storing state in a client-side cookie is to complete the following steps:

1. Create a new instance of the HTTPCookie class as follows:

   ```
   Dim MyCookie as New HttpCookie("MyCookieName")
   ```

2. Set the Value property of the cookie to a desired value:

   ```
   MyCookie.Value = "MyValue"
   ```

3. Add the cookie to the Cookies Collection of the Response object:

   ```
   Response.Cookies.Add(MyCookie)
   ```

This sets a cookie named "My Cookie" that lasts until the user closes the browser.

Using Persistent Cookies to Store State

Persistent cookies are used to store state across multiple browser sessions. In order to do this, an expiration date must occur. One method for doing this is to add the following code before adding the cookie to the Response.Cookies collection:

```
MyCookie.Expires = Now.AddDays(3)
```

A best practice for using persistent cookies is to keep the expiration date within a short amount of time, such as a few hours or days.

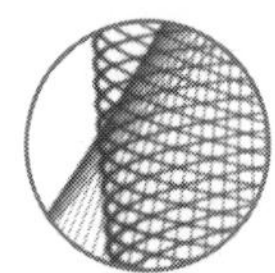

NOTE

Never store user data such as credit card numbers or other critical data that could subsequently be compromised or stolen.

Persistence on the Enterprise JavaBeans Tier

Enterprise JavaBeans residing on the Enterprise JavaBeans tier provide business logic to other tiers. Developers must be careful when deciding what functionality should be built into an Enterprise JavaBean. Frequently, developers make a mistake when defining tasks that an EJB should perform, by assigning multiple tasks to an EJB. For example, let's assume a customer is submitting an order for a large number of widgets. Fulfilling this task requires more than one trip to a database: first, to ensure the customer's status is okay and, second, to make sure the EJB checks the DBMS for available stock. These conditions present a challenge to the developer. Should these tasks be grouped together and the EJB allowed to fulfill both tasks, or should two EJBs be designated for performing the operations independently?

The best practice is to make each Enterprise JavaBean self-contained and design the logic so each EJB performs a separate task. An appropriate solution is using three Enterprise JavaBeans. One Enterprise JavaBean verifies the customer's status, the second processes the request, and the third functions as a controller. What is a controller? A controller is an Enterprise JavaBean called by a JSP application. The controller calls the EJB to validate a customer's status. Based on the results, the controller either sends a rejection notice or calls the appropriate EJB to process and fulfill the order.

Designing a Maximized Data Exchange

JSP programs and Enterprise JavaBeans communicate frequently during application execution. They may exchange individual chunks of data or exchange what is called a *value* object. This is an efficient method of transmitting data in bulk. In contrast, transmitting individual units of information is inefficient and increases network overhead. Therefore, a best practice is to keep exchanges of remote data to a minimum. This is accomplished by placing components on the same server to exchange information.

Inheritance in J2EE and .NET

Much has been written about using traditional inheritance. Unfortunately, inheritance promotes class dependencies, thereby violating the object-oriented practice of designing classes so they are independent. There are two kinds of classes—base classes and derived classes. Keep in mind that an object of the subclass has access to some or all data and member functions of the base class, including all data and methods of the derived class. The relationship between a base class and the derived class is referred to as *coupling.* This is not a good practice. It is prudent to encourage strong cohesion and loose coupling, a best practice. Always program to interfaces rather than using traditional inheritance. Both J2EE and .NET are component based and program to interfaces—a strong factor in their success because the components are designed as reusable units of data. Declaring classes as abstract makes it mandatory for developers to redeclare the classes and provide their own implementations.

A best practice is to identify commonality between objects and place those features in a base class. Place the noncommon features in a derived class. Where there is a function that is common among real-world objects, place the function in an interface. As long as the class conforms to the function's signature, the developer is free to provide a unique implementation. Try to minimize inheritance in an enterprise application. Instead, use composition when an object is a *type-of* rather than a *kind-of* object. A type-of object should inherit commonality from the base class.

Securing an Enterprise Application

BEA's Web Logic Container or IBM's WebSphere Container provides low-level system functionality such as managing security. This is always preferable to providing an individual's methods of securing an enterprise application. It is better to allow the containers to perform their routine, but essential, security tasks.

Developers must always secure a J2EE application in a web services environment. Sun and the Java community have developed numerous ways to secure enterprise applications. The following is a partial list of elements Java uses:

- Java Security Domain Controller
- Java Security Guard
- Java Security Key
- Java Security Principal
- Java Security Privilege
- Java Security Access Control

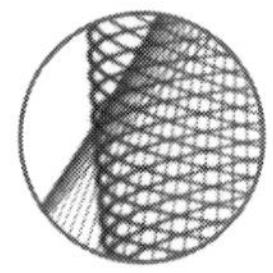

NOTE

Refer to J2EE: The Complete Reference, *by Jim Keogh (McGraw-Hill/Osborne, 2002), as an invaluable resource for learning more about the various methods of securing a web application in J2EE.*

Applying ASP.NET Code Access Security

Access control is the process of determining who can access specified resources on a server. This includes both authentication and authorization. Developers have numerous methods for providing security in ASP.NET. You can use SSL to protect communications, Windows-based authentication, or Passport authentication. Yet another method is using Forms-Based (Cookie) authentication.

ASP.NET provides a new feature called Code Access Security (CAS). CAS is Microsoft's answer to preventing untrusted code from performing undesirable actions on systems, resulting in compromise of mission-critical data. CAS allows developers to specify the level of security a given application must have. It gives you the option of using the <securityPolicy> and <trust> tags in the Web.config file. ASP.NET offers a preconfigured set of Code Access Security templates mapped to trust levels in Machine.config. Depending on the level of trust specified in the <trust> tag, the proper set of Code Access Security permissions is applied to the application. This feature provides fine-grained control over application security.

Using a Trusted Connection in SQL Server

Security should receive top priority in an application, and ASP.NET provides many important methods for guaranteeing tight security. Developers can select *impersonation* as a means of providing tight security. Trusted connections use Windows security to connect to an SQL Server database without the need for providing a user ID and password. A best practice is to set up a trusted connection by taking the following steps:

1. Configure the application to use Windows authentication.
2. Add the <identity> tag to the configuration file, which enables ASP.NET to impersonate the identity of the client submitting the request:

   ```
   <identity impersonate="true">
   ```

3. Add all desired Windows accounts to the SQL Server security database.

4. Add Trusted_Connection=yes to the connection string used to gain access to SQL Server:

```
"server=(local)\NetSDK:database=IFCE;Trusted_Connection=yes"
```

5. Select one of the accounts previously added to the SQL Server security database and log in to the ASP.NET application.

Best Practice: Applying Security Measures

Typically, all client applications request access to resources. A *client view* is a set of restrictions on resources that a client can access, embedded within an application. By assigning clients to a group or specific role and granting or denying access to specific resources, you control client requests. For example, a client view might include specific databases, tables, or rows.

An alternative to a client view is a controller, which limits access to a resource. This is known as a *resource guard*. A client request contains an ID that is compared to a client's configuration. Access is either permitted or denied on the basis of the client's configuration file.

Applying a best practice in this context means using security measures provided by an operating system such as Windows or a DBMS or network. In a J2EE JVM environment, it is best to call on a servlet to intercept a client's request, process it, validate it, and redirect the request to a specified EJB for fulfillment. Finally, use a Java Server Page to return the results to the client.

In .NET, you should use the Code Access Security features to limit access to code and resources. By employing permissions, you can define what a user can access.

If client access is limited to a particular DBMS, it is prudent to assign multiple users to a group profile and then assign permissions to that group. If this is not acceptable, remove the logic embedded within an application and use an external resource guard. The resource guard becomes shareable by multiple clients.

Providing an IFCE Business Solution in Visual Basic .NET

Web services can be called from any front-end application. This means both Windows forms and web forms can invoke the same services. In fact, .NET web services can be called by non-Microsoft applications. As we have observed in previous chapters, a developer building a J2EE can call a web service built in Microsoft .NET because web services are universally accessible. Application interoperability is the key.

Currency conversion is a service frequently needed by corporations participating in a financial business. A consumer can walk into a local bank branch or a business such as the Automobile Association to buy or sell foreign currency. IFCE provides such services. Let's build a web service in Visual Studio .NET to provide a currency conversion service.

Open Visual Studio .NET to create a project of the type ASP.NET web service. Name the project CurrencyConverter and ensure that the server selected for hosting the web service has a web server running IIS 4.0 or higher and containing a copy of the .NET Framework. Once the project is loaded, a blank designer appears. Use Solution Explorer to view how Visual Studio creates the project and presents a hierarchical tree listing the following items:

- References to System namespaces as follows: System, System.Data, System.Web, System.Web.Services, and System.XML.
- The AssemblyInfo.vb namespace, which includes information about the assembly, such as file name and path.
- The Global.asax config file, which specifies the System.Web.HttpApplication namespace. It maps values in the application configuration file <appSettings>.
- Service1.asmx, named by Visual Studio with the .asmx extension. This extension specifies a web service.
- The Web.config file, which consists of tags and attributes.

The following config file has been generated for the CurrencyConverter Web Service:

```
<?xml version="1.0" encoding="utf-8" ?>
<configuration>
  <system.web>
   <!--  DYNAMIC DEBUG COMPILATION
 Set compilation debug="true" to insert debugging symbols (.pdb information)
 into the compiled page. Because this creates a larger file that executes
 more slowly, you should set this value to true only when debugging and to
 false at all other times. For more information, refer to the documentation
 about debugging ASP.NET files.
   -->
   <compilation defaultLanguage="vb" debug="true" />
```

```
    <!--  CUSTOM ERROR MESSAGES
Set customErrors mode="On" or "RemoteOnly"
to enable custom error messages, "Off"
to disable.
Add <error> tags for_u101 each of the errors you want to handle.

"On" Always display custom (friendly) messages.
"Off" Always display_u100 detailed ASP.NET error information.
"RemoteOnly" Display_u99 custom (friendly)
messages only to users not running on the local Web server.
This setting is recommended for security purposes, so
that you do not display application detail information to remote clients.
    -->
    <customErrors mode="RemoteOnly" />

    <!--  AUTHENTICATION
          This section sets the authentication policies
 of the application. Possible modes are "Windows",
          "Forms", "Passport" and "None"
          "None" No authentication is performed.
          "Windows" IIS performs authentication
 (Basic, Digest, or Integrated Windows) according to
 its settings for the application. Anonymous access must be disabled in IIS.
          "Forms" You provide a custom form (Web page)
 for users to enter their credentials, and then
           you authenticate them in your application.
 A user credential token is stored in a cookie.
          "Passport" Authentication is performed
 via a centralized authentication service provided
 by Microsoft that offers a single
logon and core profile services for member sites.
    -->

    <authentication mode="Windows" />
    <!--  AUTHORIZATION
          This section sets the authorization policies
 of the application. You can allow or deny access
 to application resources by user or role.
 Wildcards: "*" means everyone, "?" means anonymous
          (unauthenticated) users.
    -->
    <authorization>
```

```
        <allow users="*" /> <!-- Allow all users -->

            <!--  <allow     users="[comma separated list of users]"
                             roles="[comma separated list of roles]"/>
                  <deny      users="[comma separated list of users]"
                             roles="[comma separated list of roles]"/>
            -->
    </authorization>

    <!--  APPLICATION-LEVEL TRACE LOGGING
Application-level tracing enables trace log
 output for every page within an application.
Set trace enabled="true" to enable application
 trace logging.  If pageOutput="true", the
trace information will be displayed at the bottom of each page.
Otherwise, you can view the
application trace log by browsing the "trace.axd"
page from your web application root.
    -->
<trace enabled="false" requestLimit="10"
pageOutput="false" traceMode="SortByTime"
localOnly="true" />
<!--  SESSION STATE SETTINGS
 By default ASP.NET uses cookies to identify
 which requests belong to a particular session.
 If cookies are not available, a session
 can be tracked by adding a session identifier to the URL.
To disable cookies, set sessionState cookieless="true".
    -->
    <sessionState
            mode="InProc"
            stateConnectionString="tcpip=127.0.0.1:42424"
          sqlConnectionString="data source=127.0.0.1;Trusted_Connection=yes"
            cookieless="false"
            timeout="20"
    />

    <!--  GLOBALIZATION
This section sets the globalization settings of the application.
    -->
    <globalization requestEncoding="utf-8"
responseEncoding="utf-8" />
```

```
  </system.web>
</configuration>
```

The structure of the Web.config file is XML based with the following format:

```
<?xml version="1.0" encoding="utf-8" ?>
<configuration>
   <system.web>
     <elementName1>
        <childElementName1
          attributeName1=value
          attributeName2=value
           attributeNameN=value />
     </elementName1>
     <elementName2>
        <childElementName1
          attributeName1=value
          attributeName2=value
           attributeNameN=value />
     </elementName2>
    </system.web>
</configuration>
```

Each Web.config file should contain the standard XML declaration. The file also contains opening and closing <configuration> tags. Nested within the configuration tags are the <system.web> opening and closing tags. Following these tags are the attribute tags associated with a specific value. Refer to them as *elements*.

Returning to the development of the web service, right-click on the Service1.asmx file in the Solution Explorer and select Rename. Then name the file CurrencyConvert.asmx. Select "click here to switch to code view" to open the code-behind file named CurrencyConvert.asmx.vb. The following code demonstrates how this page looks:

```
Imports System.Web.Services

<System.Web.Services.WebService (Namespace := "http://tempuri.org/
CurrencyConverter/Service1")> _
Public Class Service1
    Inherits System.Web.Services.WebService
#Region " Web Services Designer Generated Code "
    Public Sub New()
        MyBase.New()
        'This call is required by the Web Services Designer.
        InitializeComponent()
```

```
        'Add your own initialization code
        after the InitializeComponent() call
    End Sub
    'Required by the Web Services Designer
    Private components As System.ComponentModel.IContainer
    'NOTE: The following procedure is required by the Web Services Designer
    'It can be modified using the Web Services Designer.
    'Do not modify it using the code editor.
    <System.Diagnostics.DebuggerStepThrough()>
    Private Sub InitializeComponent()
        components = New System.ComponentModel.Container()
    End Sub

    Protected Overloads Overrides Sub Dispose(ByVal disposing As Boolean)
        'CODEGEN: This procedure is required by the Web Services Designer
        'Do not modify it using the code editor.
        If disposing Then
            If Not (components Is Nothing) Then
                components.Dispose()
            End If
        End If
        MyBase.Dispose(disposing)
    End Sub
#End Region

    ' WEB SERVICE EXAMPLE
    ' The HelloWorld() example service returns the string Hello World.
    ' To build, uncomment the following lines,
 then save and build the project.
    ' To test this web service, ensure that the .asmx file is the start page
    ' and press F5.
    '
    '<WebMethod()> _
    'Public Function HelloWorld() As String
    '   Return "Hello World"
    'End Function

End Class
```

Note how the Web Service example is commented out. The function name is HelloWorld(). Also observe how WebMethod has a less-than symbol placed before it. This tells the compiler to treat this function as a web service and marks it as callable on the Web.

Add the following code to the file:

```
<WebMethod()> Public Function
ConvertCurrency
(ByVal dAmount As Decimal, ByVal sFrom As String,
 ByVal sTo As String) As Decimal
        Select Case sFrom
            Case "Euro"
                Return CDec(dAmount * 1.08)
            Case "Mark"
                Return CDec(dAmount * 1.64)
            Case "Sterling"
                Return CDec(dAmount * 1.65)
            Case "Lire"
                Return CDec(dAmount * 1.998)
            Case "Francs"
                Return CDec(dAmount * 1.4435)
        End Select
    End Function
```

The code creates the method named CurrencyConvert that accepts three parameters:

- Amount of currency to convert
- Type of currency
- Type of currency to convert to

The Select Case statement ascertains whether the user is converting from the euro or Deutsche mark and some other currency. In each case, the currency is converted into American currency.

Select the Build menu and choose Build CurrencyConverter. This step creates the web service on the web server.

The next step is to test the web service. Right-click on CurrencyConvert.asmx in Solution Explorer and select View in Browser. A default page is created by .NET that allows the user to submit the amount and type of currency to be converted. The CurrencyConvert Web service is now ready to be invoked by a Web Service client. Click on the CurrencyConverter link that appears on the operations page.

Here is the default page:

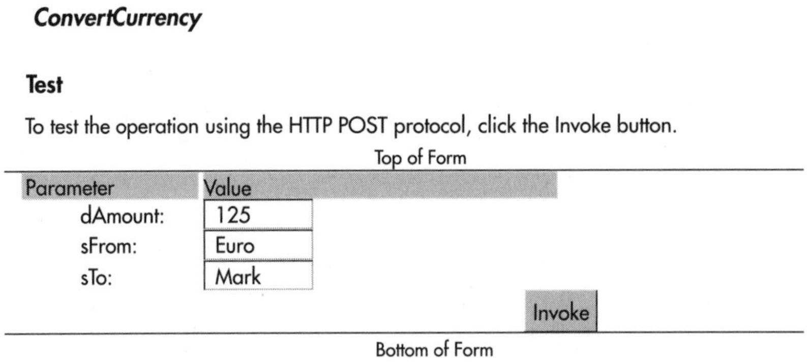

ConvertCurrency

Test

To test the operation using the HTTP POST protocol, click the Invoke button.

Top of Form

Parameter	Value
dAmount:	125
sFrom:	Euro
sTo:	Mark

Invoke

Bottom of Form

The results are displayed in Internet Explorer:

```
<?xml version="1.0" encoding="utf-8" ?>
  <decimal xmlns="http://tempuri.org/CurrencyConverter/Service1">135</decimal>
```

The SOAP headers displayed here are automatically generated by Visual Studio and are self-explanatory.

```
The following is a sample SOAP request and response.
 The placeholders shown need
to be replaced with actual values.
POST /CurrencyConverter/CurrencyConvert.asmx HTTP/1.1
Host: localhost
Content-Type: text/xml; charset=utf-8
Content-Length: length
SOAPAction: "http://tempuri.org/CurrencyConverter/Service1/ConvertCurrency"

<?xml version="1.0" encoding="utf-8"?>
<soap:Envelope xmlns:xsi="http://www.w3.org/2001/XMLSchema-instance"
xmlns:xsd=
"http://www.w3.org/2001/XMLSchema"
 xmlns:soap=
"http://schemas.xmlsoap.org/soap/envelope/">
  <soap:Body>
    <ConvertCurrency xmlns="http://tempuri.org/CurrencyConverter/Service1">
      <dAmount>decimal</dAmount>
      <sFrom>string</sFrom>
```

```
      <sTo>string</sTo>
    </ConvertCurrency>
  </soap:Body>
</soap:Envelope>
HTTP/1.1 200 OK
Content-Type: text/xml; charset=utf-8
Content-Length: length

<?xml version="1.0" encoding="utf-8"?>
<soap:Envelope
xmlns:xsi="http://www.w3.org/2001/XMLSchema-instance"
xmlns:xsd="http://www.w3.org/2001/XMLSchema" xmlns:soap=
"http://schemas.xmlsoap.org/soap/envelope/">
  <soap:Body>
    <ConvertCurrencyResponse
xmlns="http://tempuri.org/CurrencyConverter/Service1">
      <ConvertCurrencyResult>decimal</ConvertCurrencyResult>
    </ConvertCurrencyResponse>
  </soap:Body>
</soap:Envelope>
HTTP POST
The following is a sample HTTP POST
request and response.
The placeholders shown
 need to be replaced with actual values.
POST /CurrencyConverter/CurrencyConvert.asmx/ConvertCurrency HTTP/1.1
Host: localhost
Content-Type: application/x-www-form-urlencoded
Content-Length: length

dAmount=string&sFrom=string&sTo=string
HTTP/1.1 200 OK
Content-Type: text/xml; charset=utf-8
Content-Length: length

<?xml version="1.0" encoding="utf-8"?>
<decimal xmlns="http://tempuri.org/
CurrencyConverter/Service1">decimal</decimal>
```

The web service is protocol agnostic and provides interoperability 24/7 to any client residing on any platform or operating system.

Conclusion

Interoperability between Java 2 Enterprise Edition and Microsoft .NET is now available to all developers. This book has described how interoperability functions internally within J2EE and .NET, as well as externally. Third-party vendors, such as JNBridge and Intrinsyc Software, have extended interoperability by offering cross-platform integration between the two major parties. For example, JNBridgePro generates proxies facilitating access to methods, classes, and functionality on both platforms.

The goal of this book is to inform Java developers and .NET programmers of the latest technologies and demonstrate how to integrate them with existing legacy systems. J2EE and .NET support web services, thereby enabling you to build scalable, accessible distributed applications. With enthusiasm and support from the entire Java and .NET communities, the technologies keep improving at a rapid pace, to the benefit of consumers and businesses alike.

PART IV

Appendixes

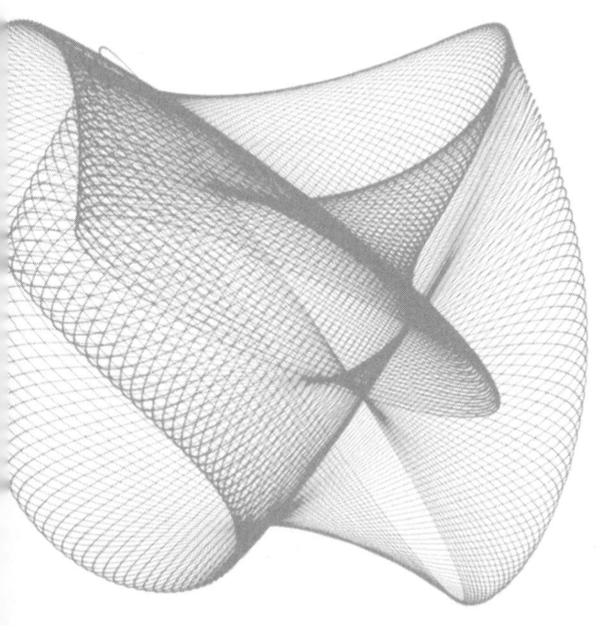

APPENDIX

A

Java Connector Architecture (JCA) Specification

IN THIS APPENDIX:

Components of the JCA

For More Information

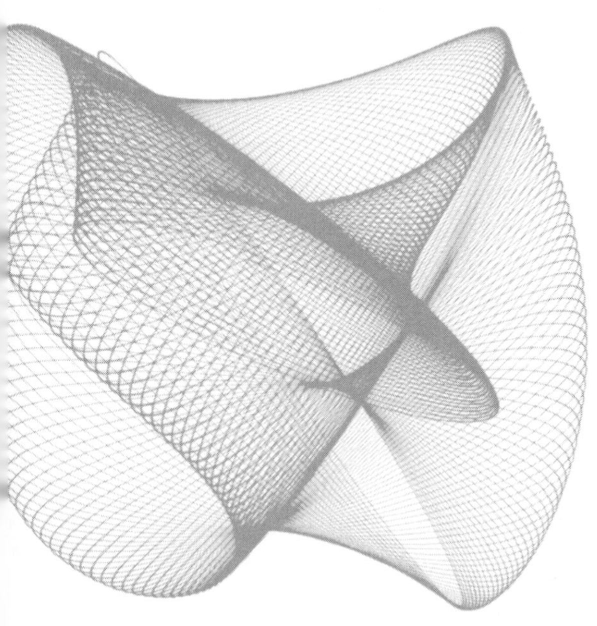

This brief overview provides basic information about the Java Connector Architecture (JCA). It explains how JCA makes the process of accessing and integrating disparate information systems much easier. One of the goals of the new J2EE connector architecture is to bring Enterprise Application Integration (EAI) into mainstream use. Although full coverage of this technology is beyond the scope of this book, the goal is to inform the reader about the JCA technology and the benefits derived from using connectors to access an Enterprise Information System (EIS).

Components of the JCA

The finalized JCA specification, version 1.5, released on October 31, 2002, provides a convenient mechanism for storing and retrieving enterprise data in J2EE. Examples of EISs include ERP (Enterprise Resource Planning), mainframe transaction processing, and database systems. The connector architecture also defines a Common Client Interface (CCI) for EISs access. The CCI defines a client API for interacting with disparate systems.

The connector architecture allows integration between J2EE servers and EISs. The architecture consists of two parts:

- An EIS vendor-provided resource adapter and an application server, such as BEA's WebLogic, that permits the adapter to plug into it.
- A set of three contracts that provide connection management, support transactions, and security. The contracts offer bidirectional communications (inbound and outbound) between an application server and an EIS, courtesy of a resource adapter.

Connection Management Contracts

A connection-level contract provides the agreement that a J2EE container must have with an adapter and refers to *establishing, pooling*, and *destroying* connections. In addition, the contract allows interested listeners to respond to events such as error handling.

All JCA resource adapters must provide two implementations with the adapter. First, a ConnectionFactor offers a vehicle for creating connections. Second, the Connection class represents the specified resource adapter's connection.

Transaction Management Contract

The transaction management contract manages transactions in two different ways. First, it permits distributed transactions to propagate transactions that begin from inside the application server to an EIS. Second, the transaction management contract can control transactions by creating local transactions as well.

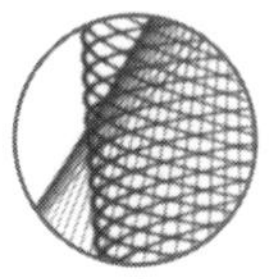

NOTE

Local transactions can only exist on specified EIS resources.

Security Contract

The security contract allows the application server to connect to an EIS by employing security properties. The server authentication process consists of a user ID and a password or certificate. The application server can use two methods to authenticate to an EIS: component-managed sign-on and container-managed sign-on.

The most efficient method of configuring security properties is using *component-managed sign-on*. This permits the developer to pass security properties every time a connection is acquired from the resource adapter. In the second method, *container-managed sign-on*, the security credentials configure when the resource adapter is deployed on the application server. Several different options are available for configuring security properties when using the container-managed sign-on procedure:

- **Configured Identity** All resource adapters use the same identity when connecting to the EIS.
- **Principal Mapping** This is the principal used when connecting to the EIS. It is based on a combination of the current principal in the application server and the actual mapping.
- **Caller Impersonation** The principal in the EIS must match the principal in the application server.
- **Credentials Mapping** This is similar to Caller Impersonation—the type of credentials are mapped from the application server credentials to EIS credentials.

Exploring the Common Client Interface

It is possible to employ JCA's Common Client Interface methodology, representing functionality similar to employing JDBC to invoke remote procedures. CCI APIs are divided into four sections:

- Connection interfaces
- Interaction interfaces
- Record/ResultSet interfaces
- Metadata interfaces

Connection interfaces refer to APIs used to establish a connection to an EIS. Interaction interfaces are related to command execution on an EIS. The Record/ResultSet interfaces encapsulate query results to an EIS. Metadata interfaces permit the querying of EIS data types.

It is significant that most recent releases of application servers, including IBM's WebSphere application server, version 5.0, and BEA's WebLogic application server, support JCA adapters for enterprise connectivity. Using JCA for access to an Enterprise Information System is similar to using JDBC (Java Database Connectivity) to access a relational database or other type of repository.

Before the emergence of JCAs, individual EAI vendors found it necessary to create a proprietary resource adapter interface for their own EAI product. This means the vendor's product required the development of a resource adapter for each EAI vendor and EIS combination. To solve that cumbersome requirement, JCA provides a way of standardizing all resource adapter interfaces.

Understanding the Role of a Resource Adapter

What is a resource adapter? A *resource adapter* is a system-level library used by an application server or a client to connect to a resource manager. The resource adapter may also provide additional services beyond the connection API. The resource adapter plugs into an application server and facilitates connectivity between the EIS, the application server, and the enterprise application itself. The application server extends its system to support the connector architecture. This ensures connectivity to multiple EISs. In addition, the resource adapter plugs into any application server that supports the JCA.

The next question naturally follows: what role does the resource manager play? It provides access to an identified collection of shared resources. The resource manager is an active participant in a transaction.

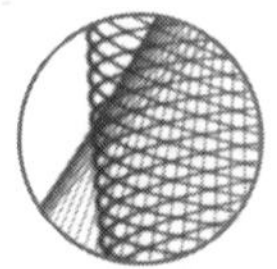

NOTE

Most EAI vendors include proprietary adapters designed to function with their own products. Those adapters allow for both asynchronous and synchronous communications with an EIS. However, JCA adapters support only a synchronous communication channel.

Data Mapping

Data mapping is easy to understand. It simply means data retrieved from a resource, such as a relational database or similar repository (this could also include Microsoft's Active Directory), and acquired in one format or another. The data requires restructuring in a format based on a business object's need. For example, let's assume the data retrieved exists in PDF format and needs transformation into XML. In order to achieve document restructuring, XML-based technologies such as XSLT exist precisely for this purpose.

It is always challenging to map data from one system to another because each business object must be mapped on both systems, an extremely time-consuming process. Fortunately, most EAI vendors provide tools to enable a developer to achieve mapping. The Enterprise JavaBeans Container Managed Persistence facility provides such mapping tools.

Understanding the Message Broker

Message brokers support both point-to-point and publish/subscribe messaging. In fact, many EAI products frequently use messaging as the connectivity layer to bind disparate systems together. A developer can implement some of a message broker's features in an EAI product by employing Java Message Service (JMS), an integral part of J2EE.

Constructing an Integration Workflow Plan

Integration can be defined as two separate processes:

- Inbound integration
- Outbound integration

Inbound integration refers to external systems initiating data requests to a system. Outbound integration means that your local system initiates requests to external systems. The following list details integration types available for both inbound and outbound messaging:

- **Message integration** This refers to transmission of data between disparate systems in a message-based format. Outbound message integration involves requesting data from a remote system in a format such as a SOAP-based XML message. Conversely, inbound integration means your system is the recipient of a request for data via a message and subsequently responds in kind with a message. Both systems are unaware of object types residing on the remote system. This is especially true for applications that communicate over the wire.
- **User interface integration** This refers to data transmitted between systems existing as a user-interface presentation. Outbound integration involves requesting a web page from a remote system. Typically, the data will be modified before displaying it as though it were part of a local system's user interface. Inbound integration entails allowing an external system to request user-interface pages residing on a local system for inclusion on a remote system.
- **Remote Procedure Call (RPC) integration of objects** RPC integration means system integration using distributed objects. This procedure involves passing data between systems as method call parameters. Outbound object-level integration suggests that a local system invokes objects on remote systems, whereas inbound object-level integration implies that a remote system calls a local system to retrieve data. The benefit derived from object-level integration is that a local object can call APIs with type safety and easily trap exceptions and errors between systems.
- **Data integration** This means data transmitted between systems exists in a data/record-oriented format. Furthermore, outbound-level integration implies that a local system requests data in record-oriented format from other systems. Conversely, inbound data-level integration means a remote system requests data from the local system in record-oriented format. Data-level integration lends itself to data mapping from one system to another. JCA belongs to this category.

For More Information

It is possible to create and implement a JCA adapter. The resource adapter represents a set of classes used by a J2EE application server to connect to a specified enterprise system. As previously mentioned, the JCA adapter's functionality is similar to a JDBC driver and how it connects to repositories.

For further information on how to create and implement a resource adapter, refer to the JCA specification, which can be downloaded from Sun's web site. Another valuable resource is *J2EE Connector Architecture and Enterprise Application Integration* by Rahul Sharma, Beth Stearns, and Tony Ng (Addison-Wesley, 2001). It covers all aspects of the JCA in depth, including detailed information on how to implement a JCA adapter. JCA is an invaluable addition to the J2EE set of specifications.

APPENDIX B

Additional Resources

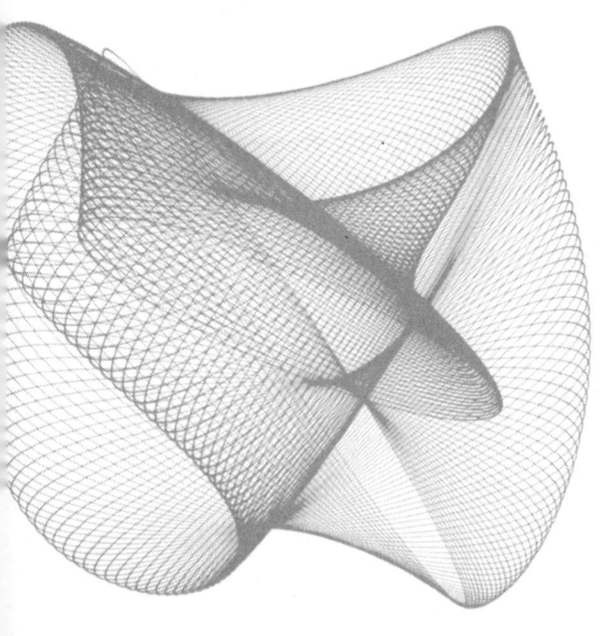

Along with recommended reading, this appendix lists the main sources for HTML, XML, XHTML v 1.0, and J2EE specifications, as well as others relevant to the main theme of this book. Although reading a specification is somewhat cumbersome, it is utterly important to do so. Within a specification lies the key to understanding that particular technology.

XML is universally accepted as the markup language of choice because it is nothing but plain old text. It is decodable by both computers and human beings. An additional benefit is that XML-marked-up text passes through firewalls on port 80. This feature alone explains why XML documents are easily transmittable over the wire.

XML pervades the entire programming world and is an essential part of both J2EE and Microsoft .NET. For example, XML plays a major part in Java deployment descriptors and many other aspects of J2EE-related technologies.

ASP.NET manifests, assemblies, PE files, config files and .asax files are constructed using XML. Schemas v 1.0, written in XML, accompany XML instance documents, enforcing business model rules and imposing document structure, as well as describing both built-in data types and user-defined types.

Web services receive support from both .NET and Sun Microsystems. XML is an essential component in building web services. Furthermore, SOAP is constructed with XML, as are WSDL, UDDI, and WSML files.

It is useful to navigate to the site for the HTML 4.01 specification and observe how it serves as precursor to the XHTML specification. The XHTML Strict Specification, v 1.0, forces developers to employ style sheets for presentation and XHTML for defining business logic. Another valuable pursuit is examining the SOAP Toolkit, viewing the latest version, 3.0, and seeing how SOAP serves as an important component in accessing web services.

One of the most valuable web sites is *http://www.w3.org* (or *http://www.w3c.org*). This site contains specifications for schemas, XSLT, XPath, XLink, XSD Schemas, and many other XML-related technologies. For example, the XSD Schema part 2 contains a complete list of data types and demonstrates how facets are applied to an element data type.

You will want to explore *http://www.w3c.org* on your own, but among the specifications found there are

- HTML 4.01 Specification
- IBM's DOM Implementation in C++
- XHTML 1.0 Specification
- XML 1.0 Recommendation
- "Schema for XML," Norman Walsh, July 1999

The Sun web site, *http://www.java.sun.com*, hosts the J2EE specification and Standard Edition specifications as well as specifications for all other Java-related technologies.

Microsoft resources are listed on their main web site at *http://www.msdn.microsoft.com*, which contains links for all of their products. The Microsoft .NET Framework can be downloaded free of charge from their site. It is essential to have the Framework installed on your local drive before you can receive support for .NET.

At *http://www.schema.net*, you will find

- Schema.NET
- SOAP Toolkit version 3.0

And at *http://www.xml.com/axml/testaxml.htm*, you can find Tim Brady's "Annotated XML Specification."

Switching to resources in print, each title listed here provides specific information on some aspect of the main theme of this book. A particular volume may focus on designing reusable components or designing interfaces, or it will discuss access of remote objects. They have all served as invaluable guides to my understanding of major platforms and their technologies.

- Appleman, Dan, *Moving to VB .NET*, Springer-Verlag, 2001
- Broemmer, Darren, *J2EE Best Practices*, John Wiley & Sons, 2003
- Brownell, David, *SAX2*, O'Reilly, 2002
- Burke, Paul, et al., *Professional SQL Server 2000 XML*, Wrox Press, 2001
- Carlson, David, *Modeling XML Applications with UML*, Addison-Wesley, 2001
- Castro, Elizabeth, *XML for the World Wide Web*, Peachpit Press, 2000
- Chappell, David, *Understanding .NET*, Addison-Wesley, 2002
- Chappell, David, and Tyler Jewell, *Java Web Services*, O'Reilly, 2002
- Duthie, G. Andrew, *Microsoft ASP.NET Step by Step*, Microsoft Press, 2002
- Gamma, Erich, et al., *Design Patterns*, Addison-Wesley, 1996
- Keogh, Jim, *J2EE: The Complete Reference*, McGraw Hill/Osborne, 2002
- Kotok, Alan, and David Webber, *ebXML, The New Global Standard for Doing Business over the Internet*, Sams, 2001
- Liberty, Jesse, and Dan Hurwitz, *Programming ASP.NET*, O'Reilly, 2003

- Meyers, Scott, *More Effective C++*, Addison-Wesley, 1996
- Mitchell, Scott, et al., *ASP.NET: Tips, Tutorials, and Code*, Sams, 2001
- Monson-Haefel, Richard, *Enterprise Java Beans*, O'Reilly, 2001
- Onion, Fritz, *Essential ASP.NET with Examples in C#*, Addison-Wesley, 2003
- Peltzer, Dwight, *XML: Language Mechanics and Applications*, Pearson Addison Wesley, 2003
- Roman, Ed, et al., *Mastering Enterprise Java Beans*, John Wiley & Sons, 2002
- Sceppa, David, *Programming ADO*, Microsoft Press, 2000
- Schmidt, Eric, *Using Schema and Serialization to Leverage Business Logic*, MSDN Library (Microsoft Corporation), 2002
- Scribner, Kenn, and Mark Stiver, *Understanding SOAP*, Sams, 2000
- Sharma, Rahul, et al., *J2EE Connector Architecture and Enterprise Application Integration*, Addison-Wesley, 2001
- Short, Scott, *Building Web Services for the Microsoft. NET Platform*, Microsoft Press, 2002
- Troelsen, Andrew, *Visual Basic .NET and the .NET Platform*, Springer-Verlag, 2001
- Tulachan, Pravin, *Developing EJB 2.0 Components*, Pearson PTR, 2002
- Utley, Craig, *The Programmer's Introduction to Visual Basic .NET*, Sams, 2002
- Williams, Kevin, et al., *Professional XML Databases*, Wrox Press, 2000
- Yawn, Michael, *J2EE and JAX*, Prentice Hall, 2002

Index

A

B

C

D

E

F

G

H

I

J

K

L

M

N

O

P

Q

R

S

T

U

V

W